'*Raw, funny, nostalgic, and knife-sharp*'

PETER CAREY

'A great, great book' RODDY DOYLE

Donald Antrim

The Afterlife

A tangled true story of heartbreak, hysteria and relative insanity

'*Vividness and warmth worthy of Charles Dickens*'

LA TIMES

www.littlebrown.co.uk

THE BEST OF **THE BEST OF YOUNG AMERICAN NOVELISTS**

CHRISTOPHER COAKE
WE'RE IN TROUBLE

DARA HORN
THE WORLD TO COME

NICOLE KRAUSS
THE HISTORY OF LOVE

CONGRATULATIONS TO OUR AUTHORS FROM HAMISH HAMILTON, VIKING AND PENGUIN

JONATHAN SAFRAN FOER
EXTREMELY LOUD AND INCREDIBLY CLOSE

OLGA GRUSHIN
THE DREAM LIFE
OF SUKHANOV

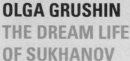

GRANTA 97, SPRING 2007
www.granta.com

EDITOR *Ian Jack*
DEPUTY EDITOR *Matt Weiland*
MANAGING EDITOR *Fatema Ahmed*
ASSOCIATE EDITOR *Liz Jobey*
EDITORIAL ASSISTANT *Helen Gordon*

CONTRIBUTING EDITORS *Diana Athill, Simon Gray, Isabel Hilton,
Sophie Harrison, Blake Morrison, John Ryle, Sukhdev Sandhu, Lucretia Stewart*

FINANCE *Geoffrey Gordon, Morgan Graver*
SALES DIRECTOR *Brigid Macleod*
PUBLICITY *Pru Rowlandson*
MARKETING AND SUBSCRIPTIONS *Gill Lambert*
IT MANAGER *Mark Williams*
TO ADVERTISE CONTACT *Kate Rochester, ksrochester@granta.com*
PRODUCTION ASSOCIATE *Sarah Wasley*
PROOFS *Lesley Levene*

PUBLISHER *Sigrid Rausing*

GRANTA PUBLICATIONS, 2-3 Hanover Yard, Noel Road, London N1 8BE
Tel +44 (0)20 7704 9776 Fax +44 (0)20 7704 0474
e-mail for editorial: editorial@granta.com
This selection copyright © 2007 Granta Publications.
In the United States, Granta is published in association with Grove/Atlantic Inc,
841 Broadway, 4th Floor, New York, NY 10003

TO SUBSCRIBE go to www.granta.com
or call +44(0)20 7704 0470 or e-mail subs@granta.com
A one-year subscription (four issues) costs £27.95 (UK), £35.95 (rest of Europe)
and £42.95 (rest of the world).

Granta is printed and bound in Italy by Legoprint. The paper used in this publication meets the
minimum requirements of American National Standard for Information Sciences—Permanence of
Paper for Printed Library Materials, ANSI Z39.48-1984.

Design: Slabmedia. Cover image: Paul Elliman
Granta would like to thank Nadia Aguiar, Kimberly Burns and Beth Chimera for all their
help with Best of Young American Novelists.

ISBN 978-0903141-92-5

GRANTA 97

Best of Young American Novelists 2

Faber and Faber congratulates

AKHIL SHARMA

author of *An Obedient Father*
for being selected as one of *Granta's*
Best of Young American Novelists

INTRODUCTION

When *Granta* published its first Best of Young Novelists selection in 1983, the words 'young' and 'novelists' were an unusual combination. Few people in Britain connected serious fiction with youth. Publishing was felt to be a mature or even elderly trade. Cartoonists drew publishers as men in tweed waistcoats who smoked pipes, and the typical successful novelist as a well-settled householder in Hampstead, Oxford or a country rectory. Plenty of writers didn't conform to the caricature—1983's Best of Young British Novelists welcomed a generation that included Rushdie, Martin Amis, Ishiguro and McEwan—but only in the worlds of music and fashion did youth tend to be taken as an absolute recommendation, a quality to flaunt. It was, perhaps, a mark of publishing's conservatism that in 1983 *Granta*'s definition of a young novelist was one under the age of forty.

We held to that rule over the next twenty years. *Granta*'s Best of Young British Novelists for 1993 and 2003 and its first Best of Young American Novelists in 1996 all took forty as the cut-off point. For the second Best of Young American Novelists we have lowered it by five years—everybody in this issue was born after 1970 and the oldest of them turned thirty-five in 2006. We reasoned that as people seem to be writing (and publishing) fiction sooner—it's increasingly seen as a career choice by Americans in their early twenties, who attend universities to learn it—they have at least in theory a head start on their predecessors and should be getting better, quicker. We also reasoned that, had we stuck to forty as the upper age limit, several writers in the 1996 selection (Sherman Alexie, Elizabeth McCracken, Edwidge Danticat) might need to be included again, and that the selection of others aged between thirty-five and forty (Dave Eggers and Jhumpa Lahiri are two examples) would give the list too great a sense of establishment and déjà vu.

We made one other change. In 1996 there was a pyramid of judgement in which five regional judging panels read and sifted the work of authors who lived in their region—West, Midwest, South, Mid-Atlantic and New England—and then submitted shortlists to the national judges, so that the final list of twenty was chosen from fifty-two writers rather than a few hundred. I came to the process late as a national judge and the recently appointed editor of *Granta*, and for reasons I can never understand the national judges were denied sight of a few writers who certainly (and not just with hindsight) should have been on the national shortlist. Where were Nicholson Baker, David Foster Wallace, Michael Chabon, Richard Powers, Donna Tartt? Not present: discarded by folks elsewhere. This time I decided that all the mistakes would be our own—that we wouldn't be outsourcing anything to judges with God-knows-what axes to grind in California or Kansas. *Granta* asked for submissions early in 2006 and received nearly 200 books and manuscripts from publishers and agents. Editors at *Granta* read all of them, if not always all of all of them, and by spring had the elements of a shortlist which with some later additions ran to seventy-five writers. The judges were free to call in books from any writer who had been excluded from the shortlist and reinstate them for consideration, or to put forward any writer we had somehow completely overlooked. One or two did so. There were six judges: A. M. Homes and Edmund White, novelists and memoirists; Sigrid Rausing, *Granta*'s publisher; Meghan O'Rourke, culture editor of *Slate*; Paul Yamazaki of City Lights bookstore in San Francisco; and me as the chair. We read through spring and summer and into the fall.

What kind of picture of new American writing emerged? I would say a very different one from the first exercise in 1996. In that year the novelist Robert Stone, one of my fellow judges, memorably wrote that 'an almost obsessive pursuit of "authenticity", and a *narodnik* romance with land and ordinary people' was still evident in the work of young writers, despite the fact that many of them were suburbanites. (Or perhaps because of it; as Stone wrote, 'The European-descended writers could be described as post-ethnic and post-regional, in other words beyond the forces that informed much American writing in the past. Aware of this deprivation, they write in pursuit of it.') A cruder and unfairer way of putting this would be to say that writers wrote about trailer parks with little experience of living in them, and that the influence of Raymond Carver and 'realism' lay heavy on creative writing schools.

However merely voyeuristic it may have been, that interest in social class has ebbed. A few years ago Zadie Smith noted in her introduction to an anthology of stories by young Americans (*The Burned Children of America*, 2003) that their tone could be summed up by one word—'sad'—and that 'fear of death and advertising' were two prominent concerns. Things seem to have moved further down that road, certainly so far as death is concerned. In story after story, novel upon novel, he appeared with his hood and scythe, sometimes suddenly in a car smash but more often in the long prelude of cancer or dementia. There were the dead, there was the memory of the dead, and sometimes there were the post-dead, surviving in the Life Hereafter. 'Why so sad, people?' asked Zadie Smith. It would be easy to reach for 9/11 or even our awakening to environmental apocalypse as the cause—or more trivially, literature often being prompted by other literature, the earlier success of Alice Sebold's *The Lovely Bones*. I don't know. Death is a preoccupation at both ends of life, among children, who haven't learned to ignore it, and among adults whose age or health brings them close to the inevitable fact. In prosperous societies not torn apart by civil conflict, it usually seems furthest away between the ages of, say, fifteen and forty. But many of our books written by writers within that age group were infused by loss and the feeling that present things would not go on forever. Reading them reminded me of the boom in spiritualism and Ouija boards that followed the First World War, or Powell and Pressburger's eerie film *A Matter of Life and Death*, which tried to console the bereaved of the Second.

They also gave the impression of America as a very uncertain country. This may be what it has recently become, but fiction doesn't always catch up with reality so quickly. The condition of *just being an American*, especially when not in America, produced an interesting anxiety in several writers (for example, Tom Bissell and Tony D'Souza). Just as America is no longer so confident, American writing is no longer so snugly self-contained, as other judges were quick to notice. Meghan O'Rourke wrote, 'I was struck by the degree to which American writers are looking outward... There's a sense now that to be an American fiction writer is to deal with America in the world—and the world in America. If in the past American fiction dealt with the rest of the globe by trying hard to assimilate it, today it deals with it by going outward towards it.' Edmund White noted 'what might be called the Peace Corps novel, written about the encounter of the young privileged American with the developing world. Often his idealism is sorely tested by cynical insurgents or by poorer but more worldly foreigners.'

All of us agreed on one thing: ethnicity, migration and 'abroad' had replaced social class as a source of tension despite the fact, as O'Rourke pointed out, that the gap between the wealthy and poor in the United States is wider than ever. 'In America all class analysis is forbidden,' said White. 'It's as if the conflict and alienation offered in, say, the British novel by encounters with members of other, lower social classes are replaced in America by contrasts of first and third world cultures.' But then a lot of what we considered the most interesting writing came from America's newest migrants. In this volume a third of the contributors were born or raised in other countries, including Russia, China, Peru, India, Nigeria and Thailand. (The 1996 volume contained only one.) This is a tremendous variety, though it becomes less various when examined through the prism of class. Of 2003's Best of Young British Novelists, sixty per cent attended the universities of Oxford and Cambridge. Anyone who expected literary production to have a broader social base in the United States will be disappointed. At least fourteen of the twenty-one Best of Young Americans were schooled in the Ivy League and universities of equal expense and reputation, such as Stanford and Oberlin. As O'Rourke said by way of explaining the thematic absence of social division, 'There are still far too many talented young writers who lack financial independence and can't find ways to make their voices heard.'

Nearly all our chosen (and unchosen) writers also attended writing school; four went to Iowa. A lot has been written about the 'factory fiction' and 'industrial production' of writing schools—I have written a share of it myself. One result of writing schools is a vast number of short stories; in London, *Granta* gets several dozen every week with US postage on the envelope. Most are none too interesting but a few are good, and deny the idea put forward recently by an American critic, Elif Batuman, that 'the American short story is a dead form, unnaturally perpetuated'. Reading the submissions, it seemed to us that many story collections deserved as much if not more attention than the novels, that there were great liveliness and insight in them and that often, given their binding structure of character and location, they were nearly novels in any case. This accounts for our extending the list to twenty-one rather than twenty and also for the number of writers on our list (seven) who have yet to publish a novel.

We met to decide the list in a New York hotel in late October. The meeting went on all day, names were traded, none of us got our own way, all of us had disappointments. Ed White regretted the omission of Benjamin Kunkel ('His novel *Indecision* was a delirious piece of imaginative writing'), Meghan O'Rourke was sad that Dean

Bakopoulos didn't find general favour (*'Please Don't Come Back from the Moon* is a really incisive and clear-headed portrait of class boundaries in America'). Paul Yamazaki was sorry about Sarah Shun-Lien Bynum and her 'very strange' book *Madeleine is Sleeping*. I missed Nick Arvin, Benjamin Markovits, Julie Orringer and, especially, Joshua Ferris, whose first novel, *Then We Came to the End,* struck me as a brilliant account of the desperations of working life and had the singular distinction among all these writers of making me laugh aloud quite often.

No list of this kind can offer anything approaching a final judgement. That is up to posterity, if there is one. In the meantime, here is our provisional and partial portrait of who was young and wrote good fiction in America in the early years of the twenty-first century. I would like to thank all the judges, publishers, agents and of course writers who made it possible.

Ian Jack, January 2007

Best of Young American Novelists 1 (1996)

Sherman Alexie	Allen Kurzweil
Madison Smartt Bell	Elizabeth McCracken
Ethan Canin	Lorrie Moore
Edwidge Danticat	Fae Myenne Ng
Tom Drury	Robert O'Connor
Tony Earley	Chris Offutt
Jeffrey Eugenides	Stewart O'Nan
Jonathan Franzen	Mona Simpson
David Guterson	Melanie Rae Thon
David Haynes	Kate Wheeler

Daniel Alarcón was born in Lima, Peru in 1977 and raised in the southern United States. He is associate editor of 'Etiqueta Negra', a monthly magazine based in Lima. His short story collection, 'War by Candlelight' (Fourth Estate/HarperCollins), was a finalist for the 2006 Hemingway Foundation/PEN Award. His first novel, 'Lost City Radio', is published by HarperCollins in the US and will be published in the UK by Fourth Estate in July. He currently lives in Oakland, California, where he is the Distinguished Visiting Writer at Mills College. Though hampered by a nagging ankle injury, Alarcón still plays soccer three times a week, striking fear into the hearts of defenders and goalkeepers everywhere. 'The King is Always Above the People' is a new story.

GRANTA

THE KING IS ALWAYS ABOVE THE PEOPLE

Daniel Alarcón

Daniel Alarcón

It was the year I left my parents, a few useless friends, and a girl who liked to tell everyone we were married, and moved two hundred kilometres downstream to the capital. Summer had limped to a close. I was nineteen years old and my idea was to work the docks, but when I showed up the man behind the desk said I looked scrawny, that I should come back when I had put on some muscle. I did what I could to hide my disappointment. I'd dreamed of leaving home since I was a boy, since my mother taught me that our town's river flowed all the way to the city.

I rented a room in the neighbourhood near the port from Mr and Mrs Patrice, an older couple who had advertised for a student. They were prim and serious and they showed me the rooms of their neat, uncluttered house as if it were the private viewing of a rare diamond. Mine would be the back room, they said. There were no windows. After the brief tour we sat in the living room, sipping tea beneath a portrait of the old dictator that hung above the mantel. They asked me what I was studying. All I could think of in those days was money, so I said economics. They liked that answer. They asked about my parents, and when I said they had passed on, that I was all alone, I saw Mrs Patrice's wrinkled hand graze her husband's thigh, just barely.

He offered to lower the rent and I accepted.

The next day Mr Patrice recommended me to an acquaintance who needed a cashier for a shop he owned. It was good, part-time work, he told me, perfect for a student. I was hired. It wasn't far from the port, and in warm weather I could sit out front and smell the river where it opened into the wide harbour. It was enough for me to listen and know it was there: the hum and crash of the ships being loaded and unloaded reminded me of why I had left, where I had come to and all the further places that awaited me. I tried not to think of home, and though I'd promised to write, somehow it never seemed like the right time.

We sold cigarettes and liquor and newspapers to the dockworkers and had a copy machine for the folks who came to present their paperwork at the customs house. We made change for them and my boss, Nadal, advised them as to the appropriate bribe, depending on what item they were expecting to receive and from where. He knew the protocol well. He'd worked for years in customs before the dictator fell, but hadn't had the foresight to join a political party when democracy came. His only other mistake in thirty years, he told me once, was that he hadn't stolen enough. There had never been any rush. Autocracies are nothing if not stable and no one ever thought the old regime could be toppled. We sold postcards of the hanging, right by the cash register: the body of the dictator swaying from an improvised gallows in the main plaza. There was a caption below: THE KING IS ALWAYS ABOVE THE PEOPLE. It is a cloudy day and every head is turned upward to face the expressionless dead man. One has the sense of an inviolable silence reigning over the spectators. I was fifteen when it happened. I remember my father crying when he heard the news. He'd been living in the city when the man first came to power.

We sold two or three of these postcards each week.

In the early mornings I wandered around the city. Out in the streets, I peppered my speech with words and phrases I'd heard around me, and sometimes, when I fell into conversations with strangers, I would realize later that the goal of it all had been to pass for someone raised in the capital. I never pulled it off. The slang I'd picked up from the radio before moving was disappointingly tame. At the shop I saw the same people every day, and they knew my story—or rather, the one I told them: a solitary, orphaned student. When do you study? they'd ask, and I'd tell them I was saving up money to matriculate. I spent a good deal of time reading, and this fact alone was enough to convince them. The stooped customs bureaucrats in their faded suits came in on their lunch break to reminisce with Nadal about the good old days, and sometimes they would slip me some money. For your studies, they'd say, and wink.

There were others—the dockworkers, always promising the newest, dirtiest joke in exchange for credit. Twice a month one of the larger carriers came in, depositing a dozen or so startled Filipinos for shore leave. Inevitably they wandered into the shop, disoriented, hopeful, but most of all thrilled to be once again on dry land. They grinned and yammered incomprehensibly and I was always kind to them. That could be me, I thought, in a year, perhaps two: stumbling forth from the bowels of a ship into the narrow streets of a port city anywhere in the world.

I was alone in the shop one afternoon when a man in a light brown uniform walked in. I'd been in the city three and a half months by then. He wore his moustache in that way men from the provinces did and I disliked him immediately. With great ceremony he pulled a large piece of folded paper from the inside pocket of his jacket and spread it out on the counter. It was a target from a shooting range: the crude outline of a man, vaguely menacing, now pierced with holes. The customer looked admiringly at his handiwork. 'Not bad, eh?'

'Depends.' I bent over the sheet, placing my index finger in each paper wound, one by one. There were seven holes in the target. 'What distance?'

'At any distance,' he asked, 'can you do better?' Without waiting for me to respond, he took out an official-looking form and placed it next to the bullet-riddled paper man. 'I need three copies, son. This target and my certificate. Three of each.'

'Half an hour,' I said.

He squinted at me and stroked his moustache. 'Why so long?'

The reason was that I felt like making him wait. And he knew that. But I told him the machine had to warm up. Even as I said it, it sounded ridiculous. The machine, I said, was a delicate and expensive piece of equipment, newly imported from Japan.

He was unconvinced.

'And we don't have paper this size,' I added. 'I'll have to reduce it.'

His lips scrunched together into a sort of smile. 'But thank God you have a new machine that can do all that. You're from upriver, aren't you?'

I didn't answer him.

'Which village?'

'Town,' I said, and told him the name.

'Have you seen the new bridge?' he asked.

I said I hadn't, and this was a lie. 'I left before it was built.'

He sighed. 'It's a beautiful bridge,' he said, allowing himself to indulge briefly in the image: the wide river cutting through green rolling hills that seemed to stretch on forever.

When he was done reminiscing, he turned back to me. 'Now, listen. You make my copies, and take your time. Warm up the machine, read it poetry, massage it, make love to it. Do what you have to do. You're very lucky. I'm happy today. Tomorrow I go home and I have a job waiting for me at the bank. I'll make good money, and I'll marry the prettiest girl in town, and you'll still be here breathing this nasty city air, surrounded by these nasty city people.' He smiled for a moment.

'Got that?'

'Sure,' I said.

'Now tell me where a man can get a drink around here.'

There was a bar a few streets over, a dingy spot with smoky windows that I walked by almost every day. It was a place full of sailors and dockworkers and rough men the likes of whom still frightened me. I'd never gone in, but in many ways it was the bar I'd imagined myself in when I was still back home, plotting a way to escape: dark and unpleasant, the kind of place that would upset my poor, blameless mother.

I took the man's target and put it behind the counter. 'Sure, there's a bar,' I said. 'But it's not for country folk.'

'Insolent little fucker. Tell me where it is.'

I pointed him in the right direction.

'Half an hour. Have my copies ready.' He noticed the plastic stand with the postcard of the dictator's hanging and scowled. With his index finger, he carefully flicked it over, so that they all tumbled to the floor.

I let them fall.

'If I were your father,' he said, 'I would beat you senseless for disrespect.'

He shook his head and left, letting the door slam behind him.

I never saw him again. As it happened, I was right about the bar. Someone must not have liked the looks of him, or maybe they thought he was a cop by the way he was dressed, or maybe his accent drew the wrong kind of attention. In any case, the papers said it was quite a show. The fight started inside—who knows how these things begin—and spilled out into the street. That's where he died, head cracked on the cobblestones. An ambulance was called, but couldn't make it down the narrow streets in time. There was a shift change at the docks and the streets were filled with men.

Shortly after my encounter with the security guard, I wrote a letter home. Just a note really, something brief to let my parents know I was alive, that they shouldn't believe everything they read in the newspapers about the capital. My father had survived a stint in the city, and nearly three decades later he still spoke of the place with bewilderment. He went there shortly after marrying my mother, and returned a year later with enough money to build the house where I'd been raised. The city may have been profitable, but it was also a frightening, unsteady kind of place. In twelve months he saw robberies, riots and a president deposed. As soon as he had the money together, he returned home and never went back. My mother never went at all.

In my note I told them about the Patrices, described the nice old couple in a way that would put them both at ease. I would visit at Christmas, I promised, because it was still half a year off.

As for the target and the dead man's certificate, I decided to keep them. I took them home the very next day and folded the certificate carefully into the thin pages of an illustrated dictionary the Patrices kept in their front room. I tacked the target up on my wall so that I could face it if I sat upright in bed.

One night a storm rolled in, the first downpour of the season, and the rain drumming on the roof reminded me of home. I felt suddenly lonely, and I shut my left eye and pointed my index finger at the wall, at the man in the target. I aimed carefully and fired at him. It felt good. I did it again, this time with sound effects, and many minutes were spent this way. I blew imaginary smoke from the tip of my finger, like the gunslingers I'd seen in imported movies. I must have killed him a dozen times before I realized what I was doing, and after that I felt a fidelity to the man in the target I could not explain. I would shoot him every night before sleeping, and sometimes in the mornings as well.

One afternoon, not long after I'd sent my letter, I came home to find the girl—Malena was her name—red-faced and teary, in the Patrices' tidy living room. She had just arrived from my home town, and her small bag leaned against the wall by the door. Mrs Patrice was consoling her, a gentle hand draped over Malena's shoulder, and Mr Patrice sat by, not quite knowing what to do. I stammered a greeting and the three of them looked up. I read the expressions on their faces, and by the way Malena looked at me, I knew immediately what had happened.

'Your parents send their best,' said Mrs Patrice, her voice betraying grave disappointment.

'You're going to be a father,' her husband added, in case there had been any confusion.

I stepped forward, took Malena by the hand and led her to my room in the back without saying a word to the Patrices. We sat for a long while in silence. There had never been anyone besides me in the room, except for the first time the Patrices had shown me the place. Malena didn't seem particularly sad or angry or happy to see me. She sat on the bed. I stood. Her hair had come undone and fell over her face when she looked down, which, at first, was often.

'Did you miss me?' she asked.

I had missed her—her body, her breath, her laughter—but it wasn't until she was in front of me that I realized it. 'Of course,' I said.

'You could've written.'

'I did.'

'Eventually.'

'How long?' I asked.

'Four months.'

'And it's—'

'Yes,' Malena said in a stern voice.

She sighed deeply and I apologized.

Malena had news—who else had left for the city, who had gone north. There were weddings planned for the spring, some people we knew, though not well. A boy from my neighbourhood had joined the army, was rumoured to have escaped basic training and gone to live with a woman twice his age in a slum on the outskirts of the city. It sounded far-fetched, but it's what everyone was saying. As I suspected, the murder of the security guard had been a big story, and Malena told me she herself hadn't been able to sleep, wondering what I might be doing, whether I was all right. She'd visited my parents, and they'd tried to convince her not to travel to the city, or at least not alone.

'Your father was going to come with me.'

'And why didn't he?' I asked.

'Because I didn't wait for him.'

I sat beside her on the bed, so that our thighs were touching. I didn't tell her that I'd met the victim, about my role in his misfortunes, or any of that. I let her talk: she described the small, cosmetic changes that our town had undergone in the few months I'd been away. Mayoral elections were coming up, she said, and everyone looked forward to the campaign with the usual mix of anxiety and despair. The owner of the cement plant was going to run. He would likely win. There was talk of repainting the bridge. I nodded. She was showing already, an unmistakable roundness to her. I placed the flat of my palm against her belly and then pulled her close. She stopped talking abruptly, in mid-sentence.

'You'll stay with me. We'll be happy,' I whispered.

But Malena shook her head. There was something hard in the way she spoke. 'I'm going home,' she said, 'and you're coming with me.'

It was still early. I stood up and walked around the tiny room; from wall to wall, it was only ten short paces. I stared at my friend in the target. I suggested we see the neighbourhood before it got too dark. I could show Malena the docks or the customs house. Didn't she want to see it?

'What is there to see?'

'The harbour. The river.'

'We have that river back home.'

We went anyway. The Patrices said nothing as we left, and when we returned in the early evening, the door to their room was closed. Malena's bag was still by the front door, and though it was just a day bag with only one change of clothes, once I moved it, my room felt even smaller. Until that night, Malena and I had never slept in the same bed. We pressed together, and shifted our weight, and eventually we were face to face and very close. I put my arm around her, but kept my eyes shut, and listened to the muffled sounds of the Patrices talking anxiously.

'Are they always so chatty?' Malena asked.

I couldn't make out their words, of course, but I could guess. 'Does it bother you?'

I felt Malena shrug in my arms. 'Not really,' she said, 'but it might if we were staying.'

After this comment, nothing was said, and Malena slept peacefully.

When we emerged the next morning for breakfast, my landlords were sombre and unsmiling. Mrs Patrice cleared her throat several times, making increasingly urgent gestures at her husband, until finally he set down his fork and began. He expressed his general regret, his frustration and disappointment. 'We come from solid people,' he said. 'We are not of the kind who tell lies for sport. We helped settle this part of the city. We are respectable people who do not accept dishonesty.'

'We are church people,' Mrs Patrice added.

Her husband nodded. I had seen him prepare for services each

Sunday with a meticulousness that can only come from great and unquestioned faith. A finely scrubbed suit, shirts of the most pristine white. He would comb a thick pomade into his black hair so that in the sun he was always crowned with a gelatinous shine.

'Whatever half-truths you may have told this young lady are not our concern. That must be settled between the two of you. We have no children ourselves, but wonder how we might feel if our son was off telling everyone he was an orphan.'

He lowered his eyebrows.

'Crushed,' Mrs Patrice whispered. 'Betrayed.'

'We do not doubt your basic goodness, son, nor yours...'

'Malena,' I said. 'Her name is Malena.'

'...as you are both creatures of the one true God, and He does not err when it comes to arranging the affairs of men. It is not our place to judge, but only to accept with humility that with which the Lord has charged us.'

He was gaining momentum now and we had no choice but to listen. Under the table, Malena reached for my hand. Together we nodded.

'And He has brought you both here, and so it must be His will that we look after you. And we do not mean to put you out on the streets at this delicate moment, because such a thing would not be right. But we do mean to ask for an explanation, to demand one, and we will have it from you, son, and you will give it, if you are ever to learn what it means to be a respectful and respectable citizen, in this city or in any other. Tell me: have you been studying?'

'No.'

'I thought not,' Mr Patrice said. He frowned, shook his head gravely and then continued. Our breakfast grew cold. Eventually it would be my turn to speak, but by then I had very little to say, and no desire to account for anything.

Malena and I left that afternoon.

I went to the shop first to arrange my affairs, and after explaining the situation to Nadal, he offered to help me. He loved doctoring official paperwork, he said. It reminded him of his finest working days. We made a copy of the original certificate and then corrected it so that the name was mine. We changed the address, the birth date, and typed the particulars of my height and weight on a beat-up Underwood Nadal had inherited from his days in customs. He whistled the whole time, clearly enjoying himself. 'You've made an old man feel young again,' he said. We reprinted the form on bond paper and, with great ceremony, Nadal brought out a dusty box from beneath his desk. In it were the official stamps he'd pilfered over the years, more than a dozen of them, including one from the OFFICE OF THE SECRETARY GENERAL OF THE PATRIOTIC FORCES OF NATIONAL DEFENCE—that is, from the dictator himself. It had a mother-of-pearl handle and an intricate and stylized version of the national seal. I'd never seen anything like it. A keepsake, Nadal told me, from an affair with an unscrupulous woman who covered him, twice weekly, in bite marks and lurid scratches, and who screamed so loudly when they made love that he often stopped just to marvel at the sound. 'Like a banshee,' he said. She maintained similar liaisons with the dictator, and, according to the woman, he liked to decorate her naked body with this same stamp. Nadal smiled. He could reasonably claim to have been, in his prime, extraordinarily close to the seat of power.

'Of course, the king is dead,' Nadal said. 'And me, I'm still alive.'

Each stamp had a story like this, and he relished the telling—where it had come from, what agency it represented, how it had been used and abused over the years and to what ends. Though Malena was waiting for me, we spent nearly two hours selecting one, and then we placed the forged document, and the target which I'd removed from my wall that morning, in a manila envelope. This, too, was sealed with a stamp.

Nadal and I embraced. 'There'll always be a job for you here,' he said.

Malena and I rode home that day on a groaning, inter-provincial bus. She fell asleep with her head on my shoulder, and when I saw the city disappear and give way to the rolling plains and gentle contours of the countryside, I was not unhappy. The next morning I presented the documents at the bank in the town just across the bridge from mine. 'We've been needing a security guard,' the manager said. 'You may have heard what happened to our last one.' He blinked a lot as he spoke. 'You're young, but I like the look of you. I don't know why.' And then we shook hands; I was home again.

My son was born just before Christmas that year, and in March the papers began reporting a string of bank robberies in the provinces. The perpetrators were ex-convicts, or foreigners, or soldiers thrown out of work since the democratic government began downsizing the army. No one knew for certain, but it was worrisome and new, as these were the sorts of crimes that had been largely confined to the city and its poorer suburbs. Everyone was afraid; most of all me. Each report was grislier than the last. Half an hour upriver, two clerks had been executed after the contents of the vault had disappointed the band of criminals. They hit two banks that day, shooting their way out of a police perimeter at the second one, killing a cop and wounding another in the process. They were said to be travelling the river's tributaries, hiding in coves along the heavily forested banks. Of course, it was only a matter of time. We received sizeable deposits from the cement plant once a week and many of the workers cashed their cheques with us on alternate Friday afternoons.

Malena read the papers, heard the rumours and catalogued the increasingly violent details of each heist. I heard her tell her friends she wasn't worried, that I was a sure-shot, but in private she was unequivocal. Quit, she said. We have a son to raise. We can move back to the city.

But something had changed. The three of us were living together in the same room where I'd grown up. She smothered our son with so much affection that I barely felt he was mine at all. The boy was always hungry, and I woke every day before dawn when he cried, and watched as he fed with an urgency I could understand and recall perfectly: it was how I'd felt when I left for the city almost exactly a year before. Afterwards, I could never get back to sleep, and I wondered how and when I'd become so hopelessly, so irredeemably selfish, and what, if anything, could be done about it. None of my actions belonged to me. I'd been living one kind of life when a strong, implacable hand had pulled me violently into another. I tried to remember my city routines, but I couldn't. Nor could I recall a single dirty joke of the dozens I'd heard from the dockworkers at the shop, or the pattern of the wallpaper in the Patrices' tidy living room. The name of the street that ran parallel to the port had escaped me, as had the sound of the dauntless Filipinos chattering among themselves on those days they came ashore to visit the kind, ornamented women of the capital.

The rest of the world had never seemed so far away.

By late summer the gang had hit most of the towns in our province. It was then that my father suggested we go to the old farm. He would teach me how to use the pistol. I began to tell him I knew, but he wasn't interested.

'You'll drive,' he said.

We left town on a Saturday of endless, oppressive heat, the road nothing but a sticky band of tar humming beneath us. We arrived just before noon. There were no shadows. The rutted gravel road led right up to the house, shuttered and old and caving in on itself like a ruined cake. My father got out and leaned against the hood of the car. Behind us, a low cloud of dust snaked back to the main road, and a light breeze brushed over the grassy, overgrown fields but seemed somehow to avoid us, so that all we could feel was the relentless heat. My father took out a bottle, drank a little and pulled the brim of his cap down over his eyes. The light was fierce. He was seven years old when my grandfather died and my grandmother moved the family into town. He passed me the bottle; I handed him the gleaming weapon. He loaded it with a smile and, without saying much, we took turns firing rounds at the sagging walls of my grandfather's house.

An hour passed this way, blowing out what remained of the windows, and circling the house clockwise to try our onslaught from another angle. We aimed for the cornices just below the roof, and hit, after a few attempts, the tilting weathervane above so that it spun maniacally in the still afternoon heat. We shot the numbers off the front door and tore the rain gutter from the corner it had clung to for five decades. I spread holes all over the facade of the house. My father watched, and I imagined he was proud of me.

'How does it feel?' he asked when we were finished. We sat leaning against the shadowed eastern wall.

The gun was warm in my hand. 'I don't know,' I said. 'You tell me.'

'You're no good with that pistol.' He took his cap off and laid it by his side. 'You've got to shoot like you mean it.'

'I don't.'

'It's all right to be scared.'

'I know,' I said. 'I am.'

'Your generation isn't lucky. This never would have happened before. The old government wouldn't have allowed it.'

I shrugged. I had a postcard of the dead general buried in a bag back home. I could show it to my father any time, at any moment, just to make him angry or sad or both, and somehow, knowing this felt good.

'Are you enjoying it?' he asked. 'Are you enjoying being a father?'

'What kind of question is that?'

'It's not a *kind* of question. It *is* a question. If you're going to take everything your father says as an insult, your life will be unbearable.'

'I'm sorry.'

He sighed. 'If it isn't already.'

We sat, watching the heat rise from the baking earth. It seemed like a strange thing to have to deny to my father. I mentioned the bridge, its new colour, but he hadn't noticed.

He turned to face me. 'You know, your mother and I are still young.'

'Sure you are.'

'Young enough, in good health, and I've got years of work left in me.' He flexed his bicep and held it out for me to see. 'Look,' he said. 'Feel it if you want. Your old man is still strong.'

He was speaking very deliberately now, and I had the feeling that he'd prepared the exact wording of what he said next. 'We're young, but you're very young. You have an entire life to lead. And you can go, if you want, and look for that life elsewhere. Go do things, go see different places. We can take care of the child. You don't want to be here, and we understand.'

'What are you talking about?'

'Your mother agrees,' he said. 'We've discussed it. She'll miss you, but she says she understands.'

I wasn't certain I understood. For a moment I stared at him. 'And Malena?'

'She'll want for nothing.'

I picked up the gun, brushed the dust off it. I checked to make sure it was unloaded and passed it back to him.

'When?' I asked.

'Whenever.'

And then we rode home and spoke only of the weather and the elections. My father didn't care much for voting, but he supposed if the owner of the plant wanted to be mayor, he could be. It was fine with him. It was all fine with him. The sky had filled with quilted, white clouds, but the heat had not waned. Or maybe it was how I felt. Even with the windows down, I sweated clean through my shirt, my back and thighs sticking fast to the seat. I didn't add much to the conversation, only drove and stared ahead and thought about what my father had said to me.

I was still thinking two weeks later when we were robbed.

It was no better or worse than I'd imagined. I was asked to say something at the manager's wake and, to my surprise, the words would not come easily. I stood before a room of grieving family and shell-shocked friends, offering a bland remembrance of the dead man and his kindness. I found it impossible to make eye contact with anyone. Malena cradled our son in her arms and the evening passed in a blur, until the three of us made our way to the corner of the dark parlour where the young widow was receiving condolences. She thanked me for my words; she cooed at our boy. 'How old?' she asked, but before Malena or I could respond, her face reddened and the tears came and there was nothing either of us could say. I excused myself, left Malena with a kiss and escaped through a back door, into the warm evening. The town was shuttered and quiet. I never made it home that night and Malena didn't look for me. □

GRANTA

PARAKEETS

Kevin Brockmeier

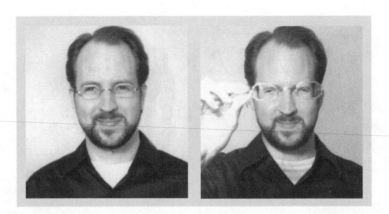

Kevin Brockmeier was born on December 6, 1972 and raised in Little Rock, Arkansas, where he still lives today. He is the author of two novels, 'The Brief History of the Dead' (John Murray/Pantheon) and 'The Truth About Celia'; a short-story collection, 'Things That Fall from the Sky' (Pantheon); and a trio of children's books. He has taught creative writing at the University of Iowa, the University of Arkansas at Little Rock, and Grinnell College. His minor eccentricities are legion. 'Parakeets' is taken from his forthcoming collection of stories, 'The View from the Seventh Layer'.

Once there was a city where everyone had the gift of song. Gardeners sang as they clipped their flowers. Husbands and wives sang each other to sleep at night. Groups of children waiting for the school bell to ring raced through the verses of the latest pop songs to get to the pure spun sugar of the choruses. Old friends who had not seen each other in many years met at wakes and retirement parties to sing the melodies they remembered from the days when they believed there was nothing else in the world that would ever grip their spirits so and take them out of their bodies. Life was carried along on a thousand little currents of music, and it was not unusual to hear a tune drifting out from behind the closed door of an office as you passed, or even from the small back room of the art museum, which was almost but never quite empty. The people of the city did not always sing with great skill, but they sang clearly and with a simplicity of feeling that made their voices beautiful to hear. And because they loved what they sang, no matter how painful or melancholy, a note of indomitable happiness ran through their voices like a fine silver thread.

In this city there lived a mute, the only person who was unable to lend his voice to the great chorus of song that filled the air. The mute had spent his entire life in the city, and everyone from the members of the school board to the stock boys at the grocery store knew who he was. In some communities there is a man who sells whistles by the courthouse or paper kites down by the river. In others there is a woman who decorates her home with multicoloured lights and streamers every holiday. Usually these people are no more than small figures at the periphery of everyone's attention, but when they die, it can be more surprising than the death of a prominent leader or a renowned artist, because no one has ever regarded them carefully enough to consider what their absence might mean.

The mute was of that age where his hair had turned white and his shoes no longer seemed to fit him properly. Some of his neighbours believed he was deaf—an understandable mistake. He was not deaf, though, only mute, and from time to time he liked to sit in a chair on his front porch and listen to the people around him chatting with each other as they took their afternoon walks. They would say things like, 'I'm telling you, buddy, the second my pension kicks in, it's off to the tropics for me.' And, 'Peter asked me out for dinner tonight, dear thing. I think he's finally going to pop the question.' And, 'That's the deaf man, Sarah. He can't hear you, but that's no reason you can't be friends with him. Why don't you go wave hello?' It comforted him to listen to these conversations. He had never married or fathered children, and behind the door of his house, there were only the quiet tapping of his footsteps and the endless chirping and fluttering of the parakeets.

The mute had gotten his first pair of birds when he was still a young man, purchasing them from a pet vendor he met in the city park. One morning he had seen them preening and tilting their heads in the sunlight, and that was all it took. The colour of their feathers seemed to call out to him: the jewel-like greens and yellows of their wings, the shaded blue around their necks, but most of all the lovely soft purple above their beaks. It was not until he released the parakeets into his living room and watched them hop from the back of the chair on to the curtain rod, and from the curtain rod on to the shelf beside the mirror, that he felt something slipping loose inside him and realized how much he had needed their companionship.

One of the parakeets turned out to be a male and the other a female, and soon he had five birds to take care of. The next year he bought two more from the pet vendor and watched another three hatch from their eggs. It wasn't long before he had so many birds that he knew he had better make new arrangements for them. He hauled the good furniture out of the parlour and attached dozens of little swings, perches, ladders and mirrors to the walls. He put a wooden gate in the doorway. He even installed a pair of recessed skylights in the ceiling so that the birds could watch the shadows of the clouds move across the floor. In the end he believed he had managed to create the kind of space a parakeet might enjoy.

He loved each and every one of his birds, and as the flock grew in size, he learned various tricks to distinguish them from one another. It was only from a distance, he realized, that their bodies seemed to blur together in a single shifting net of brightly coloured wings and tails. When you looked more carefully, you noticed that one of the birds had a particular way of tucking her head under her wing while she ate. Another liked to stand by the window after the sun went down, pecking at her reflection in the glass. Another wore a set of markings on his back that looked like two-day-old snow with dapples of wet grass beginning to show through. Every bird was unique.

He enjoyed watching their lives play out inside the walls of his house, and he took tremendous satisfaction in being able to feed and take care of them. It felt good to be needed by something with a working voice and a beating heart. He often wondered if the other people in the city knew how much happiness a creature so small could bring.

When did he first start giving the birds away as presents? No one could remember, least of all the mute. But a time came when he might be expected to turn up at any public celebration with a bamboo cage in his hands and a bag of fresh seed in his pocket, smiling and nodding in that richly communicative way of his. He became a fixture at birthday parties, baptisms, inaugurations and weddings. There was always singing on such occasions, of course, a boundless wave of pop songs and old standards. As he listened to all the love and sorrow wrapped up inside the harmonies, he wished more than anything that he could join in, but the only thing he had to offer was his parakeets.

With every bird he gave away, he included a set of instructions that ended with the sentence, 'Parakeets are natural mimics, and if you treat your bird as you would a human being, it is likely that he or she will learn how to talk.' Some of the people who accepted the birds from him were busy or practical-minded sorts who had little interest in keeping a pet, but were too polite to tell him so. They stowed the parakeets away in a dimly lit corner of their spare bedroom, or even set them loose in the woods at the edge of town. Others appreciated the birds as no more than a spectacle or a diversion, something to feed every morning and take out whenever they happened to grow bored. Only a few cherished them as much as the mute did. Still, most of the people who kept the birds were able to teach them such simple phrases as 'Good morning', 'What's your name?' and 'I love you.' A number of the birds were clever enough to learn a more complicated set of expressions: 'It's a cruel, cruel world,' for instance, and, 'How about this weather we're having?' One man successfully showed his parakeet how to say 'I prefer the music of Brahms' whenever anyone turned on the radio. Another taught his bird to say 'Hubba-hubba' every time a red-headed woman came into the room.

There was one particular bird who was able to reproduce almost any sound he heard, but when his owner coached him to repeat the phrase 'I don't understand the words they're making me say' he refused to utter so much as a syllable.

31

Kevin Brockmeier

For every parakeet the mute gave away, two more were born into his parlour. Some of the birds died of illness or old age, but there were always new birds to replace them, and the flock showed no sign of diminishing. It began to seem to the mute that the rules of time had been suspended inside the aviary—or if not suspended, then at least reshaped. When he brought his first pair of birds home from the city park, they had not been much older than children, he now realized— and neither, for that matter, had he. Then something changed, and he began to settle into the rhythm of his days and nights. His grandparents died, and later his parents. The long history of a lifetime fell into place behind him. And the birds, it seemed to him, were still not much older than children.

Sometimes he stood at the gate, watching them flit about between their perches, and allowed his mind to wander. He couldn't help thinking of his childhood, particularly those times when he would sit at the back of his classroom during choir practice. He remembered what it was like to listen to everybody singing, to feel the music scaling and building inside him, higher and higher, climbing towards the open air, until it became so powerful that he was almost sure it would not give way this time, though invariably it did. He used to shut his eyes and sway back and forth behind his desk. Anyone could see what was happening to him. The truth was that he, too, had the gift of song—it was just that he could not make use of it. One of his teachers had the idea of giving him a tambourine to shake, and that helped for a while, but the rattling sound it made was not quite what he was looking for. Later he thought about learning to play a real instrument—a flute, maybe, or a clarinet—but as it turned out he did not have the talent for it.

The mute gazed at the birds until his memory faded away. Then he went to the front porch to wait for his neighbours to take their afternoon walks.

No one who has ever lived closely with a flock of birds and come to know their eccentricities could say that they are not intelligent. The parakeets were curious about this man who never spoke, who filled their seed dishes every morning and fed them sweetcorn, grapes and chopped carrots in the evening. Sometimes he stood behind the bars of their cage with a faraway look in his eyes and made a sound like the wind puffing through a long concrete pipe. Sometimes he fluttered his fingers at them, giving a friendly chook-chook-chook noise with the tip of his tongue. What did these activities mean?

The birds studied the mute as though he were a puzzle. And because they had always understood the world best by participating in it, after a while they began to imitate him. They mimicked the clang that went echoing down the hall when he dropped a pot in the kitchen. They jingled like a pair of silver bells when his alarm clock went off in the morning. They duplicated the sound of his footsteps tapping across the wooden floor, the sigh that came from his chair when he sank into the upholstery and even the small back-and-forth sawing noise of his breathing as he drifted off to sleep.

The mute noticed the various sounds the birds were making, and occasionally he said to himself, 'That was me popping my knuckles just now,' or, 'That was me slicing this apple in half,' but generally speaking the thought did not occur to him. He had never listened as carefully to himself as he had to other people. He began to imagine that the reason the birds were raising such a commotion was because they were restless or unhappy, and eventually he decided to move the aviary's gate to the end of the hall so that they would have more room to spread their wings. A few weeks later he moved the gate again, this time into the entrance of the dining room, and a few weeks after that he installed it in the area between his study and the master bedroom. Finally, the only spaces he had left for himself were the kitchen, the bathroom and the sitting room by the front door, where he managed to squeeze not only his lamp and his bed, but also the smallest of his dressers.

He never would have believed that a houseful of birds might be enough for him one day, and yet here he was, an old man, and though he had longed for many things over the years, and had sometimes, like everyone else, felt an overwhelming sadness he could not explain, he had also experienced periods of great calm and radiant joy, and he did not believe that his life had been empty.

One morning he was cleaning the dishes when his heart gave out. There was no pain, just a sudden flooding sensation in his arms and legs that made him feel curiously light-headed. What was this? he wondered. What was happening to him? He sat down on the floor, lifted his hand for a moment and then he closed his eyes.

Perhaps it was later that day, at the banquet in honour of the mayor's wedding anniversary, or perhaps it was the next afternoon, when the butcher's son finally graduated from law school, but it did not take long before the people of the city began to ask themselves where he had gone. They had grown accustomed to seeing him at one social occasion or another, making his way through the crowd with a handmade bamboo cage and the chattering little bundle of a parakeet. A few people thought to wonder if he was all right. They told a few others, who told a few more, and soon they all gathered together and set off down the road towards his house. They knocked on the door. When he did not answer, one of them said, 'He probably doesn't hear you, remember? The man's always been deaf as a post,' and so they tested the knob and found it unlocked.

None of them had ever been inside the house before. How could they have guessed how many parakeets there would be, or how their voices, calling out in mourning or celebration, would fill the air? In a thousand different tones, a thousand different inflections, they reproduced all the sounds of the mute's daily life, from the steady beat of his footsteps to the whistle of his coffee pot to the slow, spreading note of his final breath. It sounded for all the world like a symphony.

□

GRANTA

THE COMPLAINT
Judy Budnitz

Judy Budnitz was born in 1973 and grew up in Atlanta, Georgia. She is the author of a novel, 'If I Told You Once' (Flamingo/Picador US) which was shortlisted for the Orange Prize, and two short story collections: 'Flying Leap' (Flamingo/Picador US) and 'Nice Big American Baby' (HarperPerennial/Vintage US). She has received grants from the Lannan Foundation and the National Endowment for the Arts. Budnitz now lives in San Francisco with her husband and her nice big American nine-month-old son. 'The Complaint' is taken from a novel-in-progress.

'Thank you for holding... What is the nature of your complaint?'
'I've been waiting on the line here for forty-five minutes. What's wrong with this department? I have half a mind to lodge *another* complaint about lodging *this* complaint.'

'Go ahead.'

'Let me speak to your supervisor.'

'I am the supervisor.'

'Well, I... Let me speak to someone else. I don't like your tone.'

'I don't like yours either.'

'This is an emergency and you don't seem to even care. The building behind mine—I can see it from my window—it's absolutely streaming with vermin. I can see them streaming in and out of there, in broad daylight, bold as brass. It's disgusting. The people living there don't even seem to care. They practically hold the doors open for them.'

'What's the address?'

'I don't know if it even has an address. It's the alley behind my own building, 4027 M Street... I wouldn't even care—if people want to live like animals that's their right—but I'm afraid they're going to spread to our building, and we can't have that, we just can't.'

'Alley behind M Street.'

'And there are children over there, it's not clean for the children. If you're an adult you can make the decision about whether you want to live with rats or not, fine, but the children don't get to choose.'

'Do you have documentation of the vermin? Photographs, or droppings?'

'Good God in heaven, am I supposed to go collect rat droppings before you people do anything?'

'According to the rulebook, yes.'

'I shouldn't have to... Haven't there been other complaints? I *know* there have been other complaints. We have been calling and calling you people...'

'When we get the necessary quota of complaints, we'll come and check it out.'

'And how many complaints is that?'

'We can't tell you. Departmental policy. And don't try calling back ten times a day. We'll know it's you.'

'I would never...'

'Or you can gather some droppings and bring them in. Remember, the bigger the droppings means the bigger the rat that made them and the bigger the problem. So if you really want to prove this is an emergency, you might want to dig around for the biggest ones you can find.'

'Well, I…'

'And we go by weight, not volume, so you might want to weigh them first. Looks can be deceptive.'

'I'm going to lodge a complaint as soon as I hang up the phone. I'm going to call the Office of Complaint right now…'

'Go ahead. They can't fire me, and I can't get demoted any lower than where I'm at right now.'

Rick hangs up the phone when he can't hold back his snickers any more. The new guy is gaping in open amazement, Tamara rolling her eyes in disgust. Claude's big lips want to smile, but he tries to freeze his face. It isn't funny, they all *could* get demoted. There *is* one department worse than theirs—the Office of Complaint. He's seen those guys in the cafeteria, so full of despair they can't even bring themselves to complain about it. They're too low to steal the office supplies. The suicide rate puts a constant strain on personnel. He looks at the plastic-bagged dead rat on his desk. It's ten inches long, not including tail, with long yellow teeth and toes the colour of human skin, and a surly, hateful expression in its gummy eyes. He needs to label the bag and send it over to the lab for testing, but he's forgotten what it needed to be tested for. He thinks keeping it on his desk might help him remember.

'You know she's going to call back. And when she does I'm going to give her hell. That was nothing.'

'You should give the new guy a try,' Tamara says. 'You're supposed to be training him.'

'Nuh-unh.' The new guy shakes his head vigorously. 'It's way more funnier when he does it.'

'M Street,' Tamara repeats, and glances over at Claude.

Claude moves the rat aside and takes a list out of his desk drawer. He adds a tick mark to the tally next to an address. There are already several bundles of ticks marked off. A few more and they'll have to go out there and make a show of doing something.

The final call comes a few days later, just as they had settled into their chairs for the long night shift, with their mugs of tea or coffee or cabbage soup. Claude, unable to decide, had all three on his blotter, their odours clouding the air above his desk.

Again, a complaint about a building infested with vermin. There have been complaints upon complaints. Marching in and out of the place in broad daylight, bold as brass. The neighbours fear it will spread. They'll have to go in, right away, and clear the place out.

'Right now?' says the new guy.

'Element of surprise,' says Rick.

'I know that place,' Tamara says. 'By the reservoir. It's a dump. It ought to be wiped off the face of the earth.'

'I never noticed it,' says Claude.

'Well, you wouldn't, would you?' Tamara says. 'You don't notice anything.'

They put on their gear, Claude helping the new guy with the clamps and snaps because he still can't do anything for himself, and Rick helping Tamara ball up her frizzy hair and stuff it down her collar, though she shrugs off his hands as soon as he's done, and they load the tanks of chemicals into the van and Claude gets Alice out of her kennel. A messenger from headquarters bikes over with a master key. Rick drives and Tamara sits up front with the map shouting the directions at him. Claude and the new guy sit in the back, keeping the tanks upright, their breath fogging up the plastic panels in their hoods.

Alice straddles Claude's left foot and leans her head between his knees, panting asthmatically. Both of her eyes are more or less on the same side of her snout, though only one works. Her lips droop off her jaws like fraying hems, baring black gums and occasional teeth like old hardened pieces of chewing gum. Her nose has an inside-out aspect, pink and peeled and raw, and she always wheezes. Claude wonders if working around the chemicals for all these years has made her face the way it is.

They keep turning around and doubling back, unable to find the street that leads to the place, the new guy swaying and pantomiming carsickness in the windowless van, until eventually they discover there is no street, only a dirt track that leads between dumpsters behind a complex of dark brown apartment buildings, over a rise and down into a depression of mulchy earth that drags at the tyres of the van and carries in the tang of sewage and feet and armpits when they slide back the doors.

'Aaaaah,' the new guy breathes deeply, his hood sucking up against his nostrils.

'How do people live like this?' Tamara mutters.

The building's a big rectangular block, eight or ten storeys tall. Claude is used to sizing up buildings but can't say how many, exactly; it has sagged and warped, like Alice's face, and the windows appear to have slid and settled in unaccustomed places. It's made of brick, brown brick that shines wet and soft like slabs of clay. Black soot-stains frame the windows and long trails of rust hang from the vents poking from the walls. There are weird structural bits—struts, girders—poking out that seem naked and vulnerable—you know you're not supposed to be seeing them—like bones working their way through the skin.

'Who's that?' says the new guy.

'Where?' says Claude.

'Nothing,' he says, waving off into the darkness. 'Thought I saw someone.'

Claude sees it too, a flash of light-coloured shirt bobbing in the distance.

'It's a free country,' Tamara says. 'People can walk around.'

A jaunty veranda sticks out in front over the entrance. A waist-high chain-link fence encloses a patch of dirt and playground equipment before the doors. Rick steps over the fence, nearly snagging the crotch of his jumpsuit, and begins searching the front of the building.

'It's around the back,' Tamara says, her hood rolled up level with her nose and smoke dribbling from her mouth. She'd spotted the alarm box as soon as they drove up, but had held off mentioning it so she could get through this one cigarette. It's not like there's a big rush. These people and their rats aren't going anywhere.

Rick's the one with the key that opens the box. He stomps around to the back, his booties flapping around his ankles. A moment later, a feeble jangling begins. There's no way that's going to get them out, Claude thinks, but almost immediately yellow squares of light blink on in the facade above them, here, there, then all of them, and Claude can hear the familiar thump and bumble and murmur and blurt of people waking in a panic. Alice heaves her big wheezing head forward, her throat clicking like a latch, and he wraps another loop of her leash around his wrist.

A shadow darkens the door, and then it swings open and out steps an elderly woman with her hair full of curling pins and her arms full of houseplants. She stops short when she sees them, then takes in their uniforms and ID badges and with an offended air shuffles past them and settles herself on the nearest bench.

First they come out in ones and twos and threes, then in clumps, some running, jerky, panic-stricken, hair in wild tufts. Some come walking, with bags and arms full of papers and trinkets and favourite clothes. An immensely pregnant woman toddles out with a half-eaten hard-boiled egg in one hand and a jar of relish in the other. Others clutch scraps of truncated activity—books, television remotes, beer cans, video-game consoles, a torn foil square, a condom wrapper halfway breached, which a man holds delicately on his palm as if it's his last one. Claude glances round but can't tell for whom it's intended.

Some come out half dressed, others fully dressed, and most have thought to put on their shoes. But there is one woman in nothing but a thin nightgown that clings to her nipples. Everyone is looking at her. She keeps raising her hands distractedly to her hair, bunching it up on the top of her head and then letting it fall, self-consciously unselfconscious, making no effort to cover herself.

'She's not wearing any underwear,' chants the smaller of the two boys in matching flannel pyjamas. It's the same thing Claude is thinking, but he starts to tell the boy to hush. Then he thinks it isn't his place; it's a parent's job to tell him to hush, so he waits, but no parent speaks and the words hang in the air, echoing themselves: she's not *wear*ing any *under*wear.

'Bet you noticed *that*, didn't you,' Tamara mutters in his ear. 'Slut. Guess she just *forgot* to get dressed before running outside in the freezing cold.'

They watch as a woman in an overcoat and slippers approaches with an afghan blanket in her arms. At first she heads towards her nightgowned neighbour, the blanket proffered, but then she abruptly changes course and veers towards the two boys, who now stand staring up at the building as if waiting for it to burst into flames. The elder holds the upper arm of the younger in a way that appears gentle, but as if he might dig in his fingernails at any moment. The smaller is tensed, as if waiting for a signal. The woman hesitates, then drapes the blanket around both of their shoulders. 'There,' she says, 'now you're nice and warm.'

She waits, but the boys do not thank her or even look at her. Again Claude feels the urge to say something and quashes it. Where are their parents? They have to be somewhere in the pen, milling about. The woman in the overcoat sighs and turns away. As soon as she does the boys shrug off the blanket, leaving it in the dirt, and go to stand next to a dented metal pony on a spring. Neither mount it; they put their hands on the worn metal, as if it is a holy relic, and continue to watch the building.

Rick goes through the place first, unlocking all the apartment doors with the master key. You'd think people fleeing in a hurry would leave them open, but no, most people have taken the time to lock their doors, as if there were something precious inside. They divvy up the apartments by floors and split up, dragging hoses and nets and wheeling the tanks behind them.

The first few apartments Claude inspects have the air of people who haven't budged in years. He knows by the first whiff: floral dusting powder, doilies, family pictures, old furniture stained by decades of heads and elbows, a bowl of fruit arranged just so in the centre of the kitchen table, but when you look closer there are ants crawling on it. Glasses of water on bedside tables, some with teeth in them, cabinets stuffed with yellowing papers and bits of this and that. People have an instinctive tendency to arrange their homes exactly the same way—Claude can walk into any kitchen and know where the pots are, or the drawer full of coupons and dried-out ballpoint pens and Scotch tape and kitchen detritus. He can walk into any bedroom and find the secret stash of softening candy bars, the dirty magazine.

In one apartment he finds the rubber-banded wad of cash right where he thought it would be. He wants to take just a few bills and put the rest back, but his rubber gloves stick to the rubber band and he can't get it off so he pockets the whole thing.

There are no signs of vermin—no droppings, no gnawed electrical cords, no holes, no smell. Not a one. It doesn't surprise him. He knew, as soon as he saw the kind of people who came streaming out the doors, that the complaints were not really about vermin.

Most of the places are full of clutter and dust and old things, yet at the same time they have an air of impermanence, as if they have been moved from another place, a more spacious place, and arranged here in a hasty unsuccessful attempt to recreate it. A certain sparseness to the clutter, like a flea market at the end of the day when the good things are gone and everything left has been fingered and shaken and put back down willy-nilly.

He sifts through an apartment that contains a jungle of houseplants and an elephantine upright piano covered in carvings of scrolls and bulbous grapes and pineapples, with massive Roman columns supporting the keyboard and iron lamps mounted on either side of the music rack, which holds thick exercise books and a pointer like a radio antenna. The wooden bench before it is worn and faded in the shape of two sets of buttocks, and there's a dark stain running from the centre of one set to the front edge, as if a nervous player, or many, had given vent to their nervousness.

There is a constant fleeting movement in the corner of his vision that is making him uneasy. Not rats—he knows a rat's stutter and dash. This is more cat-like (a parrot? A ferret? Who knows what these people keep as pets), or something else entirely. He checks the valve on the tank and makes sure it's tightly closed. The chemicals can do funny things to your head. Rick and Tamara have gotten him to huff it a few times, on slow nights, but always in a controlled environment: the office, with the doors locked, the phones unplugged, and all papers and stray bagged rats hidden in drawers. The first breath makes colour seep into the room from the floor upwards, and then vibrations run through the air in warm bursts, like a subway train passing somewhere, and Tamara sits on Rick's lap, or his, her tense back gone bendy and her thighs heavy and cushiony against his (like bags of wet cement, he remembers thinking once, as if this were a beautiful thing), and he runs a finger along her cool eyelids, top and bottom, as if to soothe away the wrinkles there, and all is forgiven. They haven't done it for a long time now.

Up on the top floor of the building he checks an apartment that might belong to the two boys he noticed outside. There are boy-toys scattered about in unlikely places—army men in the refrigerator, Lego under the bookshelves. There's a bedroom with small twin beds, a blanket tent, a burnt-out night light shaped like a stubby rocket. An algae-scummed fish tank next to the TV.

The fridge door is covered with alphabet magnets spelling out POO and DAM and BUUGER, and a painting of a brown creature with claws and fangs, with a dotted line connecting its chest to a gun held by a small smiling boy-figure with glasses. And there is one photo, down at small child's eye level, of, yes, those two boys both wedged on to a woman's lap. Her plaid skirt has ridden up so you can see a knee and a bit of thigh. There is no fat on that knee; it is not bony but not lardy either. Claude holds the picture close and still can't see her face clearly, but he can see that she has long hair.

He hears a steady low murmur of noise and pushes open the closed door to the second bedroom, half expecting to find the woman lying in bed, her knee displayed invitingly. She's not, but there are plenty of woman-leavings. A cloying, hairspray-and-perfume odour clouds the air above a big, sloppy, pink-sheeted bed, and a vanity table, and a bureau crowded with bottles and hair-clogged brushes. Brown hair? Red? Somehow it is hard to tell. A small pink television sits on a slender ice-cream-shop chair talking buzzily to itself. Scarves and strings of beads hang around the vanity mirror; glossy women's magazines lie on and under the bedclothes. There is a red heart-shaped cardboard box full of crumpled papers beside the bed. He slides his fingers in among the papers and gropes around until he feels something solid. He works his hand under his hood and slips the thing into his mouth. He feels the smooth chalkiness of stale chocolate. When he bites, a limp cherry slides down his throat like a dead guppy. He thinks of the murky tank in the living room. But he reaches into the box for another.

He looks at his feet, kicks at the clothes on the floor. He picks up a bra. It is delicate and lacy, with none of that nasty padding; it's pale pink, and rosette-trimmed, and enormous. He presses it under his hood and sniffs. It smells like dusty carpet. He drops it and picks up another, this one silky and black and trimmed with red ribbons. On this one, the cups are distinctly smaller than the first. He picks up a third—he isn't sure what it is, at first, because it has a front closure and looks strange splayed out on the floor like a snare waiting for an unsuspecting foot—and this one is floral-patterned and the largest of them all. How many women live here?

He wonders if there is a husband, a man of the house. There are no signs of one in this pink, cloying room with ridiculously high-heeled shoes littering the carpet and windowsills, and the open box of tampons by the bed (By the bed? Don't women keep those things in the bathroom?).

He goes into the bathroom and finds face powder spilled in the sink, filmy stockings hanging in the shower to dry. He puts out his hand to let the stuff slither over his glove, and he notices the stockings are the kind you see in magazines, separate legs that require straps and snaps and a garter belt. He checks the medicine cabinet for razors, men's deodorant, anything smacking of maleness, and finds nothing. The drains are clogged with long sodden hairs. Something swells in his chest, an anxious, buoyant sort of hopefulness.

He stands in the living room, raring to go, longing to stay. The pink room beckons him. There's something off about it all, theatrical, sweet edging towards rancid—the room of someone who wants to be, and is no longer, or possibly never was, a quintessential teenage girl. He'll take just one thing, a memento, a bra, panties, to puzzle over later, at home. He dashes into the bedroom, snatches something off the floor and hustles out, his tank banging behind him.

The thing in his hand is soft and spongy. In the elevator he looks down and sees that it is a boy's athletic sock, thick and white with three green stripes. He sniffs it. The boys are young enough to still have that sweaty-puppy smell that he knows from his nephews, rather than a teenager's sour funk. He puts it in his inner pocket with the wad of money.

Downstairs he finds the other three (and Alice) inspecting every inch of the lobby with unusual diligence. He brushes past them, pushes through the front doors and eagerly pulls off his hood to breathe the night air. Outside the residents are standing in resigned clusters, or pacing in circles, or draped half asleep over the playground equipment. But the minute they take in his expression, and his empty collection bag, their faces change. He can see it happen, the accusatory tightening of eyes and lips rippling through the crowd. His own face feels clammy and numb, a moist slab. He looks for the two boys and sees the smaller brother shiver dramatically and the older one put an arm around his shoulders. Nearby adults cluck in a maternal chorus. There's a general pressing forward of bodies. Claude backs up a step and waits for the others. He'll let Tamara or Rick handle this. Maybe Rick's big mouth can keep the residents at bay, at least long enough for them to get back to the van. □

SOUTHBANK CENTRE

DISCUSS THE BURNING ISSUES OF THE LONDON BOOK FAIR, JUDGE THE ORANGE PRIZE FOR FICTION AND BE THE FIRST TO HEAR PAT BARKER'S NEW NOVEL.

MONDAY 16 APRIL
Tracy Chevalier

William Blake:
Still Burning Bright

William Blake is at the heart of Tracy Chevalier's exhilarating new novel, *Burning Bright*. 18th-century London is brought to life with flames, funerals, circus feats and seductions, and all the drama and detail for which Chevalier is so acclaimed. Tracy reads from the book and discusses her work with John Mullan.

Purcell Room, 7.45pm

London Book Fair at Southbank Centre

TUESDAY 17 APRIL
Margaret Atwood, Andrew O'Hagan, Stephen Page and Erica Wagner

Digitise or Die: What is the Future of the Author?

What is the future of the book, its author and readers, in the age of new technology?

Queen Elizabeth Hall, 7.30pm

London Book Fair at Southbank Centre

MONDAY 4 JUNE
From Jane Austen to Catherine Tate: The Rise of Female Comic Writing

Unpick the funny bone of women's writing with a panel of top women writers. How does it differ from men's writing? Is it funnier, gentler or crueller?

Purcell Room, 7.45pm

Orange Prize for Fiction at Southbank Centre

TUESDAY 5 JUNE
Orange Prize Readings 2007

Hear the writers shortlisted for this year's Orange Prize. Introduced by Muriel Gray, Chair of the judges, the authors read from their books, answer questions and sign copies of their work. On the eve of the award, hear the books being judged and judge for yourself.

Purcell Room, 7.45pm

Orange Prize for Fiction at Southbank Centre

MONDAY 2 JULY
Pat Barker

One of our most daring writers, Pat Barker launches her new novel, *Life Class*, with a reading and discussion in her only London show. *Life Class* is a breathtaking return to the subject for which she is best known: World War One. Pat Barker won the Booker Prize for *The Ghost Road*, the first part of the bestselling *Regeneration* trilogy.

Purcell Room, 7.45pm

NOW BOOKING
Ticket Office: 0871 663 2500
www.southbankcentre.co.uk

Pictures from left to right: Tracy Chevalier; Margaret Atwood; Andrew O'Hagan; Erica Wagner; Muriel Gray; Pat Barker.

GRANTA

THAT FIRST TIME
Christopher Coake

Christopher Coake is the author of a short story collection 'We're in Trouble' (Penguin/Harcourt). The stories previously appeared in journals such as 'Five Points', 'Epoch', 'Gettysburg Review' and 'The Southern Review'. In 2006 he was awarded the Robert Bingham Fellowship for best debut fiction from PEN American Center, and is currently at work on a novel set in turn-of-the-last-century Colorado. Coake, a native of Indiana, lives in Reno, where he teaches creative writing at the University of Nevada. (He does not gamble.) He lives with his wife, Stephanie Lauer, and together they care for two very needy dogs. When the above photo was taken, he was suffering from flu. 'That First Time' is a new story.

Bob Kline was sitting at his computer, reading and then deleting a number of old letters from his soon-to-be ex-wife Yvonne, when he received an email from a sender he didn't know. Its subject line contained a name—Annabeth Cole—he didn't recognize either. The email read:

> Is this the Bobby Kline who went to Westover High in 1988? If so, I'm sorry to tell you that Annabeth Cole died several months ago. She wanted you to know. If you have any questions, call me. Sorry to bring bad news.

At the bottom of the message was a number and a name: Vicky Jeffords.

Bob stared at the email for a long time, not understanding it at all, eyes still damp and blurred from the hour he'd spent reading Yvonne's old love letters. In the early days of their marriage her job had kept her travelling, and she'd sent him dozens of them, each one impossibly sweet. *I'm just looking out over the ocean and missing you.* He tried now to pull his thoughts together.

Annabeth Cole? He was the Bob Kline this Vicky wanted, but as far as he could remember, he'd never gone to school with an Annabeth. He dug for a while in his closet, pulled out his yearbook. He didn't see an Annabeth—or a Vicky, for that matter.

He went to the kitchen of his apartment and opened a can of beer. Then he punched the number from the email into his cell phone. A woman answered after two rings.

This is Bob Kline, he said. You emailed me—?

Bobby! she said. This is Vicky. Thanks for calling.

Her voice was completely unfamiliar.

Sure, he said. Listen—I'm the guy you want, but I have to say I'm a little confused. I don't remember going to school with an Annabeth.

Annabeth *Cole*, Vicky said.

Help me out. How did I know her? Did I know *you*?

After a few seconds of silence, she said, Not as well as you knew Annabeth. You slept with her once. If that narrows it down any.

I did?

She and I went to East Oaks. She met you at a—

And then Bob knew. *Annie?* he said. Holy shit.

He sat down hard on the couch and put a hand over his eyes. Annie. It had been what—eighteen years? He'd forgotten her last name. And if she'd ever told him her full name was Annabeth, he'd forgotten that too. A picture of her came into his mind: a small, slender girl, long sandy-coloured hair, glasses. He'd only known her a week, if that. They *had* slept together, just once, when he was seventeen.

She's dead? he asked. How?

Cancer. Non-Hodgkin's lymphoma.

Vicky told him the story while he stared at the beer can on his knee. She had been Annabeth's—Annie's—best friend since grade school. And Bobby had met Vicky soon after he met Annabeth—did he remember? At the pizza place? He told her he did, but this was mostly a lie. He remembered a girl, sitting across the booth, while he flirted with Annie. A place-holder shape in his memory. Was she tall? Maybe blonde?

Vicky told him she went to stay with Annabeth in Chicago for the month before she'd died. Towards the very end they talked a lot about the old days, and about what to do when Annabeth was gone, and Annabeth had written Bob's name on a list of people who might want to hear the news. Then Vicky tracked him down on the web.

There are a lot of Bob Klines, she said. You're a hard man to find...

Vicky then told him about the service, three months past, but he didn't listen. When she was quiet again he said, Look, I guess I don't remember Annie and I...ending up on the best of terms. Back then.

I don't either, Vicky said.

Was she—was she still angry with me?

It was a stupid question, and he knew it the moment the words were in the air.

Vicky said, Well, you were her first time.

Yeah, he said, rubbing a knot at the base of his skull.

And it was kind of intense. I mean the whole thing. She was pretty messed up, after you dumped her.

Yeah, he said again.

Vicky said, Well. She thought you might remember her. And that you'd want to know.

I do, he said. Thank you. Listen, Vicky—

He could barely believe he was saying this.

I'm not like I was then. I mean, I was seventeen. She was such a sweet girl. If I could do it over—

Hey, Vicky said, we were kids.

He couldn't even picture the outlines of the girl Vicky had been, but he could see her now, on the other end of the phone: a woman with her head in her hand, tired and sad. He wanted to say something else to her, to console her. But while he was thinking of what that might be, she said, I should go. I'm sorry, Bobby.

When she'd hung up Bob went to the patio doors and opened the blinds. He lived in an apartment overlooking downtown Indianapolis, fifteen floors up. The sun was setting, and the city lights were coming on, which was more or less the best thing that happened to him any more. He'd been separated from Yvonne for six months, and hadn't been doing much since but working and then coming home to sit out on the balcony at night, drinking and watching the lights, telling himself he'd done the right thing.

His head was pounding now. He decided the circumstances called for a switch from beer to bourbon. For a little impromptu wake.

Bob picked up a bottle and glass from the kitchen, and took them both outside on to the balcony. A helicopter darted overhead. Next door he could hear a lot of people talking, the sound of music playing—jazz. He had classy neighbours on that side.

He finished the bourbon in his glass and tried to find grief for poor Annie in his swimming head. He couldn't. It was somewhere outside of him, but faint, like the music he could just hear through the walls from next door.

Annie Cole. He'd broken her heart. Not on purpose, but all the same he had. He meant what he'd said to Vicky—she had been a sweet girl, and he'd been stupidly cruel. When he'd thought of her these past eighteen years, it was to wish her a happy life, a good husband, a big yard with kids and dogs. Had she told him she wanted those things? Or had he simply given them to her, in his mind? He couldn't remember.

He lifted his glass, first to the party next door, then to the big glittery mirror-windowed office building across the street, where a few sad souls still worked; in this light he could just see them, ghostlike, through the reflective glass. To Annie, he thought. He wasn't a religious man, but for her sake he hoped there was a heaven, someplace far away from sickness, from people like him.

A week went by. Bob's settlement hearing with Yvonne was coming up in another two. As the day pulled closer he grew more and more impatient, more restless.

He ran his own business, a house-painting company. As he worked that week, balanced carefully on his ladder, he found himself thinking more and more about Annie Cole. He'd been so shocked to hear the news that he'd asked Vicky almost nothing about her. In his head she was still the tiny slip of a girl he'd known for a week in high school; he couldn't picture her as a grown woman, let alone someone pale, bald, suffering. Dying, and then dead.

Then, Bob remembered: he might still have a picture of Annie, packed away in storage. She'd sent one to him, after, and he didn't think he'd ever had the heart to throw it out. When he came home from work that night he unlocked his basement storage cage and dug out the box labelled HIGH SCHOOL. He lugged it upstairs and emptied it on the living-room floor. He set aside his diploma, and a bunch of old report cards, all relentlessly unexceptional. For the first time in years he looked at his senior prom picture, with Yvonne. In her gown she looked fabulous, proud; he looked confused, maybe even a little scared. But then he'd been stoned that night.

Scattered on the bottom of the box were several loose photos. Sure enough Annie's was one of them: a wallet-sized picture, well tattered. In it she leaned against a tree, wearing a baby-blue sweater and a tan skirt. She was smiling shyly, and wasn't wearing her glasses. Her hair fell thick and glossy over her shoulder. On the back of the photo was a girl's handwriting: *To Bobby. I'll never forget. Love, Annie.*

By the time Annie sent him this picture he'd known he'd never speak to her again. He set it down on the carpet, right next to the prom photo. And there they were: the triangle Yvonne had never known about.

Bob had already been in love with Yvonne the summer he and Annie met. That was the whole problem. Yvonne, his first girlfriend, the first person *he'd* slept with. That summer—1988—they'd briefly broken up, while she prepared to leave Indiana for college in Maryland. Bob's folks had just split, and for complicated reasons he had to spend the summer

in his father's house in little East Oak, fifty miles from Westover. There
Bob had a jumbled basement room with its own bathroom and exterior
door. His father was away a lot on business, and Bob was in a town
he didn't know well, and in which he wouldn't stay past summer's end.
Everything, even the ground under his feet, felt impermanent.

He worked part-time in a restaurant, and met a lot of East Oak
kids there. He was a decent-looking guy, and thanks to friends back
in Westover he always had pot, so he found himself, that summer,
strangely popular. He took advantage. In the month after Yvonne
broke things off, he brought three different girls back to his basement
room. Why not? He didn't know then whether what he felt was
freedom or despair. When he was in his room, smoking a joint, or
stripping off the panties of a girl he'd just met, he was able to believe
it was freedom.

He'd met Annie at the East Oak park, while he was waiting with
his friend Lew for their turn at a game of pickup hoops. Annie sat in
the grass next to them with a friend—it must have been Vicky—
watching boys she knew on the other team. Who had talked first? Bob
couldn't remember. But they'd introduced each other, chatted, joked.

He looked down at the picture in his hands. He would have
noticed Annie's hair first. And then—her voice. He remembered it.
Deep, a little husky—like she smoked, even though she didn't,
usually. He remembered her long thin legs, her white tennis shoes.
He and Lew got up to play their game, and when he came back
twenty minutes later Annie had left. But she'd written her number
on a slip of paper and tucked it beneath his keys.

Bob called her that afternoon and a couple of nights later they
met up at the Pizza King downtown. Annie brought Vicky and he
brought Lew. Bob sat next to Annie in the booth. She was wearing
a short skirt, and was laughing and wild and flirty, turning in the
seat to face him and, once, putting her hand on his knee.

Later that night, down in his basement room, he was shocked
when Annie told him it was her first time. Why me? he asked her.
You barely know me.

Annie, curled up beside him on the bed, laughed and blushed and
said, I feel like I do. Like you're right for me.

Bob put down the photo. Against whatever judgement he had left,
he called Yvonne. She didn't answer. He left her a message: A friend

of mine from high school died. It's thrown me for a loop. I'd really like to see you before next week—

He realized what he was saying and quickly hung up. Then, without setting down the phone, he dialled Vicky's number.

While her phone rang he stood out on the balcony, 150 feet above the city streets. Off to the east a thunderhead had massed; lightning flickered down over the suburbs. If it rained tomorrow there'd be no painting; he'd have nothing at all to do. The thought filled him with panic.

Vicky, he said when she answered. It's Bob Kline.

Oh! I thought the number looked familiar.

Is it a bad time? I can let you go.

No. I'm fine, really. How are you?

I don't know, he said. Leaves blew on to his balcony, from some place in the city that had trees. I guess I'm a little curious, he said.

He listened to the long silence.

Is it all right if I ask about her? he said. I don't want to put you in a bad spot—

No! Ask. Please.

Her voice was strange. Was she crying? He couldn't tell.

He said, I forgot to ask whether she was happy. I want to know if she—if she was in a good place.

Yes, Vicky said. Until she got sick, she was very happy.

Was she married?

Yes.

Nice guy?

Yeah. They were good for each other.

Kids?

No. She wanted them. But no.

Bob stood and leaned against the rough concrete wall of the building. Rain was starting to fall through the glow of the patio light, the drops appearing frozen for an eye-blink.

What did she do? he asked.

She was a lawyer.

He laughed.

Is that funny?

I'm in the middle of a divorce, he said. Or at the end, I guess I mean. I make a lot of lawyer jokes.

She was a prosecutor.

Well, I've steered clear of those, he said, taking a sip of his drink. I guess that's all right.

She was quiet on the other end. He said, Hey, I can let you go. I'm just shooting the shit now.

It's all right, Vicky said. I'm—I get a little defensive about her.

Can I ask another question? Do you mind?

Sure.

Was it— He ran a hand through his hair. Did she suffer? Was it bad?

Another long quiet. It was cancer, Vicky said.

You were with her.

Yes. Me and Rick and her folks.

That must have been—

It was hard.

He said the next part quickly, meaning every word of it: I don't know you, or even her, really. But it sounds to me like she was real lucky in her friends.

The line was so empty that he had to check the screen on his phone to make sure he hadn't lost the call.

Thanks, Vicky said. A little burble of sound in the machine next to his ear. It's—it's been rough. I miss her.

Bob wanted to say, I do too—but that would be stupid. Up until a week ago he hadn't missed her at all. But he did, now that he thought about her. He missed the girl touching his knee at the Pizza King. That feeling of invitation.

Listen, he said. You said you live in Indy?

Yeah.

You want a drink? I'm just sitting around here thinking about this. If it'll help—I mean if you want to—I'm glad to meet you someplace.

He hadn't planned on saying that, but once he had, he hoped dearly Vicky would say yes. But why would she? She didn't know a thing about him except that he'd screwed over her friend in the eleventh grade. He paced back and forth and wondered at his own stupidity.

But then Vicky said, Sure. Okay.

It turned out she lived not very far from him, out in the neighbourhoods to the east, right underneath the lightning and the smudge of rain. She gave him the name of a bar halfway between them.

Bob spent a few minutes in the bathroom, taking a quick shower, shaving off two days' worth of stubble, looking with dismay at his jowls, rubbing some gel in his hair. He was thirty-five, but he looked older. He had some grey at his temples. Years working in the sun had done a number on his skin. He was tanned, at least, didn't look unhealthy. Vicky would be remembering the seventeen-year-old he'd been: long, greasy hair, bloodshot eyes, a wispy goatee. Whatever he was now would have to be an improvement. He put on a nice polo shirt and clean blue jeans and black shoes.

Bob squared himself up in the mirror. After the attention, he still looked just like he felt: lonely, a little drunk, probably on his way to making a mistake.

Just before Bob walked into the bar, he realized he'd forgotten to ask what Vicky looked like. She hadn't asked him, either.

But it was a Tuesday night and the bar wasn't busy. After his eyes adjusted to the light he spotted Vicky right away, sitting at a small table against the outer wall. She was the only woman in the place who looked as though someone close to her had just died, her face a white, sad oval in the low, warm light. Whatever he looked like, she spotted him too; she stood the moment he met her eyes, offering a half-wave.

He'd been trying to remember a blonde, but Vicky was a redhead, her hair in a pixie cut, though her face was a little too round for that to work. She'd dressed in a light-green blouse and black slacks. Work clothes, he thought. On the whole she looked nice, but not done up.

Bobby, she said.

Vicky.

Then she smiled at him, crookedly, maybe happy or sad or both at once—and right there, he remembered her, sitting across the table from him at the Pizza King. The smile was the key. While Annie flirted with him, Vicky's smile had gone more and more lopsided, tipping through sadness and into panic; her laughter had gotten louder and louder. The best friend getting left behind.

He held out a hand to her, but Vicky shrugged and gave him an embrace instead, quick and clumsy. When they pulled apart she said, You haven't changed a bit.

I remembered you, he said, but I wasn't sure I'd recognize you.

Vicky laughed a little. Her cheeks were dotted with freckles, and the low neckline of her blouse showed him more. He didn't remember those, but he liked them.

So, you want a drink? she said. First round's on me.

Thanks, he said. Bourbon?

Vicky walked over to the bar and Bob sat at her table. An empty margarita glass stood next to her car keys. Beside her keychain was a small photo album, closed with a clasp. She'd brought pictures of Annie along. Bob wished he had the bourbon in him already.

Vicky came back with their drinks. She sat and sighed, and said, Bobby Kline.

You know, he said, I go by Bob these days.

Oh, right. I don't know if I can do that. You've been Bobby for eighteen years.

Fair enough. You mind if I keep calling Annabeth Annie?

Her eyes flickered up. I guess not.

And you're Vicky.

And Vicky I shall remain.

He liked her. Had he expected not to? He lifted his glass, and she followed suit; they clinked rims. Thanks for this, he said.

Well, you're buying the next one.

I will. But I mean meeting me.

She shrugged, smiled her half smile. I've been spending a lot of time in my head, you know? It's good to be out.

This your bar?

One of them.

It's nice.

She nodded and took a sip of her drink. Oh, Bobby, she said. I don't know if I can do small talk.

She levelled her eyes at him, which were very green.

He said, I guess now that I've got you here, I don't know what to ask.

Vicky said, You can't figure out why she wanted me to call you.

He laughed, surprised—that was it all right. Yeah, he said.

You weren't the only person I called. The only ex-boyfriend.

I'd be real sorry if I was.

Vicky kept her eyes on him. She was very good at that.

He said, I guess for my sake I was kind of hoping I wasn't...still important.

Vicky said, You were the first guy she ever slept with. You never forget your first, right?

Bob remembered Yvonne, in the back seat of his old Impala, grinning, unbuttoning his jeans, guiding his hand underneath her skirt. You better be sure, she'd told him. This is the big time.

He'd felt the warm inside of her thigh with wonder and said, I am absolutely, positively sure.

Yeah, he told Vicky. You never do.

Annabeth was obsessed with you, Vicky said. Right from the start, when she talked to you in the park. She was crushed for months, after you dumped her.

It hurt him to hear, but he had no place to hide from it.

I was an asshole, he said. I admit it.

You were a total fucking prick, is what you were.

He kept his eyes on his drink.

I'm sorry, Vicky. I wish I could have apologized to her.

So why didn't you?

I don't know. I always thought about looking her up, but at a certain point I figured the past is the past, you know?

He was lying. It had never occurred to him to call Annie, or any of the other women he'd slept with that summer, before Yvonne showed up at his doorstep and said she wanted him back. Sure, he'd treated Annie badly, but Yvonne had come back for him, and once that happened, he couldn't turn around and stare for even a second at where he'd been. Or what he'd done.

A furrow was deepening between Vicky's eyebrows.

He said, I don't want to excuse myself, okay? I feel like shit. It's why I called you. I can't stop thinking about how terrible it is that this happened.

You can't, huh.

Do you need to tell me off? he asked. Would that make it better?

No, Vicky said. Her face was clouding. It wouldn't.

Bob wished he hadn't called her, that he hadn't come. He took another drink and turned to look over his shoulder. It had gotten dark, and the rain was coming down hard.

He asked, Did she hate me?

Vicky might have been gearing up to it for a while, but after that question, out of nowhere, she dropped her head and began to cry.

Not noisily; she ducked her head and tears rolled out of her eyes, and she fumbled for a napkin.

After a while she shook her head and said, She wasn't like that.

She had to. At least a little.

Vicky jerked her head up. She wanted you to remember! Is that so fucking hard to figure out? She was dying! She shared something really special with you. Maybe she thought you might still have a heart in there, huh?

Over Vicky's shoulder the bartender was giving them both the eye. Other people were looking, too.

Vicky's voice quavered. She was the one who told *me* not to hate you—

Bob stood up. Vicky had started to sound too much like Yvonne, like every phone call he'd taken from her late at night, when she'd had to accuse him of anything and everything, and he had to agree.

Look, he said. I'm sorry. I didn't mean to upset you. I'll go.

Vicky buried her face in her hands. You don't have to go, she said. I'm sorry.

Annie was a good girl. Better than me. I'll always remember her. Okay?

Vicky didn't say anything, or lift her eyes from behind her fingers. Her shoulders shook. Bob stood at her side for a few seconds, unsure whether to say anything more, or squeeze her shoulder, or what. She still didn't move. Finally he figured he'd done enough damage and he walked out the front door. The heavy rain gave him an excuse to jog the half block to his car, to pile in and drive away as fast as he could.

Inside his parking garage he didn't get out of the car. He couldn't bring himself to go home yet. What had Vicky said? She'd been in her head too much. That was about right—so had he. If he went inside he'd call Yvonne, he knew it. Better to keep both of his hands on the wheel and manoeuvre the downtown streets. He had a little too much drink in him, so he stopped at a drive-through for black coffee and sipped it carefully while he drove.

He'd lied to Vicky. He'd said he'd always remember Annie. But he couldn't remember everything that happened, at least not in the way Annie had always believed. He remembered meeting her, remembered flirting with her. Remembered taking her to his room.

Christopher Coake

But the sex, the actual first time Annie had chosen him for—he couldn't remember any of it.

He remembered pulling a handful of beers for the two of them out of his father's refrigerator. He remembered Annie asking him if he had any pot—she said she'd heard that if you got high before you did it, it wouldn't hurt as much. He told her he did have pot, but that it might hurt anyway. It's okay, she said. I'm ready.

He remembered her body; she undressed in front of him, blushing, smiling through the thick curtain of her hair. Without her clothes she seemed even smaller, her arms and legs too thin, her chest barely bigger than a boy's. He undressed for her, feeling strangely shy.

When he took off his underwear she reached over and curled her hand around his penis, then withdrew her fingers, as though she'd done something she shouldn't have. Even then that just about broke his heart.

They hadn't rushed. But why? He'd been plenty excited. For a long time they sat side by side, naked hips touching. He put on music and they talked and shared a joint and drank the beer. Relaxing. It was hot, even after the sun went down, and they opened a window to let in a breeze.

But all the beer and the pot did its work; he remembered the two of them listening to Pink Floyd for a while, and after that the night went blank.

Then it was morning. He woke with Annie's head tucked against his shoulder, one of her legs flung across him. He nudged her awake. They were both hungover, and he took her to a diner on the interstate for coffee, which he found she'd never tried before. She made a face and joked about how sex was easier, the first time. They both joked about how much trouble she'd be in, for staying out all night without permission. It was worth it, she said. You sure? he asked. I'm sure. He dropped her off down the block from her house. When he got back home he saw the blood on his sheets, and that was really the last thing he remembered: sitting hungover out behind the house, wadding up his sheets into a five-gallon bucket full of bleach and stirring them around with a stick.

Annie called him that night, in tears, to tell him she was grounded for two weeks. She told him she missed him. He told her he missed her too. He was sure he meant it.

And then a week later Yvonne called him, for the first time in a month. He remembered that call with great clarity; he'd been hoping for it all summer, jumping to his feet whenever the phone rang. I can't do this, she told him, crying, while he listened in disbelief. She said, I can't live without you. He told her to come over, and she did. They lay together on his clean sheets, and she said, Bobby, make love to me, and if he thought about Annie Cole, or any of the other girls, it was only to hope he hadn't missed cleaning any trace of them out of the room. Yvonne took off his clothes and he took off hers and they cried together, and made love, and in the early morning he said, I think we ought to get married, as soon as we can. And she said, Of course we should. We're meant for each other. He remembered, and would always remember, kissing her then, his hands cupping her cheeks, while she pressed her entire length against him; afterward she stared into him with her big unblinking eyes.

Annie called again two days later, and that was when he'd begun to hurt her. She'd left a message on the machine: how she wanted to see him, how she was thinking about him all the time, how she was worried because he hadn't called. Yvonne was in the shower when he listened, and he was afraid she'd hear too. He hit the Erase button before the message was over.

Annie left two more messages, her voice growing sadder and sadder. The last time she cried. I can't understand this, she said, over and over. He erased it. He came home two days later and found a letter taped to his door.

No getting around it. He'd been a kid, sure, but an asshole was an asshole. He tore up the letter without opening it. After that he never heard from her again. And if he felt bad, there was Yvonne, talking about their wedding, the kids they'd have, the names they'd give them.

Yvonne used to like to say to him, I feel safe with you.

As Bob drove through the city, he imagined what it would have been like, if he'd chosen differently. If whatever had happened with Annie had made him love her, instead of Yvonne. Annie with her tiny body and her gravelly laugh. Her long silky hair. He imagined the two of them going off to school together. Marrying their sophomore year. Maybe they would have been able to have kids. Maybe they would have had something to talk about, these last five years.

But whatever they would have been, Annie would still have gotten sick and died, and he would have had to watch.

Maybe, he thought, it would be better that way—maybe it was better to love someone who died than it was to fall out of love with someone living.

Here was a first time for Vicky, one he'd never forget: the first time he cheated on Yvonne. This was three years ago. Yvonne was out of town, at her sister's. He'd started a fight just before she got on the plane, and she'd left tight-lipped, furious. He sat at home thinking about what she was saying to her sister until he couldn't stand it any more. He walked to a bar downtown and traded drinks with a woman ten years younger than him, who was only weeks away from going off to grad school. At the end of the night they shared a taxi home. While they were parked at the kerb she said, Why don't you come in? He gave her a look, and she gave it back. She said, It's what you think.

I'm married, he said.

She was twenty-two, blonde, impossible. One of the straps of her dress had fallen off her shoulder. I won't tell, she said. Come on in.

He had. And he remembered damn near everything.

Bob tried and tried to avoid it, but after an hour of driving aimlessly he found himself in Yvonne's neighbourhood, up in Carmel. She lived in a nice apartment complex, behind a gate, and at eight o'clock, after circling her block five times, he gave up and turned the wheel into the entrance. He hadn't seen her in two months. He punched her number into the security box. She answered right away.

It's me, he said.

What do you want?

To talk to you.

I don't think so. Are you drunk?

No, he said. Five minutes, that's all.

Bob—

Five minutes, he said. I don't even have to come in. We can even do it like this, if you want.

She didn't say anything. But after several seconds the gate buzzed open, and he drove slowly through. He parked in one of the Visitor slots, which, for a moment, made him want to cry.

Yvonne answered the door in a little black dress and heels. Immediately he smelled her perfume; it made him want to reach for her. She'd dyed her hair a dark maroon; the last time he saw her it was long, but she'd had it cut short. It showed off her neck. He thought she might have lost a little weight, too. Her mouth was pursed, and she didn't look at him, beyond an initial once-over.

You *are* drunk, she said. You shouldn't be driving.

I'm all right, he said. You look great, by the way.

I'm about to go out.

A guy?

She laughed and crossed her arms. Like I'd tell you?

He figured that meant no; these days she would tell him.

So what do you want? she asked. Four minutes, and I've got to go.

Bob peered at her again, trying to see the girl she'd been, the one he'd taken to prom. He could feel her anger swelling while he did.

I've just been thinking about us, he said. Trying to make sense out of it.

She laughed, without any humour. Join the club.

He said, How did this happen?

You told me you didn't love me any more, is what happened.

He ran a hand through his hair. What if it wasn't true? What if I got it wrong?

Well, it's too late for that now, she said, and glanced theatrically at her watch. That was a favourite line of hers, right up there with *Maybe you should have thought of that before you fucked all those girls.*

I did love you, he said. I know that, and you do too.

And you felt the need to drive over here and tell me?

Can I ask you something?

Two minutes.

Would you have done things differently? If you'd known?

What—if I knew we'd end up like this?

Yes.

She laughed again. Of course I would have, she said. I married you; I didn't think I was taking out a fucking lease. Seriously, Bob. Would *you* have?

I don't know if I could have stopped myself, he said. That's how in love I was.

I'm leaving, she said. Right after you.

Yvonne grabbed her purse off the kitchen table and gestured towards the door. She was still beautiful, still smarter and better than him. And Bob was everything she said he was, believed him to be. It was better for them to be apart. Better for her. He knew that.

But Yvonne was so beautiful—spectacular, really, in her dress and good shoes, smelling of flowers, her new hair shimmering around her neck. He couldn't help it.

Von, are you really going to hate me the rest of your life?

She stared at him.

He said, If I died tomorrow, would you still hate me?

Yvonne pressed her lips together and pointed at the door.

Come on, he said. Next week it's permanent. Answer me.

For a second he saw something else in her eyes, a moment of—of what? Sadness? Remorse? She still didn't answer him.

His next words surprised him. Let me kiss you again, he said. Once more, while I'm still your husband.

Uh-uh. Absolutely not.

I don't remember the last time we kissed, he said.

This was true; it had been bothering him. The last one had probably been nothing but a meaningless kiss goodbye, some morning as they left for work. His closed lips against her turning cheek.

She opened the door for him. Her voice still shaking, she said, Well I do.

Bob drove home quickly, with only one stop, at the liquor store for a bottle of Maker's Mark. There was nothing more to do tonight but get blind drunk, and if that was the case he might as well go down in style.

Inside his apartment he sat on the couch with a drink in one hand and the old pictures—Annie, he and Yvonne at prom—in the other. Both women looking up at the camera, happy, expectant. And him looking dull, stoned. Maybe a little scared. How had that skinny kid in the tux managed to cause so much pain? He looked at Yvonne, eighteen, thrilled to be alive and holding his hands. He turned over Annie's picture and read the inscription again. Why had they trusted him with anything?

His phone buzzed then against his hip; he dug it out. Yvonne, he thought. She'd probably thought up some good lines, or was going to give him the AA speech again.

But instead he saw Vicky's number on the screen. He told himself, Don't answer. Do her a favour and never speak to her again.

But he couldn't help it.

Bobby, she said. Thanks for picking up.

Did you think I wouldn't?

She sighed. I wouldn't blame you. Listen. I'm sorry. I went off on you and I shouldn't have.

Vicky, he said, touched. Come on. It was my fault, too.

This is really hard on me, she said. But I wouldn't want someone calling me on shit I did when I was seventeen, either.

It's okay, he said. My wife does all the time.

He thought he heard her lighting a cigarette. She said, It's just that I feel like I have to honour her, you know? But I'm too unstable to do it right. She wouldn't have wanted me to yell at you.

He swirled the bourbon in his glass and looked at the pictures in front of him. He said, Tell me something I don't know about her. What would she have wanted me to know?

Vicky was quiet for a while. Then she said, She would have wanted you to know she was strong.

She seemed plenty strong to me. Sure of herself.

Yeah, but as an adult. A woman. She'd want you to know she was *tough*. She grew up and put bad guys in jail. She was proud of that.

Another silence, and he knew they were coming to the end of things. After they hung up there'd be no reason for either of them to call again. But he didn't want to hang up. Vicky might be crazy, but he liked her voice on the other end of the phone. He thought again of the freckles on her chest, and wondered what kind of a man that made him.

She surprised him. Hey, Bobby, she said, do you still get high?

What?

That was your rep, she said. You were the Westover guy with the good pot. Annie was all nuts about you, and the first thing I said was, The pot guy?

Jesus, he said, leaning his head back on the couch. Yeah, he said, Sure I do. But I don't exactly have the supply I used to.

Listen, she said. I've got some. You want to come by? If we're going to talk about Annie—let's talk about Annie.

He sat up and looked at the clock. Was she really inviting him over?

Vicky, it's almost midnight.

I know. I don't sleep much. Not these days.

Half an hour later, showered, in a change of clothes and wearing aftershave, Bob knocked at Vicky's door. She lived in a nice new brownstone town house, not two miles from his apartment building. While he waited for her to open the door, he saw a tiger-striped cat watching him from the windowsill, its tail lashing. He tapped a finger against the glass; it fled instantly.

Vicky answered the door. Her eyes were red, a little glassy; she might not have waited for him to light up. Bobby, she said, with her crooked smile. Come on in.

She was dressed in a pyjama top and cut-off shorts, and was barefoot. One of her ankles was ringed with some kind of tribal tattoo. Her thighs were freckled too.

He followed her into the town house. Nice place, he said, even though it was a mess. Her living room was full of books, and every surface was dusty. Through an arched doorway he could see a kitchen counter piled with dishes. The air smelled like incense and weed and maybe some kind of Mediterranean food.

Thanks for calling, he said, trying for some kind of charm.

Thanks for coming, she said. Then she stopped and leaned forward and hugged him, as awkwardly as she had at the bar. She sniffled in his ear. She might be high, but she was still sad, too.

You want a drink? she asked. I've only got wine. Red.

I'll take some, sure.

Wine and bourbon. He might not survive the morning. From the couch, he heard the kitchen faucet come on, water splashing. Music was playing softly from speakers he couldn't see—a woman and an acoustic guitar; he couldn't make out the words. He looked over the walls. Even the spaces that weren't covered by bookshelves had books stacked against them, as high as his chest.

On the end table, next to his elbow, was a photograph in a wooden frame. He turned it to get a better look. It showed Vicky—in college, he guessed—and another woman, standing together in bikinis, on a dock someplace blue and tropical.

He'd stared a few seconds before he recognized the other woman as Annie.

He picked up the photo and peered closely. Annie hadn't remained a skinny little girl. She'd grown up and out—she'd become a knockout, in fact, tanned and curvy. The Vicky next to her—tall, angular, sunburnt across her forehead—seemed to know it, too; she was shrinking into herself, her smile as uncertain as it had been back in East Oak. She knew she was completely outmatched.

This was the picture Vicky kept out for herself to see.

She came back from the kitchen and handed him a generous glassful of wine. That's my favourite picture of her, she said.

She's beautiful.

Yeah. She always was. Vicky took the photo from him and held it against her chest. You want to see more pictures?

Did he? Vicky wanted him to, at least, and he didn't want to disappoint her. Sure, he said.

Vicky disappeared for a few seconds, then returned with the little photo album he'd seen earlier that evening, on the table at the bar.

She sat next to him on the couch and put the album between them, balanced on their knees. He resisted the impulse to put his arm around her shoulders. He hadn't picked up anything from her, that way, since arriving, and he felt a little sheepish. He wished he hadn't put on aftershave, but if she noticed it, she gave no sign.

She opened the album. That's us in elementary school, she said.

Looking at the pictures was the strangest thing he'd done in a long time. He turned the pages and watched Annie slowly age, from a little kid with braces into a tomboy, and from there into the skinny long-haired girl he remembered.

In college Annie suddenly blossomed, and not just her body; there was something in her face that hadn't been there, before. She and Vicky toasted the camera with martini glasses. Was it that she seemed calmer? A sudden intuition told him: there was someone on the other side of the camera she liked.

Then on to adulthood. Annie and Vicky sitting at a New Year's party, wearing hats. A man sat next to Annie, smiling at the camera, his hand over hers. An average-looking guy, thin, with a full beard.

Rick? he said.

That's him.

Only two pictures in the album didn't have Vicky in them. The first was a wedding picture, in black and white: Annie in her gown, caught in a swirl of activity, at the reception probably—she looked to be on a dance floor, surrounded by blurred bodies. Annie was grinning, eyes and teeth shining, her face turning back to look at the camera over her shoulder. Bob thought of the pictures he had of Yvonne, looking like that, and had to pinch the bridge of his nose.

The second picture—the last one—showed Annie sick. She was sitting on a deep couch, looking up at the camera, a blanket on her lap and a mug in her hands. She was wearing a bulky sweatshirt, but her face and her wrists were shockingly thin, and he was sure the hair on her head was a wig. Her skin was as white as paper.

Vicky said, I thought she'd be mad at me for taking that one. I don't even know why I keep it in here.

He didn't know either. He wished, looking at it, that he'd seen only the pictures of Annie happy.

Vicky said, I still think she's beautiful. Even then.

She put a hand over her mouth and began to shiver, staring down at the picture.

Bob closed the album.

It's okay, she said. You can keep looking. But tears were rolling down her cheeks.

He put his arm around her shoulders, and she collapsed—he could feel her tumbling into herself, inside, even as she leaned into him.

It's okay, he said. It's all right.

No, it's not.

You did what you could, he said, hoping it was what she needed.

I didn't.

She groaned, and then said, I loved her, Bobby. I loved her for years, and I never told her. I never told anybody.

She was your best friend, he said. She knew you loved her—

Vicky lifted her head and fixed her wet eyes on him.

That's not what I mean.

He had to turn the words over for a few seconds before he understood.

Oh, he said.

Vicky sat up and reached for a tissue from the end table, her lips trembling. Yeah.

Did she know? I mean, that you were—

That I'm what? A lesbian?

He was the stupidest man on earth. Yeah, he said.

Vicky shook her head. Annabeth knew, but I didn't—I didn't bring it up much.

Bob thought of the wedding picture: Annie twirling, with no groom in sight.

How long did you know? he asked. About Annie.

Vicky shook her head. For ever. When I got jealous of her boyfriends in high school, I figured it was just because she was more popular than me. For sure in college. After I came out.

Vicky sniffled and kneaded the pillow.

That was right when Annabeth met Rick, and after she told me she was in love with him I went to my room and threw up and was in this panic—

She looked off to the side, like she was seeing Annie, there in the corner of the room.

And then she got married, and she was happy, so I tried to keep my distance, and had my own things going on, but then when she got sick, she called me and said Rick needed help—

And you went.

Yeah.

He tried to imagine what she must have gone through. What it would have been like to be close to Yvonne all those years—loving her, but never having it returned, never being able even to say it. Look at tonight. Even now that things were over, he'd been unable to keep his mouth shut when it counted. Vicky had been quiet for twenty years.

Vicky whispered then, I'm jealous of you.

Bob's stomach sank. Don't be, he said. There's nothing to be jealous of.

She was staring at him. Sure there is, she said.

We were kids, he said. We were stoned and drunk. We didn't take home any medals, okay?

Vicky took a breath and held it. He braced himself for her anger.

But she said, Tell me about her.

You know her so much better—

Vicky's cheeks were scarlet.

No, she said. I mean—I mean *during*. When you were...together.

I can't, he said, his mouth dry.

It's the only way I'll ever know, she said. Who else could I ask? Rick?

He thought of Vicky, across the table at the Pizza King, her face just a blur in the background, while Annie touched his knee. He thought of erasing Annie's message, her voice cutting off mid-word.

Please, Vicky said.

So he took a deep breath and told her what he could. Vicky leaned closer. He told her all the details he could remember: Annie touching his knee. Twining her fingers in his as he drove to his apartment. Murmuring while he kissed her. Taking off her clothes.

Was she beautiful? Vicky asked. Like that?

He told her about the way Annie's hair looked, falling across her shoulders. The shape of her body. How, when Annie was naked, she'd asked, Is this all right? The two of them lying back against a pile of pillows, smoking a joint, Annie warm and smiling against his chest.

Vicky took a drink, her fingers white around her glass. She whispered the next question: Tell me what it was like.

Bob wanted to tell her, but he'd reached the limit of his memories.

It was great, he said.

How?

Vicky had closed her eyes, was waiting.

He couldn't remember. He really couldn't. But Vicky needed more. Then the solution came to him.

Carefully, without using her name, he told Vicky instead about Yvonne—about that first time, right after Yvonne came back to him. He told Vicky about a beautiful girl naked beneath the blankets, laughing; about the silky feel of her body; about how she never stopped moving against him, almost like water. About the surprising strength of her kisses. He told her about the sweet taste of her skin and lips. How, when they were done, she took his hand and kissed his palm, right in the centre. How she said, This is special.

Vicky's eyes were still closed. She spoke so softly he could barely hear the words: She really tasted sweet?

He thought of Yvonne's clean wet hair, smelling of apples; of the vanilla gloss she used to put on her lips.

Yeah, he said. She really did.

I knew it, Vicky said, and smiled. I just knew it.   □

GRANTA

PROCREATE, GENERATE

Anthony Doerr

Anthony Doerr was born in Cleveland in 1973 and has lived in Africa, New Zealand and Italy. His father runs a small printing business and his mother is an ecology teacher. Doerr is the author of a collection of short stories, 'The Shell Collector' (Fourth Estate/Scribner), and a novel, 'About Grace' (HarperPerennial/Scribner). He has been awarded the Rome Prize, the Discover Prize, the New York Public Library Young Lions Fiction Award and two O. Henry Prizes. His third book, 'Four Seasons in Rome: On Twins, Insomnia, and the Biggest Funeral in the History of the World', will be published by Scribner in the US in June and by Fourth Estate in the UK in 2008. He lives with his wife and sons in Boise, Idaho. 'Procreate, Generate' is a new story.

Imogene is tiny, all-white. Spun-sugar hair, pale forehead, chalky arms. Imogene the Ice Queen. Imogene the Milk Princess. A black spiderweb is tattooed on her left biceps. She is a resource allocation manager for Cyclops Engineering in Laramie, Wyoming.

Herb is medium-sized, bald, and of no special courage. His smile is a clumsy mosaic of teeth. Veins trail like root formations down his forearms. He teaches molecular phylogeny to undergraduates. He and Imogene live in a single-storey brick and cedar on five acres fifteen miles from town. Sage, most of it is, and skeleton weed, but they have a few cottonwoods in a dry creek bed, and a graveyard of abandoned tyres Herb is trying to clear, and whole bevies of quail that sometimes sprint across the driveway in the early mornings. Imogene has twenty-two birdfeeders, some pole-mounted, some suspended from eaves, platform feeders and globe feeders, coffee-can feeders and feeders that look like little Swiss chalets, and every evening, when she comes home from work, she drags a stepladder from one to the next, toting a bucket of mixed seeds, keeping them full.

In September of 2002, Imogene swallows her last birth-control tablet and she and Herb go out to the driveway so she can crush the empty pill container with the flat edge of the wood axe. This excites Herb: the shards of plastic in the gravel, the taut cords in Imogene's throat. He has been thinking about children all the time lately; he imagines himself coming home from class to find offspring on all the furniture.

Over the next thirty mornings Herb and Imogene have sex twenty times. Each time, afterwards, Imogene tilts her hips towards the ceiling and shuts her eyes and tries to imagine it as Herb described: vast schools of his sperm streaming through her cervix, crossing her uterus, scaling her fallopian tubes. In her imagination their chromosomes stitch themselves together with the smallest imaginable sound: two teeth in a zipper locking.

Then: sun at the windows. Herb makes toast. A zygote like a tiny question mark drifts into her womb.

Nothing happens. One month, one period. Two months, two periods. After four months, on New Year's Eve, wind hurling sleet across the driveway, Herb cries a bit.

'I'm just getting the pill out of my system,' Imogene says. 'This stuff doesn't happen overnight.'

Then it's 2003. Imogene begins to notice pregnant women everywhere. They clamber out of minivans at the Loaf 'n Jug; they hunker in Wal-Mart aisles holding tiny pyjamas to the light. A pregnant repairwoman services the office copier; a pregnant client spills orange juice in the conference room. What defects does Imogene have that these women do not?

She reads on the internet that it takes couples, on average, one year to get pregnant. So. No problem. Plenty of time. She is only thirty-three years old, after all. Thirty-four in March.

At Herb's prompting, Imogene begins sticking a thermometer in her mouth every morning when she wakes up. He plots her temperatures on a sheet of graph paper. We want, he tells her, to time the ovulation spike. Each time they have sex, he draws a little X on their chart.

Three more months, three more periods. Four more months, four more periods. Herb assaults Imogene's peaking temperature with platoons of Xs. She lies in the bed with her toes pointed to the ceiling and Herb rummages around on top of her and grunts and the spermatozoa paddle forth.

And nothing happens. Imogene cramps, finds blood, whispers into the phone, 'I'm a fucking Swiss timepiece.'

The university lets out. The Brewer's blackbirds return. The lark sparrows return. Imogene plods through the backyard filling her feeders. Not so long ago, she thinks, I'd be stoned in public for this. Herb would divorce me. Our crops would be razed. Shamans would stick garlic cloves into my reproductive tracts.

In August, the biology department administrator, Barb Swanson, gives birth to a girl. Herb and Imogene bring carnations to the hospital. The infant is shrivelled and squinty and miraculous-looking. She wears a cotton hat. Her skull is crimped and oblong.

Herb says, 'We're *so* excited for you, Barb.'

And he is excited, Imogene can see it; he bounces on his toes; he grins; he asks Barb a series of questions about the umbilical cord.

Imogene stands in the doorway and asks herself if she is generous enough to be excited for Barb, too. Nurses barge past. Drops of dried blood are spattered on the linoleum beside the hospital bed; they look like tiny brown saw-blades. A nurse unwraps the infant and its tiny diaphragm rises and falls beneath the thin basket of its ribs and its tiny body seems to Imogene like the distillation of a dozen generations, Barb's mother's mother's mother, an entire pedigree stripped into a single flame and stowed still-burning inside the blue tributaries of veins pulsing beneath its skin.

She thinks: Why not me?

Wyoming tilts away from the sun. Goodbye, wood ducks. Goodbye, house wrens. Goodbye to the little yellow warbler who landed on the window feeder yesterday and winked at Imogene before continuing on. The abandoned tyres freeze into the earth. The birds make their brutal migrations.

'What about you two?' Herb's brother asks. This is Thanksgiving, in Minnesota. Herb's mother cocks her head, suddenly interested. Herb's nephews clack their silverware against the table like drummers. 'You guys thinking about kids?'

Herb looks at Imogene. 'Sure. You never know.'

Imogene's bite of pumpkin pie turns to cement in her mouth. Herb's sister-in-law says, 'Well, don't wait too long. You don't want to be rolling to flute recitals in a wheelchair.'

There are other moments. Herb's two-year-old nephew climbs uninvited into Imogene's lap and hands her a book called *Big Fish, Little Fish*. 'Biiig!' he says, turning the pages. 'Biiiig fish!' He squirms against her chest; his scalp smells like a deep, cold lake in summer.

A day later Herb tugs Imogene's sleeve in the airport and points: there are twins by some newspaper machines with tow heads and overalls. Maybe three years old. They are jumping on the tips of their toes and singing about a tiny spider getting washed out of a waterspout, and when they are done they clap and grin and sprint in circles around their mother.

When Imogene was twenty-one, her parents were killed simultaneously when their Buick LeSabre skidded off Route 506 a mile from home and flipped into a ditch. There was no ice on the road surface and no coming traffic and her father's Buick was in good repair. The police called it an accident. For two weeks Imogene and Herb stood in a variety of living rooms holding Triscuits on little plates and then Imogene graduated from college and promptly moved to Morocco.

She lived three years in a one-room apartment in Rabat with no refrigerator and one window. She could not wear shorts or skirts and could not go outside with her hair wet. Some days she spent the whole day in her kitchen, reading novels. Her letters from that time were several pages long and Herb would read them again and again, leaning over the dashboard of his truck:

> There are two kinds of pigeons here. There are the thick-looking ones, rock pigeons, the ones we see back home. They moan on the roof at night. But there are also these other pigeons with white patches on their necks. They're big birds and gather in huge wheels and float above the rooftops, dark and gleaming, turning up there like big mobiles made of metal. Some mornings crows dive-bomb them and the pigeons will start shrieking and from my bed it sounds like little airborne children shouting for help.

She never mentioned her parents. Once she wrote: *No one here wears seat belts.* Another time: *I hope you're keeping bags of salt in the back of the truck.* That was as close as she came. Eventually she attached herself to a Peace Corps initiative and began working with blind women.

More than once in those years Herb stopped outside Destinations Travel in downtown Laramie and watched the four-foot plastic Earth turn in the window but could not bring himself to buy an aeroplane ticket. They had been dating only four months before her parents died. And she had not invited him.

He wrote his mundane replies: a hike to a lake, a new cereal he liked. *Love, Herb*, he'd conclude, feeling resolute and silly at the same time. He worried he wrote too much. He worried he did not write enough.

In 2004, after sixteen months of failing to get pregnant, Imogene tells her gynaecologist. He says workups can be scheduled. Endocrinologists can be contacted. Urologists can be contacted. They have plenty of options.

'It's not time,' he says, 'to despair.'

'Not time to despair,' Imogene tells Herb.

'I'm not despairing,' he says.

They have Aids tests. They have hepatitis tests. Two days later Herb masturbates into an eight-ounce specimen cup and drives sixty-six miles east on I-80 to a urologist in Cheyenne with the cup in a little Christmas bag meant for office gifts because he and Imogene have run out of brown-paper bags. The bag rides on the bench seat beside him, little Santas grinning all over it. His sample barely covers the bottom. He wonders: Do some men fill the whole cup?

The same afternoon Imogene leaves work early to have her insides scraped out with a speculum. She has radio-opaque dye injected through her cervix into her uterus and all the way up her fallopian tubes. Then she is wheeled into an X-ray room where a nurse with peanut-butter breath and Snoopy earrings drapes a lead apron over Imogene's chest and asks her to remain completely motionless. The nurse steps away; Imogene hears the machine come to life, hears the high whine of electrons piling up. She closes her eyes, tries not to move. The light pours into her.

The phone rings six days later. The doctors have discussed the *situation*. Dual-factor infertility. Imogene gets three words: polycystic ovary syndrome. Herb gets two words: severe deficits. In motility, in density, in something else. Only three per cent of his sperm are rated viable.

Herb's face appears to crumple. He sets his half-eaten wedge of cantaloupe on the counter and goes into the bathroom and shuts the door. Imogene finds herself staring into the space between the countertop and the refrigerator. There is dust down there and a single Cheerio. A groan comes from the bathroom. Then a flush. With one hand Imogene gently probes her abdomen with her fingers.

All morning she sits at her computer and drowns in memory. A bus climbs through layers of cold air, mountains the colour of cardboard, a phosphorous sky. Gazelles in a courtyard pick through rubbish. Sheepdogs doze on village rooftops.

'No parents, no husband, no children,' a blind woman once told her. Her gaze was a vacuum. Imogene did not know where to look. 'I am a tribe of one.'

Her computer screen swims. She rests her forehead on the desk.

'Are you mad? Are you mad at me, Imogene?' Herb cannot help himself: the refrain becomes almost visible, a whirl of haze, like fan blades turning in front of his face.

'I'm not mad,' she says. Their failures, she decides, were inevitable from the start. Pre-written. Genetic. Their inadequacies, their timidities, their differences from everybody else. She had always been confused, always living far from town, always reading, always saying no to junior high dance invitations. Imogene the Ice Queen. Imogene the Pipedream. Too petite, too pale, too pretty. Too easily scorched.

'Everything is fine,' she tells Herb during dinner, during *Jeopardy*. Ten years of trying *not* to get pregnant and now it turns out they never could.

Herb develops his own theory: it's the tyres out in the yard. A whole graveyard of them, seventeen metals, sixteen types of hydrocarbons, sixty-one organic compounds, and they've gotten into the well water, the shower, the pasta, and now the poisons are *inside their bodies*. Fungus, cancer, bad luck incorporated.

More tests. Imogene has a laparoscopy during which a doctor punctures her ovaries a dozen times with an electrosurgical needle. Herb masturbates into another cup, makes another hour-and-a-half drive to Cheyenne, drops his pants in front of another urologist.

Wait another six days. Get another phone call. Confirmed diagnosis. Polycystic ovary syndrome. Severe deficits. Imogene blinks. She had been thinking she could quit her job. She had been thinking she could start cooking Moroccan food, Tunisian food: an infant strapped to her chest, pots steaming atop the range. Maybe raise some hens. Instead she starts a regimen of glucophage and gets diarrhoea for a week.

This is not real suffering, she tells herself. This is only a matter of reprogramming her picture of the future. Of understanding that the line of descendancy is not continuous but arbitrary. That in every genealogy someone will always be last: last leaf on the family tree, last stone in the family plot. Hasn't she learned this before?

After school Herb walks out into the big pasture behind the house and works on the tyres. They lie so deep in places, so much dust and snow blown into them, that as he hacks out one, or the pieces of it, he inevitably finds another beneath. Sometimes he wonders if there are tyres all the way down to the centre of the world. He chops them into pieces with a maul, shovels the pieces into his truck. It's cold and there is only the wind in the grass, and the ice clinking softly in the cottonwoods. After a couple of hours, he straightens, looks at the house, small from there, a matchbox beneath the sky. The tiny figure of Imogene trudges through the sage, filling her feeders, dragging a five-gallon bucket with one arm, stepladder with the other, her legs lost in the haze.

They agree to visit a fertility clinic. It is eighty minutes away in good weather. Parked nearest the entrance is a Mercedes with the licence plate: BBYMKR.

The doctor sits behind a glass-topped desk and draws upside down. He draws a uterus, fallopian tubes, two ovaries. He draws instruments going in and harvesting eggs. On the wall is a framed poster of a giant vagina and its inner workings. Beside it, a framed photo of three chubby daughters leaning against a Honda.

'Okay,' Herb is saying. 'All right.'

Does Imogene have any questions? Imogene has no questions. She has a thousand questions.

'You draw upside down really well,' she says, and tries a laugh.

The doctor gives a quarter-smile.

'Practice,' he says.

The finance lady is nice, smells like cigarettes. They can get loans. Interest rates are swell. Her daughter did three 'cycles'. She points to photos.

The procedure, including medications, embryo lab and anaesthesiologist, will cost $13,000. On the drive home acronyms twist through their brains: IUI, ICSI, FSH, HCG, IVF. A herd of antelope stands in the scraps of snow just off the interstate, their shadows crisp and stark on the slope behind them, their eyes flat and black. They flash past: there, then gone. Herb reaches for Imogene's hand. The sky is huge and depthless.

They sign up. A box of drugs arrives. Herb unpacks it into the cabinet in their bathroom. Imogene can't look. Herb can hardly look. There are four different Ziplocs of syringes. Vials and pill bottles. Video cassettes. Two sharps containers. Four hundred alcohol wipes. Fourteen hundred dollars of synthetic hormones.

Imogene's protocol starts with, of all things, oral contraceptives. To regulate her cycle, the booklet says. She pours a glass of milk and studies the little pink tablet.

Dusk falls across the range. Herb grades quizzes at the kitchen table. The clouds deepen, darken. Imogene walks out into the yard with her stepladder and seed bucket and the pill dissolving in her gut, and the silence extends and the sky dims and the birdfeeders seem miles apart and it is a feeling like dying.

Each time she hears a syringe tear away from its wrapper, Imogene feels slightly sick. Seventeen days of an ovarian stimulator called Lupron. Nine days of follicle-stimulating hormones. Then two weeks of progesterone to prepare her uterus for pregnancy. Then vaginal suppositories. If she gets pregnant, eight more weeks of shots. Sometimes a little dot of blood follows the needle out and Herb covers it with an alcohol wipe and holds it there and closes his eyes.

After the shots, he lays out her pills, five of them. She eats toast spread with apple sauce before work and swallows the capsules on her way out the door.

'Tell me you love me, Imogene,' Herb calls from the kitchen, and in the garage, the car window up, Imogene may or may not hear. The Corolla starts. The garage door rolls up, rolls down. Her tyres hiss in the cinders. The prairie shifts under its carpet of ice.

Springtime. Imogene's ovaries inflate on schedule. They become water balloons, dandelion heads, swollen peonies. The doctor measures her follicles on an ultrasound monitor: her interior is a blizzard of pixels. Nine millimetres. Thirteen millimetres. The doctor wants them to grow to sixteen, to twenty. They root for numbers: thirty eggs, twenty embryos. Three blastocysts. One foetus.

Halfway through April, Ed Collins, the regional manager at Cyclops, calls Imogene into his office and chides her for taking off too many afternoons.

'How many doctor's appointments can a person have?' He fingers buttons on his polo shirt.

'I know. I'm sorry.'

'Are you sick?'

She looks at her shoes. 'No. I'm not sick.'

The more oestrogen that floods Imogene's body, the prettier she gets. Her lips are almost crimson, her hair is a big opalescent crown. Down both arms Herb can see the purple spiderwork of her veins.

Hormones whirl through her cells. She sweats; she freezes. She limps around in sweatpants with her ovaries stuffed full of follicles and her follicles stuffed with ova. 'It's like having two full bladders,' she says. Before potholes she has to slow the Corolla to a crawl.

Herb rides beside her with his scrotum throbbing between his thighs, traitorous, too warm. He has eighty-three protein structure papers to grade on his desk. He is fairly sure he will have to charge this month's house payment on his credit card. He tells himself: Other people have it worse. Other people, like Harper Ousby, the women's basketball coach, get their ribs sawed open and the valves of their hearts replaced with parts from the hearts of animals.

Clouds pile up at the horizon, plum-coloured and full of shoulders.

On May Day Herb masturbates into another cup and drives Imogene and his sample to the fertility clinic and the doctor goes into Imogene's ovaries, aspirating her follicular fluid with what looks like a stainless-steel hydra: a dozen or so segmented steel snakes at one end and a vacuum at the other. Herb sits in the waiting room and listens for its hiss but hears only the whirr and click of the heat register, and the receptionists' radio: Rod Stewart.

After an hour they call him back. Imogene is shivering on a chair in the RN's office. Her lips are grey and slow and she asks him several times if she threw up. He says he's not sure but doesn't think so.

'I remember throwing up,' she says. She sips Gatorade from a paper cup. He puts a pad in her panties and unties her gown and pulls her sweatpants up over her legs. Strange to think there is less of her now: she has been separated from a couple dozen of her ova.

For three days they want the eggs to grow, one cell cleaving into two, two into four. The delicacy of mitosis: a snow crystal settling on a branch, the single beat of a moth's wings.

'I was in Africa,' Imogene says. 'There were all these vultures in the sky.'

Two days later a nurse calls to tell them only six eggs have successfully fertilized, but two have become viable eight-cell embryos. Again they drive to Cheyenne. The doctor installs both embryos inside Imogene with a syringe and a long tube like a half-cooked spaghetti noodle. The whole process takes thirty seconds.

She rides back to Laramie lying across the bench seat, the sky racing past the windshield. At the doctor's instructions, she lies in bed for three days, eating yoghurt, turning her hip to Herb every twelve hours for her injections. Then she returns to work, bruised, still full, an invisible puncture wound in each ovary. She finds herself walking very carefully. She finds herself thinking: *Twins?* A week later Herb drives her back to the clinic for a blood test.

The results are negative. Implantation did not occur. No pregnancy. No baby.

Things between Herb and Imogene go quiet. Invoices arrive in the mail, one after another. For extra income Herb teaches a summer section of general biology. But he is continually losing his train of thought in the middle of lectures. One afternoon, halfway through a chalk drawing of basic protein synthesis, maybe twenty-five seconds go by during which all he can imagine are doctors scrabbling between Imogene's legs, dragging golfball-sized eggs from her ovaries.

There are snickers. He drops the chalk. A tall sophomore in the front, a scholarship swimmer named Misty Friday, is wearing camouflage shorts and a shirt with about a hundred laces in front of her breasts, like something a knight might wear under his armour. Her calves are impossibly long.

'Professor Ross?'

She chews the ends of the laces on her shirt. Herb's vision skews. The floor seems to be making slow revolutions beneath him. The ceiling tiles inch lower. He dismisses class.

Imogene and Herb buy their groceries, eat their dinners, watch their shows. One evening she crouches at the edge of the driveway and watches a mantis dribble eggs on to a stalk of weed, pushing out a seemingly endless stream of them, tapioca pearls in an amber goo. Three minutes later a squadron of ants has carried off the whole load in their tiny jaws. What, she wonders, happened to those two embryos? Did they slip out of her and get lost in the bedsheets? Did they fall out at work, go tumbling down her pant leg and get lost in that awful beige carpet?

Herb tries her in June, and again on the fourth of July: 'Do you think we could try another cycle?'

Needles. Telephone calls. Failure. 'Not yet,' she mutters. 'Not right now.'

They lie awake beside each other, speechless, and look for patterns in the ceiling plaster. Ten years of marriage and hadn't they imagined children by now? A foetus curled in an ocean of amnion, a daughter standing at the back door with mud on her sneakers and a baby bird in her palm? Seventy-five trillion cells in their bodies and they can't get two of them together.

Here is another problem: the clichés. There are too many clichés in this, armies of them. Imogene's least favourites are the most obvious and usually come from the mothers at work: You're not getting any younger. Or: I envy your freedom—you can do whatever you *want*!

Equally bad is the moment at the biology department summer picnic when Goss, the new hire in plant sciences, announces that his wife is pregnant. 'My boys can *swim*,' he declares, and pushes his glasses higher on his nose and claps Herb on the shoulder.

There is the cliché when Imogene tells Herb (Saturday night, Sunday night) that she's fine, that she doesn't need to talk about it; when Herb overhears a student in the hall call him a 'pretty ballsy professor'; when Imogene passes by two receptionists at lunch and hears one say, 'I can't even *walk* past Jeff without getting pregnant.'

Stretch marks, baby formula, stroller brands; if you're listening for something, it's all you'll hear.

'Tell me anything, Imogene,' Herb says. 'But please don't tell me you're fine.'

She keeps her attention on the ceiling. Her name hangs in the space between them. She does not answer.

The chapter about human reproduction in the textbook on Herb's desk is called 'The Miracle of Life'. Imogene looks up *miracle: An event that appears to be contrary to the laws of nature.* She looks up *fine: Made up of tiny particles.* Or: *Very thin, sharp, or delicate.*

Herb calls his brother in Minnesota. His brother tries to understand but has problems of his own: lay-offs, a sick kid.

'At least you must be having lots of fun trying,' he says. 'Right?'

Herb makes a joke, hangs up. A room away, Imogene rests her head against the refrigerator. Outside the wind is flying down from the mountains, and there haven't been headlights on the road all night, and all Imogene can hear is the whirring of the dishwasher, and her husband's low sobbing, and the hot wind tearing through the sage.

Laramie: a film of dust on the windshield, a ballet of cars turning in acres of parking lot, Home Depot, Office Depot, the Dollar Store, sun filtering through distant smoke, battered men scratching lottery tickets on a bus-stop bench. Two brisk ladies in long dresses hold salads in plastic boxes. An aeroplane whines past. Everything deadeningly normal. How much longer can she live here?

They fight. He says she is detached. He says she is not good at dealing with grief. In her eyes leaves blow back and forth. Detached, Imogene thinks, and remembers a time-lapse video she saw once of a starfish detaching from a dock post and roaming the sea floor on its thousand tiny feet.

She retreats to the garage and runs her hands through her buckets of seeds.

He chops tyres until little stars burst behind his eyes. In a parallel world, he thinks, I'm a father of nine. In a parallel world I'm waiting beneath an umbrella for my children to come out of the rain.

The summer session winds down. The swimmer in the front row, Misty Friday, wants to conference about her take-home exam. Her tank top is sheeny and her shoulders are freckled and her hair is baled up in golden elastics. The classroom empties. Herb takes a seat in the desk beside Misty's and she leans across the gap and they put their heads over a paragraph she has written about eukaryotes. Soon the building is empty. A lawnmower drones outside. Houseflies buzz against the windows. Misty smells like skin lotion and chlorine. Herb is looking at the perfect, fat loops of her cursive, feeling as if he is about to fall forward into the page, when he calls her—by accident—sweetheart.

She blinks twice. Licks her lips, maybe. Hard to tell.

He stumbles: 'All cells have what, Misty? Cell membrane, cytoplasm and genetic material, right? In yeast, mice, people, it doesn't matter...'

Misty smiles, taps the tip of her pen against the desk, gazes down the aisle.

The mountains turn brown. Range fires ring the sun with smoke. Imogene finds herself unable to summon the energy to drive home from work. She cannot even summon the will to get up from her desk. Screensaver fish swim across the computer monitor and the daylight fades to dimness and then to black and still Imogene sits in her plastic chair and feels the weight of the building settling all around her.

A person can get up and leave her life. The world is that big. You can take a $4,000 inheritance and walk into an airport and before your heartache catches up with you, you can be in the middle of a desert city listening to dogs bark and no one for 3,000 miles will know your name.

Nothingness is the permanent thing. Nothingness is the rule. Life is the exception.

It is almost midnight when she drives the dark road home, and in the garage she leans against the steering wheel before going in and feels shame draw up her torso and leach through her armpits.

It should be straightforward, she thinks. Either I can have babies or I can't have babies. And then I move on. But nothing is straightforward.

In August Herb gets an email:

> From: misty45@hotmail.com
> Subject: Neurons
> so if like you were saying the other day in class neurons are what make us feel everything we feel and each receptor works the same pumping those ions back and forth why do some things hurt and some things sort of prickle and some things feel cold?? what makes some things feel good professor ross and why if nerve fibres are what make us feel can I feel so MUCH without the receptor being stimulated at all professor ross without any part of me ever being touched at all??

Herb reads it again. Then again. It's Wednesday morning and his piece of toast, slathered with strawberry jam, remains halfway to his mouth. He imagines replies: *It's complicated, Misty,* or, *See, there are photoreceptors, mechanoreceptors, chemoreceptors and thermoreceptors,* or *Let's talk further,* or, *Friday, 4 p.m., my car, don't*

85

worry because I CAN'T GET YOU PREGNANT, but then he imagines he *could* get her pregnant, that all he'd have to do is want to, a few words here, a smile there, her twenty-year-old ovaries practically foaming with eggs anyway, so healthy, so ripe, ova almost half the age of Imogene's, basically outfitted with tractor beams, even his dying sperm, that feeble three per cent, could make it in there. He thinks of Misty's ankles, Misty's throat; a twenty year old with glitter on her eyelids and a name like a weather forecast.

From the kitchen comes the sound of Imogene's chair being pushed back. Herb deletes the message, sits red-faced in front of the screen.

Six months after Imogene returned from Morocco, they got married. He drove her to Montana for a honeymoon and led her up a trail beneath a string of ski lift towers, a drizzle coming down on her bare arms and the dry grass swishing around her knees, and the procession of lift towers running off beneath them standing silently under the rain. He'd brought a bottle of wine; he'd brought chicken salad.

'You know,' he told her, 'I think we'll be married for ever.'

Now it's 2004 and they've been married almost eleven years. He submits the summer session's final grades to the registrar and takes a corner stool at Cole's and drinks a pitcher of sweet, dark beer.

Then he drives to the Corbett Pool. A few folks in shortsleeves sit in the bleachers beneath a forty-foot mural of a cowboy. Misty Friday is easy to spot: taller than the rest of the women, sleek in a navy one-piece trimmed with white. Her bathing cap is gold. Herb sweats in his khakis. The swimmer in Misty's lane makes the turn, starts back. Misty climbs on to a starting platform, lowers her goggles. Everywhere voices echo: off the ceiling, off the churning water. *C'mon, Tammy! Go, Becky.* It feels to Herb as though he is pumping through the interior of a living cell, mitochondria careering around, charged ions bouncing off membranes, everything arranging and rearranging.

And yet everything is motionless. Misty's knees bend; her arms rise. She leaps. The chlorine in the air touches the very back of Herb's throat.

He hurries back to his truck. He tells himself it's just biology, the chemical fist of desire, his spine quaking in it like a sapling. The truth. The questions. No transgression if there is no action. Right? Misty was right to wonder how people can make other people feel without touching one another.

He starts the truck towards home. The sun sinks behind Medicine Bow to the west and sends up streamers of gold and silver.

'You never know,' Herb's mother once told him, the skin beneath her eyes streaked with mascara, 'all the things that go into making a marriage last. You never know what goes on behind closed doors.'

When Herb walks inside, Imogene is sitting at the kitchen table with tears on her cheeks. In the fading light her hair is as white as ever, almost translucent.

'Okay,' she says. 'I'll do it. I want to try one more time.'

It's early October before the clinic can schedule them in again. This time they know the nurses' names, the schedule, the dosages; this time the language is not so impenetrable. The box of drugs is smaller; they already have specimen cups, alcohol wipes, syringes. Imogene pulls down the waistband of her pyjamas; Herb drives in the first needle.

At Cyclops Engineering, receptionists string fake spiderwebs across the ceilings. Goss, the plant sciences professor, comes by Herb's office with twelve-inch subs: turkey, tomatoes, vinegar. He talks about his wife's pregnancy, how she vomits in the kitchen sink, how his unborn daughter is the size of an avocado by now.

'Isn't it crazy,' he says, 'that every student in this school, every person in town, every single human who has ever lived, existed because of two people fucking?'

Herb smiles. They eat. 'Be fruitful and multiply!' shouts Goss, and shreds of lettuce gather on Herb's desk.

Subcutaneous. Intramuscular. Herb unscrews the used needles, drops them in the sharps container. He lines up Imogene's rosary of pills. Out in the yard a few finches swoop between feeders like ghosts.

At work Imogene tells Ed Collins, the regional manager, why she will need to miss more afternoons. She lifts the hem of her shirt and shows him the spectrum of injection bruises above her panty line like slow purple fireworks.

'I've seen worse,' he says, but both know this isn't true. Ed has two daughters and a waterslide in his backyard and gets hopelessly drunk playing putt-putt golf every Friday night.

Fifteen miles away, at the kitchen table, Herb cashes in his 401K.

Again Imogene's ovaries swell. Again the season begins to turn: leaves blowing across the field of old tyres, the sky seamed with a vast, corrugated backbone of cloud.

'So our two frogs make Baby Tadpole,' Herb tells his Thursday lab, 'and Baby Tadpole will turn out like his parents but not *exactly* like them: reproduction is not replication.'

After class he erases Baby Tadpole, then the arrows of descendancy, parent frog A, parent frog B. The body has one obligation, he thinks: *procreate.* How many male *Homo sapiens* are right now climbing atop their brides and groaning beneath the weight of the species?

Tomorrow, the doctor will go into Imogene and retrieve her eggs. Herb drives home, cooks chicken breasts. The roof moans in the wind.

'Do you think they'll let me wear socks this time?'

'We'll bring some.'

'Do you think all my hair will fall out?'

'Why would it do that?'

Imogene cries then. He leans across the table and tries to hold her hand.

It starts to snow. It snows so much it seems the clouds will never empty of it and in the morning they make the long drive in a white-out and do not talk for any of it, not a single word. Trucks are overturned every few miles. The snow is hypnotic and blowing in sheets through the headlights and it looks as if the interstate has ignited into ten-foot-tall white flames. Herb leans forward, squinting hard. Imogene cradles his sperm sample between her thighs. The heads of her ovaries sway heavily inside her. Something in the way the snow swirls and checks up and swirls again reminds her of the way she'd pray for snowy days as a girl, how she'd go through an Our Father and enunciate every word and she wonders how she can be a thirty-five-year-old orphan when just yesterday she was a nine year old in moon boots.

When Herb finally pulls into the clinic, they've been in the truck three hours. He has to prise his fingers off the wheel.

The anaesthesiologist wears all black and is extremely short. They are late so everything goes very quickly.

'I'm just going to give you some candy now,' he tells Imogene through his mask, and drives the pentathol in.

Herb tries to grade lab reports in the waiting room. Slush melts in dark pools on the carpet. No matter what, he tells himself, no matter how bad things seem to be going, someone always has it worse. There are cancer patients out there incandescing with pain, and toddlers starving to death, and someone somewhere is deciding to load a pistol and use it. You ran a marathon? Good for you. Ever hear of an ultra-marathon? It might be cold where you live but it's colder in Big Piney.

After a while he gets called back in. He kneels beside Imogene in the RN's office, refilling her cup of Gatorade, watching the lights in her eyes come back on. Fifty feet away, for the second time this year, an embryologist rinses Imogene's eggs and weakens the zona pellucida and injects one good sperm into each one.

A nurse comes into the office, says, 'You two are so cute together.'

'We don't have it so bad,' Imogene hears Herb say, as he half walks, half carries her through the slush to the car. 'We don't have it bad at all.'

The sky has broken and the sun fuses the entire parking lot with light. In the truck she dozes, and dreams, and wakes up thirsty.

The telephone rings. Twenty fertilized eggs. Fourteen embryos. An entire brood. Imogene smiles in the doorway, says, 'I'm the old woman in the shoe.'

Two days later, three embryos have divided into eight cells and look strong enough to transfer. The snow melts on the roof; the whole house comes alive with dripping water.

If there's a sadness in this, Herb thinks, it's about the embryos that don't even make it three days, the ones that get discarded, lumpy and fragmented and full of cytoplasm, rated unviable. Nucleated cells, wrapped in coronas like little suns. Little sons. Little daughters. Herb and Imogene, father and mother, the DNA already unzipped, paired and zipped back up, proficiencies at piano playing and field hockey and public speaking predetermined. Pale eyes, veiny limbs, noses shaped like Herb's. But not good enough. Not *viable*.

Herb and Imogene and the birds at the feeders and Goss the plant sciences professor and Misty Friday the swimmer—all of them were once invisible, too small to see. Motes in a sunbeam. A cross-section of a single hair. Smaller. Thousands of times smaller.

'The stars,' a science teacher once told Herb, 'are up there during the day, too.' And understanding that changed Herb's life.

'Even if we get pregnant this time,' Imogene says, 'you think we'll stop worrying? You think we'll have more peace? Then we'll want to find out if the baby's got Down's syndrome. We'll want to know why it's crying, why it won't eat, why it won't sleep.'

'I'd never worry,' Herb says. 'I'd never forget.' They drive the sixty-six miles back to Cheyenne. The doctor gives them photos of their three good embryos: grey blobs on glossy paper.

'All three?' he asks, and Imogene looks at Herb.

Herb says, 'It's your uterus.'

'All three,' Imogene says.

The doctor pulls on gloves, gets out the half-cooked spaghetti noodle. He implants the embryos. Herb carries Imogene to the truck. The interstate skims past, cinders chattering in the wheel wells. He carries her up to the bedroom. Her feet bump the lampshade. Her hair spreads across the pillow like silk. She is not supposed to get up for three days. She is supposed to imagine little seeds attaching, rootlets creeping through her walls.

In the morning, at the university, Herb hands out midterm exams. His students hunch in their rows of desks, snow on their boots, anxieties fluttering in their chests.

'All you have to do,' he tells them, navigating the rows, 'is show me you understand the concepts.'

They look at him with open eyes, with faces like oceans.

Fifteen miles away, Imogene rolls over in bed. Inside her uterus three infinitesimal embryos drift and catch, drift and catch. In ten days, a blood test will tell if any of them have attached.

Ten more days. There is only the quiet of the house. The birds. The tyres in the field. She studies her palms, their rivers and valleys. A memory: Imogene, maybe six years old, had broken her front teeth on the banister. Her father was looking for pieces of tooth in the hall rug. Her mother's bracelets were cold against Imogene's cheek.

The telephone starts to ring. Out the bedroom window a pair of slate-coloured juncos flap and flutter at a feeder.

'Tell me it's going to be okay,' Herb whispers, the receiver of his office phone clamped to his ear. 'Tell me you love me.'

Imogene starts to tremble. She shuts her eyes and says she does. □

GRANTA

ROOM AFTER ROOM
Jonathan Safran Foer

Jonathan Safran Foer is the author of the novels 'Everything is Illuminated' and 'Extremely Loud & Incredibly Close' (Hamish Hamilton/Houghton Mifflin). His fiction has won numerous awards, including the Guardian First Book Award, the National Jewish Book Award, the William Saroyan International Prize for Writing and the Victoria & Albert Museum Illustration Award. In an online poll, 'Everything is Illuminated' was recently voted 'Best Work of Jewish Fiction of the Decade'. Born in Washington, DC, Foer now lives in Brooklyn with his wife, son and dog—the order of whose mentioning is random. 'Room after Room' is a new story.

She can see her breath in the room of her future.
If it were any warmer, the Polaroids that paper the walls would develop.

She moves her thumb over one of the pictures, like doing a rubbing of a grave. The warmth brings out the brown eyes of a child. They're her eyes, but how could she be a child in her own future? She rubs to reveal more—tiny blue hands—and the cold sends the eyes back into the chemicals.

The doctor told her to sleep. Instead she revisits thoughts from her childhood, as if the thoughts had never before occurred to her. The thoughts are so opaque, so veiled by chemicals, that she can't seem to have them for the second time.

She's rubbing. She's looking into the eyes of the child again. She can hear her mother telling her to dress more warmly, lest she catch a cold in her future, or worse.

Her heart is kept in a room with a very expensive security system.
When she told the combination to her doctor, he couldn't believe how mundane it was.

'Anyone who knows you could guess that,' he said, making notes on her chart.

She told him, 'It's only obvious once you've heard it.'

And besides, that's just the first level of access. There's the floor one can't touch, the matrix of lasers, the dogs that haven't been fed in days. When her eyes are red and splintered, even she fails the retinal scan.

Her doctor runs his thumbnail through the grooves in the wall.
Voices fill his skull. He can hear a childhood friend daring him to touch a hot burner, to lick a frozen pipe, a patient begging him not to let him suffer. He's ashamed of the feeling of power. He hears a dog whimpering, apples knocking against each other, a key entering a lock.

Now his wife's voice fills his head. She's young, a girl, it's long before they met. She's whispering to herself. How can he recognize a voice he's never heard?

His thumbnail traces the groove until it crosses a man's laughter. Her father's?

His nail slips back into her whisper.

Into the groove of a grown man wailing.

Into a sigh.

And then the grooves merge, for no longer than an inch, and come level to the wall: silence.

He's surrounded by the sounds of his life pressed into wax. It has to be dark. Lights would heat the walls and laughter and wailing would melt. Whispers would hang from threads of themselves, and then find relief against the floor.

The room of her body is the size and shape of her body.
She spent most of her life not noticing that she was in it. Those were the good times, when she was on assignment, in some country where no one knew her, from which she would report back on mass casualties and her own safety. But there were other times—usually in New York, usually at parties—when there was nothing that wasn't her body. She became claustrophobic in her tight self. She became self-conscious in her loose self. The size and shape of her body didn't correspond to the size and shape of her.

Everything is different now. Now she stands at the threshold of the room of her body, under the doorframe. She's looking at the bed as if through a camera. How many people have died there? The sheets are always being changed, but mattresses have memories. She's looking at her body not quite fit into the impressions left by other bodies, not quite fit into her own body's impression. She never wanted to be a wife or a mother, and is glad she never became either. She is glad she never owned life insurance or even a calendar. But she wishes there were someone who would answer many personal questions with her name.

His conscience is a room with one-way mirrors.
Everywhere he turns he sees himself. And everyone outside can see him. He doesn't know who, if anyone, is looking. But he suspects that she is looking.

He will go home tonight. His children will be playing in a large cardboard box in the living room. His wife will take a jar from the new refrigerator and comment on how cold it is. He will read ten pages of a novel, or watch twenty minutes of a sitcom, or think about his patients.

'Do you remember,' his wife will begin, and he won't even hear the rest.

'Of course,' he will say, angry that she's doing it again. It's always the same, always re-treading, using better times as accusations.

'We should think about going there again,' she'll tell him.

'Absolutely,' he'll tell her, knowing, as she knows, that there's no way they'll ever go there again.

'Your pants are hanging, by the way.'

'The plumber called.'

'Ray's sister is dying.'

'The ivy is out of control.'

'I read something interesting in the paper.'

'The wash needs to be run.'

'A couple of bulbs are out.'

The walls appear black, but aren't, they're white.

The white walls are filled with black writing: the record of everything that's happened to him so far.

His life isn't arranged in any obvious order. Some of his first hour is near the floor, some is near the ceiling. The time he lost his virginity is written around the electrical socket. He unscrews the light bulb from the lamp. The ends of the broken filament seem to want to reconnect. The only things he can find are those he doesn't go looking for.

Running into one of the corners, at eye-level, is a dog in the middle of the street. Written on the wall are the tyres of a car writing their apologies on to the asphalt.

He's a boy, watching the dog trying to lick wounds it can't reach. Its whines press into his memory, like a finger into icing. He steps towards the dog, but the room of his body collapses into rubble. He eats his dinner and goes to bed and in the morning it isn't a new day but the same day.

He's tried to erase the dog from his life. But every eraser crumbles. So he bought some white paint. But the black letters show through, no matter how many layers he brushes over them. He's tried altering words, but the tip of his pencil keeps breaking.

There are rooms she's never entered.

That's because her life is big, and she doesn't have a blueprint. No one knows her life better than she does, but that doesn't mean she knows her life. She's travelled thousands of miles, and gone through miles of film—in Zaire, in Russia, in Bolivia and Malaysia. She's not intervened—she's photographed deaths she might have been able to prevent, or at least expedite—and later used words like 'duty'.

Sometimes she hears noises coming from other rooms: laughter from below the floor, pounding at the other side of the wall, sobbing from above the ceiling, more laughter from a distant room, the ceiling straining: a dark wet spot.

'What are you thinking?' the doctor asks, two fingers on her wrist, his eyes on his watch.

'Sorry?'

'Just curious. I know how you're feeling, but what are you thinking?'

He didn't understand that she was thinking apologetically.

She says, 'You don't know how I'm feeling.'

'No, of course not.'

'I'm sorry. I'm just frustrated.'

'Nothing to be sorry about. Better you take it out on me.'

She photographed a pregnant woman being raped by a gang of rebels. In the next morning's paper, halfway into the first section, was a photo of the woman reaching out to the camera.

There are rooms he's never entered.
That's because he only uses doors. He's never dug a tunnel, or climbed a flue, or pulled a sconce from a wall and squeezed through the hole. He's never opened a window.

'I'm thinking about Jordan,' she says.

'A friend?'

'The country. I was just thinking about how much I liked it. I like thinking about it now even more than I liked being there then.'

'I've never been,' he says. 'Always meant to go.'

'Never too late.'

'Never say never.'

She laughs and asks if he would help her die.

The room of his mid-life is clammy, breadlike and mortar-coloured.

Her eyes are kept in a room papered with gauze soaked in her mother's Darjeeling steeped in her great-grandmother's china.

The room of his past is perpetually re-papered.
He doesn't know why. The paper is never peeling, or faded, or bubbling off. But every time he goes back into the room—the choices that can't be erased or painted over—he finds something different. It's disconcerting, because it's never as he remembers it. So he can never be comfortable in it, or trust it.

'Let's get married,' he tells his wife, thirty years before. They're in the shade of a tree, in the orchard behind her parents' country house. The music pouring from her father's study knocks the apples against one another.

Or, 'Marry me,' she tells him, halfway across a bridge. A glass-bottom boat passes beneath, on which tourists take pictures of the fish. In a few hours, the lake will hold the reflections of stars thousands of years dead.

Or they're in bed, stuck to the sheets, salty and breathing through their mouths. They say it at the same time.

Or neither of them said it. They never had the idea to get married, much less agreed to do so. But they find themselves, thirty years later, married.

A fraction of a millimetre at a time, the wallpaper is beginning to encroach on the room itself. The door won't open all the way any more. The boards on the floor have been lost like sand under the perpetually approaching tide.

'I'm sorry,' he tells his patient. 'It's—'

'I know,' she says. 'I know everything you're about to say. I know. But I thought you might anyway.'

'I'm sorry.'

'You don't have to be. It was unfair to ask.'

'Maybe we're not doing a good enough job of managing your pain.'

She laughs and says, 'Let's talk about something else.'

He pulls the chair up to the bed and they talk about other things, about everything that isn't her pain, which is nothing, because if pain weren't everything it wouldn't be pain, it would be discomfort. The things they talk about are just different filters for her pain, like projecting a movie through an aquarium or a stained-glass window.

He tells her about the underside of his college bunk bed—someone had carved: I'M ASLEEP.

She tells him that for years she used a flea market desk whose drawers were locked shut.

He tells her that, growing up, his family ate under a skylight, but only early breakfasts and late dinners, because the sun made the silverware too hot to touch.

She tells him about the only roll of film she never developed.

He says, 'We moved across the street once, directly across the street. We were carrying boxes, and my father told me, "Moving across the street is harder than moving halfway around the world, because you're expected to do it yourself."'

'Why were you moving across the street?'

'A better house.'

'Bigger.'

'No,' he says, 'virtually identical. My father just wanted to move. The newness hid the sameness. That it was different made it better.'

She turns to the window.

'We have a nice rapport. You and I. Don't we?'

He laughs. 'We do.'

She searches for his wrist and says, 'I can't do this myself.'

How will it end? Will the door one day not budge? Or will the tide pull back? Will it take the beach with it?

She thought the room of her loved ones was riddled with peepholes. But they are nail holes. Pictures used to hang there. She can't remember what those faces look like any more. She tries to conjure them—to rub her memories like Polaroids—but they won't come. And she doesn't rub too vigorously. As it turns out, friends haven't mattered very much in her life. The observation isn't cynical or angry.

'Do you have a will?' she asked him one afternoon, while he checked some monitors. He didn't answer for a few seconds, then looked up.

'What?'

She said, 'It doesn't matter.'

He said, 'When my first child was born we wrote something up. Nothing sentimental, just who gets what. Amazingly boring, actually.'

The wall is brittle, the holes are big. She can see into the room of her physical pain through the hole where a photo of her oldest friend once hung.

'I have a niece,' she said. 'I'm leaving her everything.'

'What's her name?'

'Her name. Oh God, it's slipped my mind. Let me tell you in a few minutes, okay?'

'Okay.'

Light shines through a cluster of holes—a constellation. There was no place on the wall where the picture of her parents looked right.

'Can you tell me a bit about your life?' she asks, turning on to her side.

'What about my life?'

'Whatever you want to tell.'

'Maybe some other time.'

'You've got a million things to do.'

'That, and I don't have anything to tell.'

'Tell. Just tell something. I know you've got to go. Just tell for a second then go.'

'*You're* the one who's been to Jordan. *You* should be telling. You'd make my stories sound so boring. But. What can I tell? I never thought I'd be a doctor. I can tell you that. When I was younger—in college, I mean—I wanted to be a musician. But I didn't want to practice. I guess it wasn't music, itself, that I was interested in, but the, I don't know, I'm saying all of this for the first time now, so it's coming out wrong. Being a musician? You know that distinction I'm talking about? I wanted to be someone who *had done*, rather than someone who *did*. You have all of these notions of things you want to have done. I don't know that I gave enough thought to the doing. Are you okay?'

Another hole—where an unimportant boyfriend's photo once hung—is large enough for her to stick her arm through. She wriggles in her shoulder, and then the top half of her body. She tumbles into her dream life.

His libido is papered with cashmere, and denim, and corduroy and silk. When he was a teenager, they were naked. In his twenties they wore scraps. Then socks and nothing, then crotchless panties, then torn stockings, then lingerie. Then skirts, then dresses. Now layer upon layer.

There was a time when he would rip his wife's shirts to get them off. Now he fingers the buttons. When did he start preferring dressed women to naked ones?

His wife asked him if he was homosexual. The answer was no, and he said no. He knew she wanted him to be furious, but he wouldn't give her that.

'And I'm not having an affair, either, if that's your next question.'

'It wasn't going to be.'

When did he recede into the cardboard boxes of the new appliances? When did he start sleeping in the mattress? Were there always so many surfaces, so many floors, ceilings and walls?

'My next question was going to be, "Why, in your only life, are you married to me?"'

He wants to be intimate with his patient, but he doesn't want to have sex with her. He wants to dress her. He wants to dress all of them: the women, the men, the children, the elderly. He wants to scrape the dogs from the street and bury them in blankets. He scrubs his hands raw before entering a room. He wants to wrap the world in layers.

'I think you've turned a corner,' he tells her. 'I think you're on your way to wellness.'

She's unconscious.

Each of her lungs is kept in its own room, with mirrored walls. The walls steam up with each exhale, and are pulled clear with each inhale.

Her last breath didn't feel like a last breath. If someone had asked her, just then, how many breaths she had left she would have guessed thousands. Or she would have laughed. Or tried to laugh.

Her last conversation with the doctor went like this:

'I'm getting used to the food here.'

'Don't.'

'It looks like a nice day. Go for a walk.'

'No time. Never any time. Maybe if you'd get better and go home…'

'Go out and tell me what it's like.'

'I'll tell you tomorrow what it's like tonight.'

'Ultimately,' she said, the tone falling out from under her words like the floor from a condemned man.

'Ultimately what?'

'Nothing.'

'What?'

She smiled and said, 'I was going to get dramatic.'

He left to check on his other patients.
She exhaled.
There were words written into the vapour on the wall.
She inhaled.

The room of his accident is papered with television screens.
The new patient didn't see the car coming, but now he can see it from
every angle, in slow-motion and real-time, forward and in reverse,
from below and above, up close and far away. He can see beneath his
own skin, his ribs breaking, his kidneys, the cavity of his chest filling
with fluid. He can see the glass in the driver's hair, the ring in the box
in the glove compartment, the music wrapped around the antenna.

And not only the accident. The screens play back everything he
never saw: his expression the first time he made love, what happened
while he slept on his brother's sofa, people reading around the pool
while he held his breath, the other side of the front door of his
childhood home, the stars at noon, the telephone wires at midnight,
letters in unopened envelopes, unwritten letters in pens.

The doctor walks into the room, looks at the chart and smiles.

'Ready to recover?' □

PICADOR congratulates

NELL FREUDENBERGER

One of Granta's Best of Young American Novelists

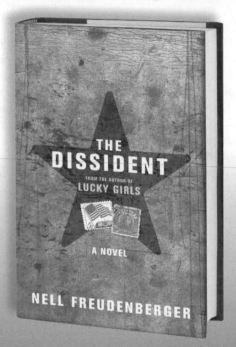

HER NEW NOVEL – OUT NOW

PICADOR presents the very best in American writing for 2007

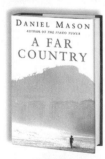

A FAR COUNTRY
Daniel Mason
Out now

EAT THE DOCUMENT
Dana Spiotta
Out now

FALLING MAN
Don DeLillo
April 2007

THE MAN OF MY DREAMS
Curtis Sittenfeld
August 2007

To read extracts visit picador.com PICADOR

GRANTA

WHERE EAST MEETS WEST

Nell Freudenberger

Nell Freudenberger was born in New York in 1975 and currently lives with her husband in Manhattan. Her collection of stories, 'Lucky Girls', and her novel, 'The Dissident', are published by Ecco Press in the US and by Picador in the UK. She has won the PEN/Malamud Award for Short Fiction and a Whiting Writers' Award. She first appeared in this magazine with 'The Tutor' in Granta 82. The story 'Where East Meets West' is meant for her grandmother, Martha Clapp Freudenberger, who died in 2005 at the age of ninety-seven and was a Latin teacher, as well as a passionate collector of silverware and passport stamps.

The Bengali girl has boots today. Not fashionable ones—I know what the fashion is from Serena, my 'keeper'. If there's anyone who doesn't deserve the beautiful name Serena—derived, of course, from the Latin, meaning calm—it's this woman. Serena's boots are pale-blue suede, with a yellow fur lining. I've seen them on the girls when we go to the beauty salon for my hair. A ninety-four-year-old woman at the beauty salon is obscene, as I've told Serena, who says it keeps my spirits up.

Not if you tell me that's the point of it.

Then she laughs: that mindless, placeholding laugh. She must weigh nearly two hundred pounds. If there's anything more foolish than an old woman at the beauty salon, it's a fat girl in blue suede boots.

The Bengali girl makes a detour on the way to the mailbox, meandering across the lawn. George must've taken her out when it first started falling, but this is the first time she's walked in it on her own. She walks gingerly, as if it's ice instead of soft powder, and looks behind her to see the tracks she's made. Doesn't she know that people are watching?

I've known George. I knew his parents, and I knew his first wife, April, and their children, Russell and Jessica. Now April lives in Florida with the children, one of whom is a drug addict. I don't know whether it's the boy or the girl. That's not because I've forgotten, but because it was Edith Overton who told me, and she sometimes has trouble with her memory.

George started baking. He would bring me cookies or bars: lemon, pumpkin and seventh heaven. I gave him the recipe for the chocolate delices, and he made those, too. He must've gained twenty pounds.

'How do you stay so skinny?' he would ask me.

'It's because I'm so old.' It looks awful, especially around my neck, which is rippled like the trunk of one of those equatorial trees. What are they called? This is a type of tree I've seen, but perhaps no one ever told me the name of it. I have an excellent memory for foreign words, even in languages I don't speak. This is a direct consequence of knowing Latin. I ought to ask my new neighbour about the tree; she would certainly know.

'I know I should lose weight, if I want to...'

George has a bad habit of not finishing his sentences. I used to penalize my students for that, and eventually they did stop. The problem seems to have gotten worse in the general population.

George would sit with me so long, I'd get tired.

'You should be out meeting women,' I would tell him. I haven't told Edith Overton I was the one who suggested that. I hope all of this isn't my fault.

First George ordered the Boflex, from cable, and then he ordered the Bengali girl. Not from cable, of course, but from the Internet: Asianladies.com, Where East Meets West. He brought a map next door to show me her country, but I know where Bangladesh is.

My granddaughter Meryl has shown me the Internet. They leave a computer here, Meryl and her father and Helen, because they can't go three days without it. They never stay longer than three days. This time two weeks from today Meryl will be here, without her parents. She's bringing a boy, the first time she's ever done this; they'll be on their way to a friend's wedding in Canada. Helen says she thinks this is 'the one'. I think that if Helen had had Latin, she wouldn't resort to expressions like that.

The boy's name is Sam, and he is a graduate of Harvard Law School. Helen, being Helen, hasn't been able to give me any further details. I notice that Serena uses the words 'farther' and 'further' interchangeably; Helen admonishes me that it's hard to find nice people in Serena's line of work, and that I shouldn't be so critical. I am eager to meet Sam.

I didn't pay attention when Meryl tried to explain the computer. I pretended, because she seemed so excited about it: *You can look up anything you want. That's called surfing. Or you can chat with people in your community of friends. Like a conference line—you know what that is, right? Here, look: this is a picture of Budapest.* It made my hands hurt just to look at the keyboard. Meryl set it up in Frank's office, on his desk, with all the wires coming out of it, blue on one side and black on the other. She moved his typewriter to the corner of the desk, leaving a faint, discoloured square, then glanced at me to see if I minded. I pretended to be examining Budapest. The Chain Bridge looks exactly the same as it did when Frank took my picture there, in my new Burberry raincoat, in 1962.

'Can I...?'

'Move it wherever you want,' I told her. It's a strange thing to dissemble in front of your own granddaughter.

The Bengali girl is still standing by the mailbox. What could have come for her? She's reading it right out there in the cold. I wonder whether she has a boyfriend in Dhaka, whom she'll eventually try to bring over here unbeknownst to George. (I know the name of the Bangladeshi capital, too). That's the kind of thing that would happen to George. It's winter and so I can't tell whether she's pregnant. I'm sure she wants to get pregnant right away, to cement things. George has told me that he wants to have more children.

Because you've done such a beautiful job with the ones you have. But I sit on my hands and don't say anything.

Now the Bengali girl is running—running!—up the driveway, back to the house, clutching the letter in her unmittened brown hand. It's like it's summer, or she's completely forgotten about the snow. If she's not careful, she'll fall, especially in brand new boots. George probably didn't tell her about the black ice we get here: you can't see it at all against the asphalt, until it's too late.

S he knocked so early on Thursday, I thought Serena had forgotten her key. I jumped a little when I saw her, because the garage was dark and so is she, and because I wasn't expecting her.

'Oh Mrs Buell,' she said, 'I'm George's wife, Amina. I'm sorry.'

'I thought you were my nurse.' That's all I could think of to say. 'She forgets her key.'

She stood there a moment, holding a foil-covered plate, until I realized that she had come visiting, like any other neighbour, and was waiting to be asked inside.

'George says he is bringing me over to see you this weekend, but I made some cookies, and I thought: If I wait, they will not be good. I can just leave them?'

George was right. Her English is good—as good as Serena's, if not better. 'Come in,' I told her. 'I'm afraid I can't offer you very much. My helper is going to Wegmans today.'

'I love Wegmans,' the girl said, putting the cookies down on the counter as if she were accustomed to visiting my house. 'They have everything.'

That's true—it's the flagship and it's over 240,000 square feet. There's a whole aisle for exotic fruits, and one for homeopathic medicine; there's a sushi counter and a French patisserie. It shocked me the first time Serena took me there; I can't imagine what it would look like to someone from Bangladesh.

The Bengali girl took off her parka, a red one that George must've bought her, and held it awkwardly in her arms. She wasn't wearing her boots. This was the first time I'd seen her up close and I guess she is pretty. Her eyes are enormous, especially behind the oversized glasses, and her mouth is full. Flaws: she has a low, simian forehead, and a large space between her nose and mouth; her features could be better placed. She does not seem to have combed her hair when she got out of bed this morning. Maybe she was too busy getting George his breakfast.

'You can put your coat over the chair, there. You might as well come into the living room and sit down—unless you have a job to get to?'

'Oh, no,' Amina said, and this got her started. 'I want to work, very much, but I can't drive. And so it has to be somewhere George can drive me. The timing is the most important thing, George says, and so every day I'm calling places. We drove around on Saturday, looking for signs. The Best Buy might be hiring. In Desh I was an English teacher.' She had an animated way of speaking, almost as if she were performing lines in a play. Not that her words seemed false: it was just that they seemed to have a greater intensity than other people's.

'George says you were a teacher too?'

'Latin,' I said, which usually stops people. Either that, or they ask whether I believe that we should continue to teach 'dead' languages in the schools. They ask this very respectfully, with a measure of self-congratulation, the same way that the receptionist at the beauty salon sometimes mentions Frank to me, proud of remembering his name.

'My great-uncle was a professor of Sanskrit in Calcutta!' The girl looked as if we'd just discovered a remarkable coincidence. 'George says that you've travelled all over the world.'

'Not to India,' I said. And then, in case that sounded abrupt: 'I travelled with my husband and our daughter, Helen.'

Amina nodded and looked up at the oil portrait of Papa over the fireplace. 'Is that your husband?'

'That's my father,' I told her. 'A Baptist minister in Corpus Christi, Texas.'

'Your father was handsome,' she said, which is true, but I wondered if she were being polite. Did she find white men handsome? There are several things I'd like to know, such as whether she corresponded with other men before she met George. Did her parents encourage her to learn the Internet to find a foreign husband? Is George the first man she's been to bed with? But I'm not sure I can ask any of these.

'Did you always know you wanted to come to America?'

'I always wanted to travel,' Amina said. 'George says you have a lot of souvenirs of your trips.'

The vitrine was right behind her, but I don't open it to just anyone. Sometimes at night, when I'm trying to fall asleep, I go through it shelf by shelf, trying to remember each object. There are the Dresden figurines, the coin from Sardis and the model of the pyramids in glass. There is the Chinese paper fan, a gift from Frank's parents, who sailed around the world in 1929. In the corner of the bottom left-hand shelf is the picture of Helen in the Ancient Theatre at Ephesus, all alone except for a stray cat at her feet. Frank took the picture, and I was standing just outside of the frame, a little too close. You can see my shadow. 'Look at your father,' I was telling her, but Helen was more interested in the cat. I put it in the vitrine because Frank liked it, even though I usually reserve that space for things of historical value. Lately I have been thinking about how that picture perfectly expresses the American attitude towards the ancient world.

I remember when we had the roll developed. Frank noticed the cat and joked, 'A very cute picture of Helen and Tabby.' (He used to call me Tabby, which I didn't mind, although I prefer Tabitha from everyone else.)

Once, after Frank was diagnosed but before we started seeing the signs of it every day, he called me into his office. He would still put on a shirt and tie every morning, and even I used to sometimes get confused, when he got up from the kitchen table and headed downstairs, instead of out to the garage. He would take the newspaper into the study, and when he was finished reading it, he would mark the mistakes. Then he would put it with the others, to take over to Mr Calthorp, the editor-in-chief, 'when I have time'. Luckily, there was never time.

'Tabby,' he said that afternoon, 'I want to show you something.'

I could see it was a stock certificate. His first investment had been in Gannett—some sort of deal for employees—and after that he'd made a few more, all Rochester companies. This one, it turned out, was from Xerox, and it was for much more money than I expected.

'This is to keep you going, when I'm gone.'

I don't remember what I said to make him yell at me. Probably something to the effect that he would be with us a long time. He wasn't the kind of husband who raised his voice very often, and so I was surprised. Not that it was always a picnic, as Helen is apt to remind me now.

'Listen, Tabby, goddamnit! While I'm—clear on it. You have to pay attention—it's Bank of America, not Rochester Savings and Loan. It's a separate account.'

He was only seventy-three then, not so old at all. I had been right there when Dr Pashman had given us the diagnosis, but Frank wasn't forgetting anything big or shocking then. It was still things like, where did we keep the paper clips, or, was it milk or sandwich bread that I needed from the store? It happened suddenly, as the doctor said it would, the way that these November afternoons turn into nights, without any kind of evening in between. You look up and the light is gone.

Where did we keep the car, he would ask; was he correct in thinking it might be upstairs, in the guest bathroom? He asked these questions formally to cover the embarrassment, which lingered long after other things had gone—a strange and useless relic—and I answered them the same way, to preserve the equilibrium between us. I believe it's in the garage, but I would be grateful if you would open the back door and check.

Ah, the garage—of course. And then a day or two later: could I tell him, by any chance, the name of the charming child in the picture in the vitrine, the one who is sitting on a large, circular flight of steps, trying to touch the kitty by her feet?

'Tabby!' Serena shouted. Serena *is* the type of person who raises her voice. She shouts my name every time she enters the house.

'I'm right here,' I said. 'In the living room.'

When Serena saw Amina, she said, 'Oh, excuse me. I didn't realize you were entertaining.' She said this in the tone you might use with two little girls having a tea party. I wished George's child bride had managed to iron her blouse before coming over. I don't care what Serena thinks, of course, but now that we spend so much time together, I can't escape hearing her opinions.

I saw Amina out the front door. 'Thank you for the cookies. I don't have much of an appetite any more, but my nurse is crazy for sweets—I'm sure she'll enjoy them.' I heard an exasperated sound from the kitchen, and was glad.

'George wants to come see you on Sunday,' Amina said. 'Maybe after church?'

There are many people in this community who visit me, some I've known for a long time. I can tell the difference between duty and genuine enthusiasm, however, and George's wife reminded me that the latter is in scarce supply.

'Yes,' I said. 'Please tell George I'll be at home.' Of course, I'm almost always at home, but the Bengali girl doesn't have to know that. I wonder if she might think I'm younger than I am.

After Amina left, I went into the kitchen, where Serena was reading an article about George Clooney in *People*. That and *US Weekly* are her favourites. I've seen George Clooney on David Letterman and he seems smart, or at least smarter than most of them. It's the magazines that are so stupid.

'That's George's new wife,' I told her. 'George from next door, not George Clooney.'

Serena ignored me, probably because of my remark about the cookies.

'He got her from the Internet.'

That caught her attention. She looked up warily: 'What do you mean, from the Internet?'

'Asianladies: Where East Meets West,' I said, with as much authority as I could manage.

'What is she?' Serena asked, forgetting her magazine. That's the kind of question that you couldn't ask in front of my granddaughter, but I knew what Serena meant.

'She's Bangladeshi. Bangladesh borders east India, and the population is primarily Muslim. After Indian independence, it was called East Pakistan, but in the early Seventies, it became its own country.' Serena didn't go to college, although she holds a certificate in Home Care. I try to give her some sort of general education when I can.

'Our neighbours are Indians,' Serena said. 'They moved in last April.'

'When Frank and I moved here, this part of Rochester was only white.' That's another thing I certainly couldn't say in front of Meryl, or even Helen. Meryl teaches at a public school in New York, and Helen tells me that most of the students there are black or Hispanic. Meryl won't even say that: she uses all the new hyphenated language, and otherwise pretends that she doesn't notice anyone's colour. Once I told her that there had been two Negro students in the first class I ever taught—Latin I, at Springfield Tech in Springfield, Missouri— and she looked so horrified that I thought she was having some kind of physical attack, menstrual cramps perhaps. I didn't realize what I'd done until Helen told me. Sometimes I wonder how we went from segregation in America—which I never supported, no matter what my granddaughter says—to pretending there's no such thing as race. It's like we've all caught Alzheimer's.

'There were Methodists and Lutherans and Baptists, and a couple of Catholics,' I told Serena. 'That was it.'

'Yeah, well,' Serena said, turning back to George Clooney, 'not any more.'

For some reason I am picturing Sam as a redhead. That probably isn't likely, because his last name is Hopper, which doesn't sound Irish or Scottish. We have Scotch in our background, as well as English and Swiss German. Meryl Hopper would be a little silly, because Meryl, of course, comes from *merle*, for bird. I don't think Hopper sounds Catholic, although you can't tell as much as you used to from a name.

Meryl and Sam will be here on Thursday morning, certainly by eleven, unless the plane is late. It's possible that they may be coming here to announce their engagement.

'They live together,' my daughter told me on the phone last week. 'You know that, so I hope you aren't going to do to them what you did to us.'

'What are you talking about, Helen? I can't understand you when you don't use antecedents.'

'Separate bedrooms! Peter was so nervous anyway, and that made it worse.'

Of course Sam Hopper is going to sleep downstairs. There's a pull-out couch in Frank's office; Peter slept on it the first time he visited with Helen, and he promised me it was very comfortable. 'They're not married,' I said. 'They're not even engaged.'

'I have something to tell you,' Helen said.

I felt a great, surprising happiness pressing out between my ribs. I had to sit down. It was nothing like when Helen told me that she was getting married, although I was glad at the time that she'd found someone as sensible—if as dull—as Peter. Meryl I trust to have chosen someone singular, like her grandfather. I felt all of a sudden that Frank had picked up another line, a conference line, and was listening in from wherever he was. 'They *are* engaged,' I said. 'Aren't they?'

'No. But would that make a difference to you?'

'No.' There was an awkward pause, in which I could hear Helen covering the receiver with her hand, but not whatever she said to Peter on the other end. My hearing is not what it used to be: I can admit that.

'I'm just glad to see her so happy,' Helen said, returning to our conversation. She seemed to consider this bland sentiment personally ennobling. 'Sam obviously makes her happy.'

'I'm sure she'll be happy in the guestroom.'

Helen sighed. 'I give up. Do whatever you want—just don't blame me if she's angry with you. Remember, I tried to tell you.'

When the doorbell rang, I was sitting on the bed, just thinking about Helen and Meryl. One of the things no one tells you about being old is how you are never allowed to do anything even remotely unusual. I have always had a habit of putting my head in my hands when I'm concentrating, and sometimes Serena will come along and find me in that posture. What are you doing? she asks, as if I were dressed up in men's clothing, or finger-painting on the walls. Thinking, I always tell her, and she says, well, why don't you come downstairs and think in the living room, where I can keep an eye on you?

'I'm coming,' I said. I didn't really think it would be Meryl and Sam, arriving four days early for a surprise. Still, I was glad I had dressed properly that morning. I pretended, going down the stairs, that I would find them at the front door: Meryl, delighted with her surprise, and her fiancé (or soon-to-be fiancé), who might be nervous. He should be nervous, because I am not Helen: 'just glad to see her so happy'. I will judge him on his own merits, which I expect to be considerable.

'Meryl?' I said, as I opened the door. There was a blast of frigid air and there, on the step, were George and his wife, all dressed up for church.

'It's George. And I brought Amina to meet you.'

'We met last week.' I had a cold feeling, nothing to do with the November morning. The girl had told me they were coming: how could I have forgotten?

'She told me!' George said. 'Is now a good time for a visit?'

I opened the door to welcome them, but that was the best I could do. Had they heard me say Meryl's name? I could imagine George mentioning that slip to his mother, who would certainly tell all her friends at Shady Woods.

'I'm expecting my granddaughter Meryl and her friend Sam,' I mentioned casually, just in case. 'They're probably coming on Thursday, but there was a chance they might arrive today. They're on their way to a wedding in Canada.'

Amina had brought a second foil-wrapped plate. 'Bengali food this time.' She smiled. 'No spice.' Her teeth were white, but very crooked.

'It's delicious,' George said. 'We had it last night—chickadee.'

The girl giggled. 'Kitcharee. It settles your stomach.'

'Whatever you say, Chickadee.'

'Please sit down,' I told them. 'My helper isn't here today. I can offer you water, ginger ale or milk.'

'You sit down.' George was in high spirits. 'I'll get the drinks. I know what Amina wants—what will you have, Mrs Buell?'

'What will you have?' I asked Amina, ignoring George. She should be allowed to choose herself. I felt sure that Sam Hopper would always ask Meryl what she wanted to drink, even if he thought he knew.

Amina looked undecided.

'Have milk,' I suggested. 'And be careful not to slouch. Unless you want to grow a hump one day like me.'

'Mrs Buell, you don't have a hump! And Amina loves ginger ale. But maybe you'd like a glass of milk?'

To be fair, Frank wouldn't necessarily have asked me what I wanted to drink, but we belonged to a different generation. I told George that I wasn't thirsty. I hoped they wouldn't stay too long.

'George says you went to Africa,' Amina said, once George was out of the room. 'He says you brought back masks.'

'My husband took me to Egypt,' I told Amina. 'The mask is originally from Kenya, though.'

'I would love to see that,' Amina said, although I hadn't exactly offered.

George returned with our drinks, setting them down on a Christmas tray. 'It's almost the holidays. We hoped Amina's parents might be able to come—but the flights. Whew!' George wiped imaginary sweat from his forehead, leaving a trail of wet there, from the drinks. 'Maybe next year.'

'I just got here,' Amina complained. 'It's too soon.' That surprised me, because I would have thought she would want to bring her parents over as quickly as possible. She'll have a baby, and then there will be aunts and cousins showing up for long vacations, until George has a whole houseful of Bangladeshis. Maybe that's what he wants.

'Do your parents write to you?' I asked.

Amina smiled and nodded. 'They have a computer now at home. Even my mother uses it.'

'I meant letters. Do they send letters, too?'

Amina looked confused.

'She means paper letters.' George turned to me. 'Mrs Buell, nobody uses snail mail these days. Amina's parents send emails— that way, she gets them right away.'

I know the expression 'snail mail', a favourite of Helen's. To avoid saying anything, I went to the vitrine and took out the mask with the pocked, wooden face. There is a small, toothy mouth with a gap, where Frank used to stick one of his Pall Malls for a joke, before he quit cold turkey. The straw beard is delicate, and so I didn't offer to let Amina hold it.

'Some of the tribal people there believe that masks can help them communicate with their dead ancestors. And these are scarabs,' I hurried on, handing her one, since she can't hurt that.

'Amina and I owe our marriage to email!' George was rattling on. 'Sometimes I wonder if she would've fallen in love with me, if I hadn't had all the extra time to think of what I wanted to say to her.'

Amina frowned. 'Of course we wouldn't have fallen in love without email.' This was the first time I saw her look cross with him. 'How could we have?'

I liked to see her showing a bit of spine. In spite of the giggling manner, she was practical. Maybe that's why I decided to say what I did. 'What was that letter you got the other day? I happened to be standing by the kitchen sink, doing dishes.' (I thought that was a nice touch, although of course Serena does the dishes.) 'I noticed you'd gotten something exciting. I thought it must've come from your parents.'

Well, I felt a little bit bad, but in a way I thought I was doing Amina a service. She should know that the tract is the kind of neighbourhood where people stand by the windows, especially women, and that if she's going to get excited about something, it would be better to do it indoors.

George was looking at Amina. 'What letter?'

She wasn't quick on her feet, at least in English. She looked from George to me, and back to George, as if one of us might give her the answer. 'A friend,' she said finally. 'One of my girlfriends in Desh.'

'What did she say?' George's voice took on an uncharacteristic sharpness, as if he were imitating more forceful husbands he'd observed, in the Southtown Plaza or on television.

'Some problems.' Amina's English seemed to deteriorate suddenly. 'With family and with the job. Money problems.' She was holding an orange bolster on her lap, fiddling with the velvet-covered button, which could snap off if she wasn't careful. I didn't say anything. I found myself hoping George wouldn't be too hard on her.

'It's a poor country.' George sighed, turning back to me. 'I knew that, of course, but I wasn't prepared. The beggar kids, always asking you for money and pens.'

I had the feeling that George was using the poor children as a shield, to cover his own embarrassment. I thought I would offer him an escape route. 'You have to forgive an old lady. If I don't take my nap, I'll fall asleep right here.'

George stood up right away, but Amina remained seated for another moment. She was staring at me through those enormous glasses, as if she were trying to communicate something urgent. When George moved towards the door, she got up and went in the other direction, to the vitrine. She was trying to replace the scarab herself.

I hurried over—to the extent that I can hurry. To my relief, she surrendered the scarab (which belongs next to a very fine set of French butter knives, crafted of silver and bone.)

The girl spoke so softly that I never would've heard her, if I hadn't been standing right there. 'Mrs Buell, I would like to—have a talk with you. Can I come visit you tomorrow?'

I don't like whispered conversations in general. My father used to say, if you can't say it out loud, best not to say it at all. I think that's sound advice, although in this case I did keep my voice down, to humour her.

'Not this week. My granddaughter and her fiancé are coming.' I didn't mean to use that word, but once it had slipped out, it was impossible to correct. 'I'll be very busy preparing the house.'

'Your granddaughter is getting married?'

For a moment, she seemed to forget the letter—which I probably ought not to have brought up. It's difficult when you get older: you forget how sensitive young people can be. 'They won't be married for a while,' I told her. 'It's not a formal engagement.'

'A secret,' Amina said wistfully. 'Where is he from?'

That was a sensible question, one that I hadn't had the chance to ask Helen. I didn't want to admit to Amina that I didn't know, and so I said, 'Harvard. The most distinguished university in America.'

'I know Harvard,' Amina said, a little offended. 'It's very famous.'

'Come on, Amina,' George said. 'Mrs Buell needs her nap.'

George opened the door, and Amina turned her large, dark eyes on me. 'I could visit after they're gone then? The week after next?'

I watched them go from the kitchen window, both of them with their heads down against the wind. That's the wind from the lake, and it can be bitter at this time of year. It was hard to tell, but I didn't think they were talking. I thought that George would probably wait until they were back inside their house to do anything.

I didn't sleep a minute on Wednesday night, and on Thursday morning Serena found me on my hands and knees in the bedroom, looking for one of the pearls that had rolled underneath the armoire.

'I thought you'd fallen, Tabby! You should've warned me.'

'How could I warn you, when I couldn't see you?' (Of course I could hear her coming up the stairs—you'd have to be stone deaf to miss that.)

'Let me help you up.' Serena puts her hands under my armpits, and I have to admit that this is her one skill: in contrast to her mind and her voice, her touch is gentle, empathic, as if she feels what you feel the minute she lays her hands on you.

Serena rescued the earring, her enormous bottom in the air. 'Say anything and I'll flush this down the toilet.'

I didn't say a word. Sam is a lawyer and could charge her with blackmail, but I decided to wait until he was on the premises to reveal my advantage. Serena left me alone with my earrings, and went down to the laundry room to do the wash, and I must've sat on the bed for some time, with my head in my hands. What I was thinking of was Frank's proposal, which Edith Overton asked me about the other day. She asked so that she could tell me about hers, once again, but I didn't mind. At this point, one more recital probably won't kill me. Buzz Overton proposed on the observation deck of the Empire State Building, a location Edith seems to regard as daringly original, and so I don't speculate about the number of young people who've decided to join their lives together on exactly that spot. Along with the ring, he presented Edith with a single yellow rose.

Frank proposed in a letter. ('A letter?' Edith always says, as if I've admitted he'd asked me in a grocery store or a parking lot.) It might not have been dramatic, but it isn't gone. A letter means I have it: the exact words in a drawer next to my bed, on stationery from the Hotel Statler in St Louis, although he was writing from Crystal City. *This is the most important letter I'll ever write.* That's true, but I wonder if he knew why at the time. When I think of how often I've held these three pieces of paper (perhaps the only surviving sheets of its pattern), I become dizzy with anxiety, imagining a reality in which the letter was lost or damaged, or one in which he failed to write at all. *To say 'I love you' isn't enough, because I'm also asking you to make the greatest sacrifice you'll ever make. I'm asking you to give up your teaching, which I know you love, in order to be my wife and, God willing, to raise our children.* (One child, as it turned out, was the extent of what God willed for us.) *How can I ask this of you? I ask myself that question, and the only answer I have is a corresponding vow. I promise to protect you, to care for you, and to devote all my energies to making you happy, as you so richly deserve to be.*

'Hello?' Meryl called from downstairs. 'Nonny, we're here!' I heard her running up the stairs, and then she was in my bedroom. But she was alone.

'Where is he?' I asked her. 'Sam?'

She laughs like me, Helen always says. 'He's right downstairs in the living room. Aren't you glad to see *me*?' She crossed the room in a couple of steps, on her beautiful, solid bones. I do think she gets prettier every time I see her, in spite of this new, shaggy haircut—a style which has perhaps not yet come to Rochester—and the eye make-up, which she doesn't need. Her skin is cream and pink, without a hint of sallowness.

'Serena said you were upstairs. I thought you wouldn't want a gentleman caller in your bedroom.' She hugged me tentatively around the neck, her hands shying away from my back. I don't blame her: the curve is disturbing if you're not used to it.

When she pulled away I glanced at her left hand: nothing.

'I hope you like him. But if you don't...'

'Why wouldn't I like him?'

'I'm just saying—be nice to him. He might be a little nervous.'

I was pleased, although I tried not to show it. 'Nervous of an old lady? What's wrong with him?'

'*Nonny.*'

'I like him already,' I said, which was true.

It took me longer than it did Merry to get downstairs, of course, and I had the strangest feeling, as if I were sixteen years old, in my father's house in Corpus Christi, and John Lindsey Button was waiting in the living room to take me to the Calvary Baptist Spring Carnival. There's a mirror in the hall, and ordinarily I try not to look in it—but this time I did check, as if I might see brown curls and a lace collar, as opposed to this egg-white-stiff permanent wave.

But it was not John Lindsey Button. Nor was it the lanky carrot-top Sam Hopper, whom I'd been inventing so confidently over the past six weeks. This young man was standing in front of the green velvet chair by the window, looking out at the bare rose bushes. He wasn't tall, maybe no taller than Merry; his hair was thick and black. His build was stocky, muscular, just the opposite of what I had pictured, and his complexion was somewhere between cinnamon and mud.

'Nonny,' Merry said. 'This is my boyfriend, Samaj.'

The young man came forward to shake my hand. 'Call me Sam— everyone does, except Meryl. It's so nice to finally meet you.'

My first feeling was relief, because I knew that I had been wrong about the engagement. What Helen had called to tell me was suddenly very clear: I saw that no one had lied to me about Sam/Samaj, and that no one had told me the truth, either.

I didn't want to look at Merry, who I knew was testing me in the same tiresome way she would when she was a child, putting ice cream in the shopping cart to see if I would notice. Instead I looked at Samaj, and there was something that passed between us, not friendly exactly, but an understanding, like two prisoners confined to the same cell.

'Very nice to meet you, too.'

'I apologize for being late,' he said. 'We decided to rent a car instead of flying. We're going to drive to Toronto for the wedding tomorrow.'

'So we have to leave a little earlier than we thought,' Merry said casually.

'Will you be able to stay for lunch?' I saw my two meals with Merry slipping into one. She has never been a breakfast-eater.

My granddaughter shook her head. 'We have to be on the road by noon, at the latest.'

At my age I should be used to the way that real life jerks not only the rug, but the whole floor out from under you on a regular basis. It doesn't care about your age or the density of your bones. I saw that Merry had noticed my hesitation with Samaj, and was punishing me.

'Tonight we'll have dinner at five-thirty,' I said, moving past this disappointment. 'Did you meet my helper, Serena?'

'Who do you think let them in?' Serena shouted from the kitchen.

'We'll have to make do with what she prepares,' I said, breaking my policy about whispering. 'It won't be anything to write home about, I'm afraid.'

'Samaj could help,' Merry said. 'He's a great cook.'

'Great is definitely stretching it. But I could certainly give her a hand.' He said this seriously, as if it mattered to him that we all have an accurate conception of his culinary skills.

'Let's put our stuff upstairs first,' Merry said. 'I have to hang up my dress for tomorrow night.' She turned to me. 'Where would you like us?'

'You can sleep where you always sleep.' (That guest room, next to my bedroom, I always think of as Merry's room.) 'And your friend can sleep in Frank's office.' (I was not being nasty. I was unsure of how to pronounce his name, and I thought it better not to attempt it out loud. My aptitude for foreign words does not extend to non-Latinate language families.) 'There's a sofa bed,' I told him. 'Peter tells me it's comfortable.'

Merry rolled her eyes. 'She means my dad. What year was that?'

'That was in 1974,' I said, glad to show off my memory for dates a little.

'Only thirty-two years old! You'll sleep like a baby.'

'Why shouldn't it still be comfortable? Almost no one has slept on it since then.'

Samaj seemed impatient with the two of us. 'It'll be fine.' There was an uncomfortable silence, in which I decided to try to be agreeable. Of course, that's what got me into trouble.

'You're the first young man Meryl has introduced to me.'

'That's not true, Nonny.' I was surprised to see that my granddaughter was blushing. 'You met Charles.'

'The drunk!' I was just remembering, and didn't necessarily mean to say that out loud.

Samaj looked as if he were suppressing a smile. My granddaughter sighed. 'He had a couple of beers. At a *barbecue*. And I didn't introduce you on purpose. He just happened to be there.' She turned to Samaj, 'That was on Long Island, a long time ago.'

'That's okay. I see I'm going to have to rely on your grandmother for information about your past loves.'

'Anyway,' Meryl said, 'Samaj doesn't drink.'

'Or not much,' Samaj clarified. 'I have to admit, I do have a beer now and then. But not very often.'

'Is that because of your religion?'

It was a perfectly reasonable question. I might've asked the same thing of the Bengali girl, if I weren't already sure of the answer.

My granddaughter's response, however, was not reasonable. 'Nonny! Oh, my God, Sam—I'm so sorry.' (I noticed that she called him Sam when she was distracted.) 'Which religion do you assume he practises? Have you even asked him?'

'I don't assume. That's why I was asking.'

'I don't practise any religion.' Samaj hadn't reacted either to my question or to Merry's outburst. His voice was calm and even. 'I just don't like the taste.'

'I'll show you your bed—so to speak,' Meryl said, not looking at me. 'It's this way.' Samaj nodded politely, but I was surprised to see a hint of appraisal in that look—as if *he* were here to take the measure of *me*. One thing I can't help remembering about the young man on Long Island, Charles, was that he had appeared to worship Merry; even in his inebriated state, his eyes followed her everywhere. I assume that sort of devotion wouldn't survive a marriage, but I've sometimes wondered whether it might be a good way to start—along with picnics and yellow roses and things—if only to provide a buffer against everything to come. Doting was not Frank's style, nor did it seem (from my brief period of observation) to be characteristic of Samaj.

While they were downstairs making up his bed, I put my hands into the pockets of his jacket, hanging in the hall closet, which were lined with fleece. I didn't find anything, not even a pack of matches. Of course, most young people don't smoke now, so Samaj doesn't deserve any special credit for that. Although I can't stand drinking, smoking is one of the faults I can forgive in a man most easily.

The sofa bed was not the only source of the difficulty during Helen and Peter's unfortunate visit in 1974. Part of the blame did fall on Frank, who could be somewhat abrupt; it is even possible that my husband's manner may have contributed to Peter's asthma attack, on that first evening we spent together as a family. But fathers are notoriously protective of their daughters, and to be fair to Frank, there were some extenuating circumstances. Things at the paper were not going well. There were cuts and, as the managing editor, Frank was the one who had to make them. Dumbing down the paper didn't make him happy, but it was the lay-offs that killed him; on the night that Helen and Peter arrived from the city, he had given notice to a good friend, a man who had been to our house for dinner countless times.

Things didn't go well from the beginning. Peter, a confident talker, brought up topic after topic; Frank concentrated on his food. When the dinner was finished, he crossed his arms and squinted at the pattern on the wallpaper. (The wallpaper in the dining room is beautiful: a green-and-white scene of plantation house, dock and willow, repeating over and over on a pale ivory ground. But Frank was not admiring the wallpaper, or even seeing it. He was thinking of Ed McCurdy, who ought not to have lost his job.) Peter was talking about *his* job, which was in television, a field my husband despised. I was glad that Frank didn't seem to be listening, and I smiled encouragingly at Helen, who clearly wasn't happy about her father's behaviour.

'There's a lot television reporters can learn from print journalists,' Peter was saying. 'As more and more people decide to get their news from TV, telejournalists are going to have to get more rigorous. The standards are going to have to go up, and we can learn a lot from people like you.'

Frank suddenly turned to Peter, as if he'd been waiting for this opportunity all evening. 'Can you define for me, "telejournalists"?'

'Oh...sure,' Peter said, unaware that he was being baited. 'It's just the word we use for the reporters—the on-air reporters, mostly, although I guess technically all of them are telejournalists.'

Frank nodded, as if he were assimilating this information. I knew that look, and I thought it was time to intervene.

'Peter,' I said, 'would you like to help me with the strawberry shortcake?'

'You help, Helen. Peter and I are discussing telejournalism.'

Peter, who had risen to help me, now sat down again awkwardly, crumpling his napkin in his hand.

'Because it's always seemed to me that those men are just actors reading the news. Just a bunch of pansies, reading from a script.'

Peter gave an uncomfortable laugh. 'Well, they're involved to different degrees. Our nightly anchor, Mr Glenn, for example—'

'And that if it's as you say, that "more and more Americans" are getting their news from these men—and I use that term loosely—then this country is headed for trouble. Serious trouble.'

'Well, Sir, I can understand, from your perspective—'

'It's not *my* perspective, son. It's just a goddamned fact.'

'Frank,' I said, because I do not like swearing, and I never want anyone to forget that this is a Baptist household.

'I'm sorry, Tabby, but the country is going to hell, and this character, along with his *telejournalists*, is trying to hurry it into an early grave.'

That was when Peter starting breathing heavily, and then gasping for breath, and Helen started to sob, and our wedding platter, on which I had arranged the shortcake, somehow slipped from my hands and smashed to the floor. That was not nerves. It was the beginning of the arthritis, although I didn't recognize it then. That night especially, Frank and I were still the adults, and our child, on the point of marriage, was still a child. At the time, it would've been impossible to believe that our health would begin to decline in these various ways, and that within two years, we would hold a grandchild in our arms.

I noticed the Bengali girl midway through dinner. It must've been thirty degrees, but she had come out of the house for no apparent reason. I watched her lock the door: she was wearing the red parka, but she hadn't pulled up the hood, and I thought of how cold her bare ears must be. I could see that George's car wasn't in the driveway yet; it was only a little after six, and he must not have been home from work.

Unlike Peter, Samaj was not a big talker. Meryl had to get him started by telling me how they met. She had been in graduate school at Boston University, getting her Masters in education; in her free time, she would jog along the Charles River with friends from her programme.

'We would pass him every day, sitting on the same bench by the river, reading. The bench was on the opposite side of the river from the college, so I figured he was a law or business student.' I could see that Merry was still angry at me, but that she wanted to tell me the story, too. One thing my granddaughter has never lost is the transparency of childhood: you can always see on her face exactly what's going on in her head. I admire that quality, rare enough in adults these days.

'I was running with Katie—you remember Katie, don't you, Nonny? And she dared me to talk to him.'

'Oh, yes?' I said. I knew how important it was for me to listen to this account, but I was distracted by the Bengali girl, who was standing absolutely still underneath George's outside light. For a moment, I wondered if she were drunk. I couldn't think of any other reason for someone to stand outside in weather like this.

'Finally one day I did it.'

Finally I understood. She was watching us. With the chandelier on high, and all of the candles lit, she could see the three of us clearly. I was sitting at the head of the table and Meryl was on my left. From where Amina was standing, she would have a clear view of both me and my granddaughter; only Samaj, sitting with his back to the window, was concealed from her.

'Tell her,' Merry instructed.

'She asked what I was reading.' I noticed that he was allowing his pot pie to get cold. These pot pies come frozen, and no one can mess them up—not even Serena.

'He was reading a biography of Einstein,' Merry said. 'I thought that was cool.'

'I wrote my undergraduate thesis on the Manhattan Project,' Samaj said.

'Samaj was an American history major, before he went to law school.'

'That was an especially dark moment in American history,' I said. 'What made you choose it?'

'All American history is dark,' Meryl said. 'And they still teach the early colonial history as if it's so glorious. When really we were in the process of conducting this enormous genocide.'

'I'm interested in the scientific part of it, actually,' Samaj said. 'The history of fission. If I'd been smart enough, I would've liked to be a physicist.'

I thought I was imagining things when I saw her coming towards us. There was no way a girl like Amina would interrupt this dinner, after I had specifically told her not to disturb us.

'Of course you're smart enough,' Merry said. 'Samaj graduated fifth in his entire law school class.'

Perhaps she saw George's car coming towards the house and she was going down the driveway to meet him? But Amina kept coming in our direction, until she disappeared into our garage. A moment later, the kitchen doorbell rang.

'Who is that?' Merry asked. 'Tell me it isn't George from next door—the most boring man in the western hemisphere.'

'I believe it's his wife,' I told them. For some reason I couldn't move.

'Would you like me to get the door, Mrs Buell?'

'No,' I said. 'Maybe she'll go away.'

'Nonny.' Merry giggled, 'We can't do that.' She was pleased, although she didn't know the source of my reluctance. I wasn't sure

I knew myself. I trusted Amina not to reveal what I'd said about an engagement, since I'd told her it was a secret. At that time, I had worried about what Sam Hopper would think when he saw what kind of neighbours I had. This was not, as my granddaughter would allege, because I have anything against Bangladeshis *per se*—but because of the manner in which the marriage took place.

Now that Sam was Samaj, however, it was almost as if the worry had been inverted: what would Amina think of me for not revealing Samaj's origins, when she had asked specifically? His background was certainly relevant, if only because of its similarity to her own.

'It's the kitchen door,' Merry told Samaj. 'It sticks, so pull hard.' Then she turned to me. 'Her name is April, right?'

'George and April are divorced,' I just managed. 'This is his new wife, of only a few months.' I heard the door open, and then Samaj inviting her in. I imagined her surprise, on seeing him, but when the two of them appeared in the dining room, I could tell that Amina was completely absorbed by her own concerns. Of course she must've noticed Samaj's colour, but whatever the reason for her visit, it was too pressing to allow her to concentrate on anything else.

'I'm sorry to interrupt, Mrs Buell. I don't want to bother you.'

'Is something wrong?'

Amina looked unhappily from me to my granddaughter. She shook her head. There was nothing to do but make an introduction.

'Amina, this is my granddaughter, Meryl, and her friend, Samaj Hopper.' (I did the best I could with it.) 'This is George's wife, Amina...'

'Barker,' Amina supplied, as if I didn't know George's last name. Had I been aware of her maiden name, I would've used it, if only to avoid the kind of name that tells you nothing at all.

'It's so nice to meet you,' Merry said. 'There are never any young people around here.'

'There are the Cruikshanks across the street,' I said. 'They're right about your age.'

'Here,' Merry said, ignoring this. 'Have my seat, next to Nonny. You can join us for dessert.' I could see that she was immediately curious about my neighbour, probably wondering why I hadn't mentioned Amina until now.

'Oh, no,' Amina said. 'I won't stay. George is home at every minute. Mrs Buell, if I could talk with you for just...?'

Merry and Samaj exchanged glances at this request, but they stood up politely. I could only imagine how odd this visit would look to them. 'Then we'll get started on the dishes,' Merry said. 'You guys can sit here and chat a little.'

Amina looked down at her hands while Meryl and Samaj cleared the table; she refused to take off her coat. Only after the two of them had disappeared into the kitchen—laughing about something unrelated to us—did Amina allow herself to speak.

'Mrs Buell, I am sorry.'

'George will be home at *any* minute,' I corrected. It's the teacher in me, I can't help it.

Amina nodded. 'But I have to tell you...' Her voice trailed off. She was overheating in her parka and her cheeks were flushed; I was surprised by how pink such brown cheeks could get.

'When you saw me...'

'Yes?' I was trying to be patient, but Amina seemed to have picked up George's habit of not finishing sentences.

'...in the window...' She was glancing at the window now, probably watching for the lights of George's car. 'That letter—is not a bad thing.'

'The letter you got from Bangladesh?'

Amina shook her head miserably. 'It was *not* from Desh. But now George is asking me every day.'

'I'm sorry,' I said. 'I shouldn't have asked in front of him. I didn't know it was a secret.'

Amina was close to tears. 'It is *not* a secret. I am telling him, when—'

'Nonny?' Meryl stuck her head in. 'Sorry—does this go in the dishwasher?' She was holding a piece of the Francis First wedding silver, which I only bring out on special occasions. Like me, Merry will never make much of a housekeeper, but I do hope she'll learn to recognize these things, which will one day be hers.

'Of course not,' I told her. 'That's the Francis First.'

Merry nodded, and the swinging door closed again behind her. Of course, you could hear everything from in there.

'My learning permit,' Amina said. 'From the Department of Motor Vehicles.'

I was confused. 'You're going to learn to drive?'

Amina managed a small smile. 'My lessons start tomorrow.

127

That's why I had to tell you. You might see me out there on the wheel.'

'*At* the wheel,' I said. 'Or behind it. Why don't you want to tell George?'

'He thinks I might have accidents. Or get lost. He thinks we should wait some time. But how can I have a job without driving?'

I could not help remembering when Frank bought the Cadillac: I was Amina's age, newly married as she is. Of course the tract is a safe place to practise, since it's rare to see anyone going above thirty miles an hour. But driving is one of those things—like the ablative case, or nursing a baby: just because you know how to do it yourself doesn't mean that you can explain it to other people.

'You can't keep accidents from happening,' I said, surprising myself. 'George will have to take that chance.'

Amina put one hand on my arm. 'Mrs Buell—thank you,' she said, as if I had offered to teach her myself. 'It is not a secret—but only until I get my licence.'

I observed her strategy: putting the thanks before the favour, so that it was very difficult to say no. 'Who will teach you to drive?' I asked Amina, who was getting up, admiring the lace tablecloth that Merry and Samaj hadn't noticed.

Amina smiled that overlarge, crooked smile. 'Edith Overton.'

'Edith Overton!'

'Do you know her? She is so generous, even with her own car.'

'Generous' is not the word I would use for it. Edith Overton is eager to be seen driving up and down the street, performing a charitable act, so that everyone will notice how she still has her licence. This is in spite of the fact that she's only seventy-three—I had my licence nearly ten years longer than that.

'Be careful,' I told Amina, as I walked her to the kitchen door. 'I have driven with Edith Overton.'

'Would you like to take some shortcake with you?' Merry asked. I could tell she was disappointed that Amina wouldn't be staying. 'Here, I'll wrap it up in some foil.'

But Amina was all of a sudden distracted. 'I think that is…' And I could hear George's car too, easing carefully into the driveway.

She looked at me. 'But if I could have my plate?'

I was glad I'd told Serena to wash the Bengali food down the drain, so Amina wouldn't have to see me do it. I showed her where the plate was, and Samaj reached up to the cupboard to get it for her.

'Thank you.' Now that she had her plate, her excuse, she lingered. 'I hope you have a very wonderful stay in Rochester,' she said, examining Samaj. I thought she was trying to place him, as I had, only with more specific information at her disposal.

'Thanks.' Samaj didn't seem as charmed by Amina as Merry was; in fact, he looked as if she bored him.

'Excuse me,' she said suddenly. 'Are you from India?'

'My father is Indian—Bengali, actually,' Samaj said slowly. 'But my mother is American. She's from Iowa.'

'That is interesting!' Amina said. She gave one more reluctant look around my kitchen. 'I hope to meet you both again,' she said, before hurrying down the steps, out the garage and across the lawn to George.

Meryl was fascinated by my neighbour. She wanted to know how old she was; how long she'd been living next door; where George had met her. I answered the first two questions and skimmed over the third. We sat in the living room, balancing our shortcake on our laps.

'Someone must have introduced them,' I told Merry and Samaj. 'Someone in their community of friends.'

Merry looked at me strangely. I took a large bite of shortcake. After all, I couldn't say that I knew exactly how Amina and George had met. Presumably there were many women like Amina on the computer, many men like George. What had caused them to pause on each other's photograph, and start typing back and forth across their screens?

'But who would've introduced them?' Meryl asked. 'I have to say, I didn't think George was the type.'

'What type?' Samaj asked. I hadn't thought he was paying attention. I wondered if that was a lawyer's strategy—pretending to be distracted and then surprising you with a question.

'The cradle-robbing type. There must be fifteen years between them.'

'Only twelve, I think,' I said. There were ten years between me and Frank, and that turned out to be a good thing: how else would I have had the energy to care for him?

'Samaj's father is from West Bengal,' Merry told me. 'That's the Indian part, but people speak Bangla on both sides of the border.'

She gave the word a foreign-sounding long A—to be even more authentic, I suppose.

'Where does your father live now?' I asked Samaj.

'I don't know, exactly. We aren't in touch.' He said this nonchalantly, as if not being in touch with your living father was a completely ordinary state of affairs.

'Samaj was born in south India,' Merry said. 'In Kerala. His mom brought him back to the States when he was five.'

'Is "Hopper" your mother's maiden name?'

Samaj nodded. 'I'm really from Iowa City. To be honest, I hardly remember anything about India.'

'Samaj and I are hoping to travel in Bengal next summer,' Merry told me. 'As soon as he can take enough time off.'

'Either Iowa City or Calcutta—we haven't decided. Both have their attractions.' I thought this was a joke, but I wasn't sure. I noticed that Merry seemed annoyed.

'You remember some things,' she prompted him. 'Like those white lizards. The ones that would sometimes fall into your bed at night. And walking along the backwaters with your parents.'

Samaj didn't confirm or deny that. Instead he turned to me, with that same, surprising focus. 'Why do you think your neighbour decided to look for a foreign wife?'

'I suppose he couldn't find an American one.'

Samaj nodded in agreement. 'But why from Asia, do you think? Do you think he had a thing for Asian women?' There was something not quite sincere about these questions, although Samaj's voice was perfectly neutral. I had the feeling he was leading me in a particular direction, and I had the impulse to answer very simply, to avoid making a mistake.

'I suppose that was just who he met.'

Samaj frowned. 'But presumably he would've met a large number of American women before that. Perhaps none of them were interested in what George had to offer? No offence to your neighbour, of course. Maybe it makes most sense to think of it in economic terms, like any other commodity—just following the law of supply and demand. If there's a glut, say, of marriageable women in Bangladesh and not enough men who can support them, then they simply begin to export them here.'

I looked at Merry to see how she was taking this reference to people as commodities—just her sort of subject—but my granddaughter didn't seem to be listening. She was looking out the picture window at the house behind ours, which used to belong to the Gelbs. She had played with the Gelb children during the summers when she was nine and ten; the four of them (two boys and a girl, plus Merry) would disappear into the cornfield where the tract ends for hours at a time, until I worried about what they could be doing in there. I knew children of that age sometimes experimented with sexual games, 'playing doctor', et cetera; Frank told me not to worry, but I was terrified that something might happen to Merry while she was under our protection.

'What were you doing?' I demanded once, when she reappeared at the back door especially late, dirt on the knees of her jeans. I remember that she answered the way children do, patiently but with no expectation of my comprehension—the same way a foreigner will, if you ask them to say something in their language.

'We were playing spaceship,' she told me. 'We landed on Alpha-Omegatron, the farthest planet from the earth. It doesn't have any gravity. You float around in the air all day, and if you want to visit someone, you have to swim through the clouds. It's more than a trillion miles from earth, so that's why it took me so long to get home.'

That night I kept my clothes on. I wanted to go down and check the boiler. Helen tells me not to worry, that if anything happens she'll take care of it. But before Helen takes care of it the orange light could go off, and the pipes could freeze, and it would take thousands of dollars from the Bank of America account to fix it.

I waited until I thought the two of them would be asleep. Our floors creak, unless you walk extremely slowly, heel, toe, heel, toe, like a book I used to read to Helen about Indian braves. There's no limit to how slowly you can do things, as long as there's no one there to get impatient. This is one blessing that goes along with being alone at my age.

I must not have noticed the light in Frank's study on my way down, but when I started back upstairs from the basement, I saw the glow coming from underneath his door. Then I heard Samaj moving around in there.

'Mrs Buell, is that you?'

'Don't mind me,' I said. 'I don't sleep well these days. I was just checking on the boiler.'

Samaj came to the top of the stairs and held my arm for the last few. This is the sort of assistance I don't need, although I know it is meant kindly. I can do it, if people will only let me take my own time.

'Do you always stay up so late?'

'I was doing some work,' Samaj said. 'I guess I forgot the time.'

'What kind of work?'

'Some research for a case. We're defending a company that manufactures tiny parts for computers. There's a class-action suit against them—it's pretty boring, actually.'

'Do you have to surf the Internet for that?'

We had stepped into Frank's study. 'Meryl said I could use the computer in here—I hope that's all right. She said you didn't use it very much.'

He said this with a perfectly straight face, acknowledging the possibility that Meryl had been mistaken, that I, at ninety-four, had become a computer whiz in secret. I thought that was cheeky.

'It's for Meryl and her parents,' I told him. 'Of course I don't know how to use it.'

'Oh,' Samaj said. 'Well, it's easy. I could show you if you want. You sit here, in front of the computer,' he said, pulling up a stool for himself.

'I'll just watch.'

'It's better if you do it yourself. Otherwise you won't remember.'

'I have an excellent memory,' I told him. 'I always have had, and I haven't lost any of it. I'm lucky in that way, at least.'

Samaj nodded. 'There's something about the computer, though. It helps to learn it with your fingers. Do you touch-type?'

I was glad to be able to say I did. Frank believed that everyone ought to know how to drive and how to type; after I stopped teaching, when Helen was born, he bought me a book. While she napped, I went through the exercises page by page. I am thorough— one of the qualities Frank always told me he admired—and after only five weeks, I was at sixty words per minute. 'Except that these days my hands bother me a bit.'

Samaj nodded. 'Then I'll type and you'll tell me what to do. What should we look up first?'

'Asian ladies,' I said. Samaj looked startled. It was the first time I'd seen any uncertainty in him since they'd arrived. 'Dot com,' I remembered to add. 'Where East Meets West.'

A moment later he understood. He was quick, at least. 'That's where your neighbour met his wife, isn't it? On the Internet.'

I nodded. 'Have you heard of it?'

'I know that kind of site exists.'

'But you don't know how to find it.'

'I can *find* it,' Samaj said. 'I just wonder why you want to see it.'

'I want to see the other girls. The ones that George didn't pick.'

Samaj hit the power button and the screen turned bright blue. 'I'm just warning you—I don't know anything about this particular site. It might be disturbing for you.'

'I'm ninety-four years old,' I told him. 'I'm not dead yet.'

Samaj didn't argue with me any more. He showed me how to move the arrow to the Internet symbol: a blue 'e'. Then he showed me how you 'click', twice, with the left thumb. (He had me practise that myself, which was surprisingly painless; I have more trouble with my fingers than my thumbs.) Finally he showed me where to type the subject of my search. I'm sure that Merry is wonderful with her students, but in this case, I had to admit, Samaj was the better instructor. He remembered to reduce the process to a series of steps— which is the secret to teaching anything. With declensions, I would always ask them to choose a noun—*advena*, for example—and then make them draw the table every time, starting with the nominative, singular and plural, and working through to the ablative: *advena, advenae, advenis*; I did not allow them to skip any steps. Only that way would the pattern stay in their heads.

In only a few moments, we had found the site. The screen was lavender, with *Asianladies* in script and a picture of a white, tropical flower.

'Do you have to pay?' I asked.

'It's interesting, actually.' Samaj had taken over the keys and was typing very fast, so that the screen kept changing. The text was too small for me to read anything. 'You can scroll through all these women: here's 'An' from Nanjing, for example, and 'Kelly'—not her real name, I assume—from Mindanao. Her dream is to move to California. Bon is from Chiang Mai, and she's looking for a man who's looking for a 'traditional wife'. Samaj looked up from the screen. 'The point is that you don't have to pay to look at the women, but you do if you want to send a message to them. That's how they draw the men in.'

'Disgusting.'

'I agree with you.'

'Why would George get involved with something like this?' Perhaps I'd forgotten I was talking to Samaj; it was just what I was wondering at that moment.

'It might work out for Amina and George,' Samaj said. 'You never know.'

'Do you plan to ask Meryl to marry you?'

Samaj didn't seem especially surprised by the question. He clicked a button and all of the Asian ladies disappeared.

'If that's what she wants. We've been talking about it recently, because some of our friends are getting married.'

'Is that what you want?' They were leaving tomorrow. After that I might never see Samaj again; alternately, he would become my granddaughter's husband. Either way, I thought I had the right to ask some questions.

Samaj brushed his hair away from his face. He didn't have long hair, but a piece of it hung in his eyes. It was not unhandsome.

'I guess I'm not completely sure what the point is.'

'What the point is?'

'Of marriage. I mean, if there isn't a religious tradition that compels you to take that step.'

I should've been relieved. It did not sound like Samaj was going to ask my granddaughter to marry him. And yet I found his answer irritating: of course he wanted to marry her—how could he not?

'Were your parents compelled by a religious tradition?'

'No,' Samaj said. 'But they're divorced.'

'Was your father trying to escape an arranged marriage?'

Samaj shrugged. 'I don't think that was it. But like I said, I don't know my father very well.'

'*That's* the "point" of it!' I told him. 'So that children know their fathers.'

'You're saying I would leave my children? Unless I had a piece of paper from the county clerk, in which case I wouldn't?'

It's true I'd raised my voice at him, but I was surprised when he snapped back; it had been a long time since a stranger had been sharp with me. 'Marriage keeps families together,' I said, more gently now. 'No matter how hard it is.'

'The divorce rate in America is fifty per cent.'

I know that, of course. You can't watch the TV news without hearing all about it.

'Anyway—do you want me to marry Meryl? I haven't gotten the feeling that you like me very much.'

Every once in a while I do get the feeling that Frank is somewhere nearby, not hovering overhead like an angel, but hiding the way he sometimes did at the very end, waiting with a stupid grin for me to find him. I imagine him sitting on the occasional chair in the living room, concealed from view by my father's rosewood sugar chest. While I'm doing the laundry, I notice a dark shape in the broom closet, making himself slim behind the louvred door. I don't feel angry in these moments, the way I used to. It's comforting to pretend I might be able to ask his opinion.

'I want what Meryl wants,' I told Samaj. 'I just want her to be happy.' I was surprised to hear those particular words coming out of my mouth, words I had scorned just one week earlier. Didn't I want much more than simple happiness for Meryl, who had so much to offer to the world?

'Me too,' Samaj said, but he wasn't thinking. He didn't know what making someone happy meant. If he were to promise, it would not be in Frank's language; in fact, he would find Frank's letter insulting. He would argue that Merry had to take care of herself, protect herself—that he was her companion, nothing more. That view of marriage is wrong, although I wouldn't attempt to make Samaj Hopper understand. One person always has to take care of the other, even if it's not the one who appeared stronger at the start. There's a giver and a taker, and if you pair two takers, like Merry and Samaj, they'll eventually tear each other apart.

I wished Samaj goodnight, and he attempted to help me up the stairs, an offer I declined.

'I hope you sleep well,' he said, as I was leaving the room—a common politeness, but I thought he knew I wouldn't. I lay awake much longer than usual; it was after five by the time I finally fell asleep. When I woke up it was late, later than I'd slept in years, and

Serena was opening the blue curtains, letting in bright winter sunlight.

'You'd better get up now,' she said, 'if you want to say goodbye to them before they leave.'

I've noticed recently the way that time expands and collapses, with very little warning: sometimes I'm examining a single hour over the course of days, with my head down in my chair, and other times the events of years are compressed into moments, the blocks of colour on a folded paper fan.

My granddaughter telephoned to tell me she was engaged.

'To whom?'

Merry sighed. 'Samaj, of course. I know you don't like him, so you don't have to pretend you do. I wish you did, though.'

'Why don't you think I like him?' I'd been wondering whether Samaj had described our late-night conversation to Merry, but the next thing she said made me think he'd kept it to himself.

'I'm not sure he noticed—except for that thing about religion, Jesus. It was completely obvious to me.'

'I just think you're a little young to be married.'

'I'm thirty! And you don't think the Cruikshanks are a little young. They have two children already.'

'There's a difference between you and Lori Cruikshank. What about your career?'

'It's not like when you were young, Nonny. I'll still teach after I'm married, even if we decide to have children.'

This is the way that people ordinarily talk to me: as if I've never heard of anything that happened after 1965. I've been alive all this time—if anything, I've paid more attention over the last forty years. Still, young people can't understand that. I'm not sure I did either, when I was their age.

'I guess I should be happy Mom and Dad like him,' Merry continued. 'It's just that I was hoping...'

Well, that made me very happy, even if she didn't finish her sentence. 'I do like him,' I heard myself say, 'I think he's very smart—Harvard, after all.'

'Not everyone who goes to Harvard is smart, Nonny.'

'And he's doing well at his firm, at least according to you. You won't have to worry about money, which is very important. You might not think so now, but it is.'

'I know that,' Merry said. 'I'm not a child.'

All of a sudden she *did* sound very young, younger in certain ways than Lori Cruikshank, who takes care of those two children alone for ten hours every day, while her husband is at work.

'I hope you'll be very happy,' I told my granddaughter, and then I listened to her talk about the details of the wedding, which would take place in eight months' time in a public park in Brooklyn. I thought about that trip and it was hard to imagine how I would have the energy to make it. Of course I won't live long enough to see whether it will 'work out' for them, as it seems to for fifty per cent of American couples. That, to me, is the interesting statistic: that so many stay together, given all the things that can happen to two people these days, in our frighteningly long American lives.

Sure enough, Edith Overton is teaching Amina to drive. I can see them right outside, coming up Skytop Lane in Buzz Overton's Lincoln Continental Givenchy. I wonder what they're talking about, whether they're sharing stories of their proposals. It hadn't occurred to me that Amina's proposal would have been a letter, too (although, of course, not snail mail).

'An email!' Edith will say, horrified. 'Well, I suppose if you were halfway across the world.' Then she'll tell Amina about the Empire State Building, and the single yellow rose.

I haven't told Edith about my more recent proposal. It happened fourteen years ago in our kitchen, a year before Frank died. He was eating a boiled egg, which I had peeled for him. All of a sudden, I noticed that Frank had fallen to the floor. I rushed to help him, so that we were both crouched on the linoleum, our heads at the level of the kitchen table. Frank had fallen to his knees, one hand gripping the chair's cane seat; now he managed to get one foot on the floor, as if he were trying to stand.

'Stay where you are,' I told him. 'Don't move.'

'Tabby—'

'Where does it hurt?'

Frank put his hand to his chest, and I thought: this is it. In a way it would have been a blessing, to go quickly then and avoid the worst stage of the disease. I would have called the ambulance, and they would have come for him, and he would have died at Strong Memorial Hospital, one of the best hospitals in America according to *US News and World Report*.

At the same time that I was thinking those things, I was praying for the opposite: for that dumb, ugly muscle to keep doing its job a little longer, to give me just a little more time to prepare.

'I'll call Dr Pashman, Frank. Don't move.'

Frank looked at me with deep frustration, an expression I got used to in the last few years. I imagined his state of mind like the kind of dream in which something needs to be done or said, and the feet or the voice can't be made to accomplish the necessary action. Either that, or they insist on acting in a way completely contrary to your intention.

I don't know if that was what it was like for Frank. I didn't try to put myself in his shoes. That's something I never did with my students, and I do think it's a mistake in general. How can we presume to know what other people's experiences are like?

In any case, Frank finally spoke. He did not seem to be having a heart problem at all.

'Will you just listen for a minute?' demanded my husband of forty-seven years, his voice too loud and annoyed. 'Tabby, will you marry me?'

Edith and Amina are making a three-point turn. They're practising right in front of my house, where the tract ends in a circle. All of the snow has been cleared from the streets and driveways, and most of the rest has got dirty from everyone's boots. It's piled up on the side of the road in ashy, yellow banks. Only the cornfield is pure white and unsullied. It's likely not to snow again until late January or February; our winters, everyone says, are not what they used to be.

Amina backs up and brakes sharply. Then, unexpectedly, she rolls down her window and calls out. She lifts her hand in a little wave, even though it's impossible that she could see me. She's waving just in case I'm here, standing in front of the sink, hiding in broad daylight like a ghost. □

GRANTA

EXILE
Olga Grushin

Olga Grushin was born in 1971 in Moscow. In 1976 her father found himself at odds with the state, and her family moved to Prague, where she began writing fairy tales about 'lonely donkeys and princesses who refused to make their beds'. She returned to Moscow in 1981, and in 1989 accepted an invitation to enter Emory University in Atlanta, Georgia, as the first Soviet citizen to pursue an American undergraduate degree. Her post-graduation jobs ran the gamut—from a jazz bar hostess to an interpreter for President Carter. She wrote throughout. Her first novel, 'The Dream Life of Sukhanov' (Viking/Putnam), was a finalist for the Los Angeles Times Award for First Fiction and was shortlisted for the Orange Award for New Writers. She lives near Washington, DC with her husband and son. 'Exile' is taken from a novel-in-progress.

Odoyevsky—once Georgiy, like the noble armour-clad saint slaying the dragon on Moscow's coat of arms, now simply George, pronounced nasally, in the French manner—was striding through Paris on a March evening in 1927. Chilly rain washed over the darkening city, turning his footsteps watery and indecisive, imbuing the crowded cafes he passed on busier streets with a charmed warmth of steaming drinks, intimate conversations, an almost tangible happiness, plunging the deserted alleys of shuttered shop fronts into which he now turned into a sloshing, soggy gloom.

He walked quickly but without aim. His shoes were soaked through, and his upturned collar had grown heavy, yet he delayed going home: he owed two months' rent, and his landlord had recently acquired the nasty habit of lying in wait for his return, always emerging from his ground-floor lair in those detestable brown slippers of his, with that eternal cup of hot chocolate held in his pink, spotted hand with nauseating refinement, the little finger stuck out, at the precise moment when Odoyevsky, sneaking up the unlit staircase, his overcoat sleeves pulled down to conceal his cufflinks, would finally release his breath. He walked hardly noticing the rain, not thinking, yet abandoning himself, as he did so often, to a sort of involuntary wordless narrative of another, brilliant and joyous life in some parallel layer of consciousness, remembering other rains, the rains of his childhood, the rains of his youth: the wonderfully cosy patter against the glassed walls of the veranda where spring light would seep through the ivy and fall soft and green on the pages of a magazine as he sat copying new verses of his beloved Blok or Gumilev into a secret notebook; the rustle of a light drizzle in the garden lying before him, blue and shadowy and deeply mysterious, while he would perch on a sill in his bedroom, the window pushed open, through many a sleepless summer night, tracing the slow, brightening tread of aromatic hours and struggling with an elusive rhyme; the cold, dreary dignity of a late autumnal downpour, which would make the horses' heaving sides glisten so sleekly as his carriage flew along the canals of St Petersburg, bringing him closer and closer to that hour spent practising dance steps in the heated ballroom where, oblivious to the girls his age, in their stiff pastel-coloured dresses and with fussy bows in their hair—the girls he was obliged to lead across the candlelit floor in repetitious waltz figures—

he would watch, always watch the sombrely clad woman at the piano, her nervous fingers, her sad eyes, her absently smiling pale lips.

He never learned what had befallen her in the years that followed, but he did chance to hear of his cousin's house on Liteiny Boulevard, the place of those weekly lessons he had grown to anticipate with such terror and delight. At a New Year's Eve gathering some winters past, when he could still toast matter-of-factly to his imminent return, a guest's acquaintance, a mousy man with an erased face and a newly minted position, sojourning in Paris on some nebulous errand of the young state, had mentioned in passing that an agricultural union had come into possession of the celebrated Sergey Odoyevsky mansion. An absurd vision of burly, pitchfork-wielding peasants propping their muddy boots on his aunt's treasured inlaid tables and chopping up the piano—her piano—for firewood did much to quell the mood of feverish expectation in which he had been living ever since his escape from the Crimea; for once his own house had been gutted by fire, it was his cousin's house, in all its impossibly preserved, familiar order, with the candlelit ballroom frozen in his memory like an ancient fly in a piece of amber, to which he would see himself returning, again and again, to find her still sitting at the piano, her face not a day older than it had been that autumn of 1915, her collar still impeccably starched, her eyes at last brimming with happiness.

In his present fantasies, grown less urgent but no less frequent, he staged his triumphant homecoming at his parents' country estate. He clung to his perfect ignorance of its fate. By now the numbers of visitors from Russia had dwindled, and in the absence of hard facts he was left free to imagine that obscure green corner of the world just north of Suzdal with its slow-paced stateliness unchanged, waiting for the day when its rightful owner would step off the train at the tiny station, with that tipsy row of gas lamps he had counted so many times as a bored boy listening for the whistle of an approaching locomotive, walk the winding path through the birch grove until that first heart-stopping glimpse of the yellow facade with its white columns and the small balcony behind an elaborate railing, run up the creaking steps of the veranda—and enter the rooms, with their dear smells of dried flowers, apple pies and leather bindings…

The miserable rain of tonight threatened to wash away the last of the meaningless stage decorations of Paris, and he finally conceded that it might be prudent to seek shelter before his only pair of shoes disintegrated into shreds. A weak light flickered in a barred basement window, and, after squinting at the streaming sign above it, he descended the five or six steps and pushed at the heavy door. It offered unexpectedly little resistance and he burst inside in a misjudged explosion of water. The man at the desk glanced up over the rims of his spectacles. He was middle-aged, rotund, as dusty, sleepy and lived-in as the cramped, stuffy rooms that retreated into the dimness behind his comfortably clad back; but his eyes, comically magnified by the convexity of his glasses, moved with startling sharpness.

'*Bonsoir, monsieur,*' the man said pleasantly, pretending not to notice the puddle that had already begun to form around Odoyevsky's feet. 'Are you searching for anything in particular?'

Odoyevsky shook his head—rain flew from his hair—and walked past the man with no greeting. Once a paragon of aristocratic courtesy, he had let his manners lapse on foreign soil. Perhaps he had dispensed with the habitual trappings of his existence out of an irrational yet growing suspicion that this interlude of exile—a brief annoyance at first, now an even stretch far, far into the mists of time—this whole interruption of life as he had known it was but a tedious dream, the kind that, whenever he found himself on the brink of waking, would stealthily nudge him into a deeper realm of sleep. His instinctive response had been to strip his days down to the bare minimum necessary for survival, letting the muscles of his soul expand and contract on reveries alone, crossing the hated city of Paris between the homes of his pupils like a morose, solitary shadow—as if allowing himself simple acts of politeness or conceding some passing enjoyment would be tantamount to an open confession of defeat on his part, to a willingness to surrender to this unreality.

Bookstores, for one, were among the old St Petersburg pleasures that he denied himself here. Once in a fortnight he would duck into a small, dirty, soulless shop near his flat that sold cigarettes, shaving cream and émigré newspapers, but he had not entered a place like this in years. He moved past the shelves not stopping, not looking, propelled by a single desire to flee the damp, chilly swing of the front door. But as he penetrated deeper and deeper into the warm brown cave, the smells of old bindings stole into his lungs, and he felt a curious emotion beginning to crest in some recently unused corner of his being. These smells—these smells were so much like the long-ago smells in their country library; and the books themselves—he saw a sprinkling of Cyrillic on more than a few weathered spines.

He stooped to pick one up, recognizing, with a not unpleasant jolt, the title, the tan colouring, the golden numeral '1', of a certain book he had loved as a boy. There had been two copies of this very 1891 edition in their library—or rather, he corrected himself silently, there *were* two copies, for, of course, the library was there still. Yes, somewhere in the quiet green depths of Russia, he believed, he had to believe, in a dark-walled, low-ceilinged room, rows of leather-bound volumes still stood on their shelves, and two stout leather chairs still faced one another; and in one of them, his legs tucked under, his forehead creased in concentration, the ghost of a child struggled with heavy folios under the tranquil light of a fat little lamp, breathlessly turning age-spotted pages. There had been pictures on the library walls, he remembered, illustrations to Russian folk tales—birds with sad human faces and black wings folded across their metallic, dazzling bodies, grinning wolves, bearded men in curling red shoes; and each night, as he sat reading into the small hours, the birds with stars in place of their eyes would stare at him from their pools of darkness, and the wolves would lick their snouts with slow crimson tongues, and the shadows would deepen, changing ever so subtly, moving like low branches of fir trees in a mysterious, ancient forest; and night after night he would grow strangely oppressed, and long to walk away from this simple, quiet place, to escape into another, expansive and radiant world he knew only from books—a world full of sailing caravels, of starlight rippling under graceful arched bridges, of soaring cathedrals in remote ancient cities.

He had escaped. He had seen the blinding white sun set afire the copper jugs in the bazaars of Istanbul, had bent his head to enter the medieval cellars of the alchemists of Prague, had watched the oars fragment the trembling reflections of palaces in the waters of Venice—and had found the world wanting. Its cathedrals were dismal, echoing shells that bristled with scowling gargoyles; its canals smelled of rot; its caravels were boats nearly sinking under the weight of refugees...

'Ah yes!' a soft voice exclaimed into his back. 'A wonderful edition, this one. I acquired it only last week.'

He started. Standing in the aisle behind him, the shop owner barely reached his shoulder. Odoyevsky saw that he was still holding the book he had pulled from the shelf. He felt his fingers tighten around it, then heard his own voice asking, 'How much?' He sounded hoarse: he had not spoken for hours, was quite unused to addressing strangers, in fact.

The man thoughtfully rolled back and forth on the heels of his feet.

'Well, now,' he said, smiling a little, 'one hesitates to put a price on such a thing. Not old, of course, yet already a piece of a vanquished, cherished past. It has some very fine illustrations by Vrubel, you know. To be frank, I would be a bit sad to let it go. I was hoping to peruse it at leisure—Russian literature has always been my passion, you see. My family even resided in Russia for some years... But then, I dare say you've heard of my little shop?'

'No,' said Odoyevsky brusquely; but as he said it, he recalled the sign glistening with rain above the window and knew that he had indeed heard the proprietor's name from the parents of a pupil who at times argued, in rising voices, behind half-closed doors (for they too were trapped in their dreams, and in dreams one was heedless of privacy), debating whether to take their remaining family treasures, rescued from Russia with such trouble, to the cunning but fair Monsieur Whatever; there had been some mention of a son in Russia, too, of something that had happened perhaps... He did not remember; it hardly mattered. 'How much?'

The shop owner moved his lips with a look of mild regret and named a price.

Odoyevsky stared at the man's rotund belly, the sagging cardigan, the sparkling spectacles in a sudden convulsion of loathing. He thought of saying quite a few things in his flawless, his superior French—that Paris was an ugly city of stone expanses and trifling pastimes, with caricature cut-outs for its denizens; that the whole herd of their second-rate poets, who knew nothing about suffering and played with gusto at being poor while sipping their absinthe and ogling their women in their cafes, weren't worth a single line of Blok (starved at the age of forty-one in a non-existent place called Petrograd), a single verse of Gumilev (shot without trial at the age of thirty-five); that this was all a shameful, intolerable mistake... He said nothing. Turning to the shelf, he leafed through the book, steeling himself to send it off gently into the gaping, dusty void.

The volume fell open at the title page.

After a moment of blankness, he felt gratified by the ease with which his memory restored to him the two minuscule roundels encasing a few barely distinguishable winged figures, the verses of the epigraph in twin columns of tiny print, below the author's name and above the words 'Volume II', and all the rest—the green country haze of a June evening a decade and a half ago, dragonflies darting over a black pond, his and his brother's ruthless hands tearing at the wrappings of their identical parcels. He allowed his silent lips to shape the familiar words. He had not thought of the poem for many years now, but in another life, he recalled with a pang, he whispered it often while meandering in the delightful, enchanted fog between wakefulness and sleep, in mute, exulted expectation, as if sounding out his own destiny, his own bright release into life:

No, I'm not Byron—I'm another,
As yet unfathomed, chosen one—
Like he, a wanderer exiled by the world,
But with a Russian soul.
I began earlier, will end early,
My mind will not accomplish much;
Within my soul, as in the ocean,
Lies the burden of smashed hopes.
Who can, O my sullen ocean,
Your mysteries fathom? Who
Will tell the crowd of my thoughts?
I or God—or no one...

At once conscious of the bookseller's patient middle-aged breathing, he shut the book, a bit roughly, and thrust it into the opening between Pushkin's *Little Tragedies* and some grey monstrosity entitled *Nightingales and Axes: A Digest of Russian Classics from Pushkin to Dostoyevsky*. As he did so, the spine threw a golden flash into his eyes.

He caught his breath in surprise, then reached for it once again, ignoring the proprietary wheezing at his elbow, louder and closer now, almost grazing his cheek. Indeed, he had not been mistaken—there it was, that odd idiosyncrasy he had once found so heartbreaking: 'Volume 1' on the spine, 'Volume II' on the title page, as if the publisher had wistfully tried to smuggle another, phantom-like body of Lermontov's works into being, hoping perhaps, by a subtle switch between Arabic and Roman numerals, to confuse the fate that would deprive the genius of life just short of his twenty-seventh birthday.

Russian poets, ever the beloved of tragedy, he thought, and turned the page over.

Inside the cover, at the top, a few lines were written boldly on a diagonal. He let his eyes travel over the words, though in some dark, solitary, aching space in his chest he already knew what they said.

'To Vladimir from his father on his thirteenth birthday. Live up to your gift. Boris Odoyevsky, 1912.'

To Vladimir from Boris Odoyevsky.

For one light-headed moment he stood watching the hardwood floors darkening with the imprints of his soaked shoes, waiting for the pain to drain from his throat. Then, carefully, he shut the book, moving with slow deliberation to prevent the shaking in his hands.

'Where did you get this?' he asked.

His voice was even, he noted with a strange, suspended detachment.

The bookseller issued a delicate cough, began to retreat into the dimness of his shop.

'A gentleman brought it in the other day,' he said, smiling over his shoulder. 'Or perhaps not exactly a gentleman—but then, one can never be certain, a duke yesterday, a waiter today, perhaps a duke again tomorrow, one must be mindful of the delicacies of the situation, you understand, I am sure—though nowadays, I have to say, it looks rather less likely—'

Odoyevsky still had not moved.

'The man, did he leave a name? An address?'

'No, monsieur, and, naturally, it is my policy never to pry into—'

'What did he look like?'

'I would hesitate to say, monsieur.' No longer smiling, the proprietor stopped by his desk, ruffled some pages. 'I study books, not faces. Incidentally, if Lermontov is the object of your interest—' He paused, a tactful, insincere look in his eyes, then continued softly, 'I do, of course, have some other editions—not illustrated, you understand, but you might find them a bit more—'

All at once Odoyevsky felt suffocated by the close odours of this place, by this crowding pressure of his countrymen's presences, his countrymen's memories, this pathetic, threadbare compendium of commonplaces for sale—of leisurely childhood strolls through sun-tossed linden alleys with a treasured volume of fairy tales tucked into a governess's voluminous black purse; of spring nights redolent of lilac bushes, sonorous with the silent swell of silver poetry entering one's youthful blood for the first time; of so many bitter, lonely, greying days spent hunched over some thick classic, some fossil of a civilization destroyed, attempting vainly to hold at bay a lifetime of fortunes gone without a trace, friendships betrayed, promises squandered, places and names and words lost—a darkening, tightly pressed infinity of memories caught forever between faded covers in unlit crannies of a small shop in a dead city, emanating their mildewing smells of failure and regret and oblivion...

Once again, the futile prayer for an awakening—an awakening in his own room, in his own house, in Russia—rose to his lips like bile.

He crossed the darkness of the shop in two strides, laid the book on the desk.

'No,' he said. 'No, I want this one. I don't have the funds just now, but I have these, here—'

He struggled with the cufflinks. His brother had received an identical pair—almost identical, the difference in one monogrammed initial, the difference between life and damnation—on his, on their, eighteenth birthday.

His fingers, steady until now, grew wild and thick.

'Please,' said the bookseller in an odd, stiff voice, and moved as if to place his own hand on Odoyevsky's sleeve. Odoyevsky jerked his elbow away. 'Please,' the bookseller repeated, his hand hovering in the brown, stale air for an instant, then gone. 'I cannot accept this.'

Odoyevsky stopped his awful, humiliating fumbling, and looked the man full in the face. A great uncoiling had begun inside him, as if all the pain of his last ten years, until now wound tightly in his soul, was finally swinging free in a violent, hot, roaring arc; and for one instant, as the blood hummed in his ears, it seemed possible that he would weep, plead, fall to his knees, tell this affluent, oblivious bedbug about the woman abandoned to the vast horror of Russia— about the fates of his mother, his father, his brother—about the endless purgatory of his exile, the gut-wrenching torment of not knowing whether anything of his world still existed, existed somewhere—and this book, the terrible, divine, merciful, merciless gift of this book...

For one instant, while all this seemed possible, he listened to the violent unfolding of his heart. Then he spat out a short, fierce Russian word, turned sharply and kicked the front door.

The sleek, glistening void threw itself at him like a beast.

'Wait, monsieur, wait!' a halting voice cried behind him. 'You've misunderstood. I can't take these, but I'd be willing to extend you credit—I sometimes make exceptions—you can pay me when you can—'

Odoyevsky stood without moving on the threshold of the night.

He barely heard the rustling of paper, the slippered steps, the mention of a Russian restaurant in the Latin Quarter; barely remembered accepting the package, insisting on signing some receipt. He promised to himself he would repay the debt; he knew the bookseller was certain he would not. The ageing man's eyes, which he met for one long, awkward moment, had lost their sharpness and now swam behind his spectacles in a quivering, doubling mist. It suddenly occurred to Odoyevsky that he had not really seen the man before, had perhaps missed something important; but other men's stories, other men's sufferings were not, could not be, his burden. Looking away, he wrapped the book in his coat and with a curt 'Thank you' walked outside.

A light whiff of daffodils drifted through the damp air; the city shimmered. At the corner of the next street, he lifted his hand to his cheek. It was streaming wet; but of course, it was only the rain. □

theguardian
HAY FESTIVAL

Please join us for the twentieth festival,
25 May to 3 June 2007

www.hayfestival.com

GRANTA

PASSOVER IN NEW ORLEANS
Dara Horn

Dara Horn was born in New Jersey in 1977. She is the author of the novels 'In the Image' (W. W. Norton) and 'The World to Come' (Hamish Hamilton/W. W. Norton), and has received the Edward Lewis Wallant Award, the Reform Judaism Prize for Jewish Fiction and the National Jewish Book Awards' First Time Author Award. Horn holds a doctorate in Hebrew and Yiddish literature, and started working on her novels while in graduate school out of a desperate need to write something without footnotes. 'Passover in New Orleans' is part of a novel-in-progress, which will be published by W. W. Norton. She lives in New York City with her husband and her almost-two-year-old daughter.

I went to a hypnotist's show once, here in New York. It was years and years ago, around 1870 or so. My wife was always very superstitious, and she was the one who wanted to see the show. But I was the one who ended up on stage. The hypnotist told me and the other volunteers to close our eyes, and I felt myself swaying back and forth as he lulled us into a trance. Then he told us all that we were musicians in a concert hall, about to play the opening notes of a symphony. I later found out that I was the only volunteer to take up the violin. When I had finished the first movement, the hypnotist dismissed the others and continued with me. By the end of the evening, I had played a dozen other instruments, traded neckties with a man in the front row, barked like a dog and kissed a woman who wasn't my wife. In the final act, I climbed up to one of the box seats just beside the stage, where I fired an imaginary pistol and assassinated an imaginary president. The audience adored it.

It is an odd thing, hypnotism: a pure replacement of human will. It sounds horrible, debased, that anyone would demean himself enough to voluntarily succumb to the desires of others. But the truth is that it is a relief. To play whatever they tell you to play, and hear everyone applaud. From the moment I undertook my first mission, when I was seventeen years old, I sustained myself on such applause. And it wasn't until decades later that I understood my mistake. I thought they were applauding me, but they were actually applauding the hypnotist. And I was merely the hypnotist's slave.

That first mission was elegant. The officers removed me from the company, provided me with a real Rebel uniform (borrowed from a particularly punctilious enemy corpse who had had the gentility to bleed almost exclusively on to his hat) and then drilled me for weeks on how I would be carried by gunboat to some Mississippi island, where I would then have to insert myself into one of several barrels to be passed along to smugglers, who would then transport the goods the remaining hundred miles to New Orleans, where I would pose as a refugee from a decimated Rebel company, looking for the only kin I had left in the entire South. Once I reached my mother's cousin's house, I would have to convince her and her family that I had joined a Rebel unit and betrayed the Union out of loyalty to my parents, whose whole business was run on cotton, and in particular to my mother, whose beloved cousins had been suffering in New Orleans—

and of course my mother hadn't been able to tell them about me, because of the censoring of the mail and the blockades; in fact, no one in the family knew where I was, and now that my regiment had been destroyed, I had nowhere left to go, and had been given furlough by the command to spend an evening with family before reporting back to the nearest headquarters to be reassigned.

The goal, it was decided, was to get me to New Orleans in time for Passover—which coincided nicely with the navy's plan to capture New Orleans. This part of the plan, I'm proud to say, was my own idea. (The officers had suggested Easter, but I explained to them the limitations of that possibility.) It happens to be true—I freely informed my superiors—that every Hebrew in the world is obliged to celebrate the Passover holiday at a table with other Hebrews, and there's even a part of the Passover service right at the beginning of the meal where the head of the household has to open the door and invite all who are hungry to come and eat. The officers were quite thrilled to hear about that one. Hebrew hospitality would save the Union yet. And an uninvited guest was exactly what I would be in the home of Henry Hyams: cotton and dry-goods merchant, husband of my mother's cousin, member of the Louisiana State Legislature, relation and confidant of Judah P. Benjamin, Secretary of State of the Confederate States of America—and, of course, a repulsive traitor to these great United States. I hadn't seen him since I was nine years old, but I remembered him as a kind man, one who brought me toys and saltwater taffies from places where he had travelled, always attaching a story to each gift about what a rare treasure it was, or how the candy shop by the seaside had been about to close when he convinced the candyman to sell him the very last box of taffies. When I was a little boy, he used to lift me up high in the air when he walked through our family's door, until I was looking down at his sideburned face, laughing loudly at my new view of the world, where the adults were far below me and I had triumphed over them, all by his raising me into the sky.

My mission was to kill him.

There's a knot that you feel in your stomach when you're about to do something dangerous—when you become a bit anxious, say, about the fact that you're about to cross enemy lines and enter a place where you will enjoy an excellent chance of being not only caught, but also hanged—and then there's a different knot that you feel in your stomach when you're about to do something wrong. When you are seventeen years old, you are accustomed to believing that you simply don't know things, that there is an entire world of considerations and complications that you aren't obliged to concern yourself with, and so you tell yourself that one knot is the other knot, and that you are just terrified of being hanged. But you know the difference.

Let me tell you something about what it's like to be folded into a barrel in the back of a smuggler's boat with nothing but a small canteen of water, an even smaller tin of gruel, a chisel and a packet of poison. For the first six hours, your muscles paralyse you. For the second six hours, your thoughts paralyse you. But for the third six hours and beyond, your spirit is set free into the wide-open spaces of memory and imagination, and you start to see visions. By the evening of the second day, you have become a prophet, and by the evening of the third day, you rise from that coffin-barrel as the Messiah. I was prepared to resurrect myself and redeem the world, but unfortunately the journey from Ship's Island in Mississippi to New Orleans was only two days long.

Those first six hours inside the darkness of that barrel, into which I was folded like a message in a bottle, were agony. But it was a physical agony, which was at least a relief from the knot in my stomach, whose real origin I knew better than I could admit. After the first six hours passed, with their tortures of neck and knees and the insistent smell from the rags that I had stuffed into my uniform's crotch, my mind freed itself. I began to understand why my teachers had always insisted on rote memorization of poems and speeches and the like, and I wished I had paid more attention to my Hebrew tutors, or even to my English ones, because the ability to entertain oneself with memorized passages from the Bible (or from the *Farmer's Almanac*, for that matter) is indispensable to anyone stuck in a barrel in the bottom of a boat. I tried to recite the passage from the Torah that I had chanted at my bar mitzvah, the Song at the Sea from Exodus, and imagined myself as a new Moses, sent downriver in a basket into the heart of Pharaoh's dominion. I would enter Pharaoh's territory, I imagined, kill an Egyptian taskmaster (a slave owner, I told myself again and again, who was planning to kill Lincoln! How could I possibly be more just, more right?) and then flee back north so that

God could reveal himself to me in the burning bush of Union pride. This was just the journey in the basket, the trip down the Nile. But these were false thoughts, and I knew it. Instead, as the second six hours gave way to the third, I tried to remember everything I could about my mission, except, of course, for Henry Hyams himself. And I found myself thinking back to how it had begun.

The previous autumn, we had observed the Day of Atonement in the camp. I know it sounds improbable, a Yom Kippur service in the Union Army, but it happened. It was Abraham Mendoza's idea. Sergeant Mendoza was twenty-two years old, dark-eyed and olive-skinned, also from New York City, and, as he was thrilled to tell anyone who asked (and even those who didn't), his forebears had come to the North American colonies in 1699, after being banished from Spain in 1492 and spending the intervening centuries in some godforsaken place in Brazil—all of which made Mendoza himself a sixth-generation American, and embarrassingly proud of it. Unlike most Jews of his background, nearly all of whom had disappeared like a lost tribe into the wilderness of American Christianity, Mendoza was a bookish, traditional sort who had committed most of the Pentateuch and half the Psalms to memory in Hebrew, English and even in the Spanish-Jewish jargon, and he would quote chapter and verse about proclaiming liberty throughout the land and walking through the valley of the shadow of death any time he was giving any kind of order, oblivious enough not to notice that everyone was snickering at him behind his back. I found him insufferable and I assumed the feeling was mutual.

But one evening in the camp, I noticed him waiting behind me for the latrine. Because I was trying to ignore him, I was of course attuned to his every move. And so I heard him quite clearly when he mumbled in my direction, under his breath, '*Amcha?*'

It's a Hebrew word, *amcha*. Technically it means 'your people'. But for Hebrews, it is a code—a simple word whispered in a stranger's ear to see if he recognizes it, at which point the question is already answered. It's a perfect code, because if the person asked fails to respond, it might just as easily be disguised as a cough. And what makes it even more perfect is that only a Hebrew can use it, because no one else, except perhaps some Germans, can pronounce the guttural 'ch'. Mendoza's name and complexion gave him away immediately, of course, but I myself am quite fair, and rather tall too, not to mention that I prefer not to divulge my ancestry to everyone I meet. So he asked.

'What an eloquent sneeze,' I thought of exclaiming. Instead, I thought of my parents and lowered my own voice. *'Amcha,'* I replied.

'Wait for me on the left side of the barracks tomorrow, at eighteen hundred hours,' he said.

Before I could ask why, the line behind me had forced me to enter the latrine; by the time I was finished, Mendoza was gone.

I went to wait for him the following evening, more out of curiosity than anything else. When I arrived at the spot, I was surprised to see two other soldiers already there—Isaac Calderon and Benjamin Gratz, two sixteen-year-old enlisted men. Before I could even speak to them, Mendoza had arrived. 'We've been excused this evening,' Mendoza informed me, 'for the eve of Yom Kippur.'

Yom Kippur! I had completely forgotten about it. But Mendoza hadn't. I saw now that he had a small prayer book in his hand as he led us outside the borders of the camp and began the service in an open field. There were nineteen of us, it turned out, including some men I had never met and a few faces that surprised me. Mendoza planted his torch in the ground and lit it, and turned to the company. He announced that the service would need to be abridged. We nodded our assent, and he opened his prayer book to begin.

After the prayer was finished, we all breathed in that fall air, now dark with the first starlight, with relief and renewal. The year was fresh, unstained and beautiful as the rattle of the crickets in that open field on that cool clear night. As we returned to the camp, Mendoza began talking with me, and, unblemished by my prior loathing, I answered him. We talked about our families, our relatives near and far—holiday postcards received from distant cousins, pranks played by our fathers, foods cooked by our mothers, and all the other small details of home that lonely soldiers remember. The service that night, strange though it was, was a piece of home, and now, as we casually spoke of our mothers and cousins, Mendoza was family.

Several months later, I found myself called into the tent of the major himself, on an evening when a rumour had spread that the brigadier-general was visiting our camp. I was certain that I was going to be told that I was to receive a promotion. And when I entered the tent on that cold spring evening and saw the major, the colonel and the brigadier-general himself seated at a table before me, each with a pipe in his mouth, I felt even more certain. I could hardly stifle a smile as I greeted them and waited for the major to address me, as the brigadier-general blew a ring of smoke in the air. But it was the brigadier-general who spoke.

'Sergeant Mendoza has reported to us that you have relations in New Orleans,' he said, resting his pipe in a wooden holder on the table between us. 'Specifically, a Mr and Mrs Henry Hyams. Is that correct, Rappaport?'

I paused to breathe, tasting the smoke of his pipe. 'Yes, sir. Mrs Hyams is my mother's first cousin, sir,' I replied, both disappointed and baffled. It seemed unlikely that an announcement of a promotion would commence with a review of my family tree. And then I tried to suppress a shudder. I was only seventeen years old and my immediate thought was that my mother had somehow written to her cousins to have me sent back home.

The major noticed my trembling and smiled. 'At ease,' he said, taking up his pipe again.

I put a foot to one side and folded my hands behind my back, but I felt even more uneasy than I had felt before. My stomach shivered as he continued.

'You are hardly the only Union soldier to have family relations south of the Mason–Dixon line, Rappaport,' the brigadier-general said, as if reciting from a book. 'We wondered what your opinion might be of this Henry Hyams.'

It occurred to me then that perhaps this was a promotion after all, simply preceded by a test that I needed to pass. The illogic of this idea—that a visiting officer would ask me these questions in order to promote me, or that such an examination would require a special visit to the officers' tent at such an odd time of day, or that these questions were in any way pertinent to my future in the company—did not occur to my supremely arrogant adolescent mind. I didn't even think of Henry; the man himself was irrelevant. Instead I grinned and smartly answered, 'Henry Hyams is a slave owner and a Rebel, sir, and therefore deserving of every disdain.'

The three officers smiled. At seventeen, I could not yet tell the difference on strangers' faces between admiration and condescension, and I did not yet know that I ought always to expect the latter. I suppressed a smile of my own, certain that I had triumphed.

Another puff of smoke. 'What does he do, this Hyams of yours?'

I winced at the 'of yours'. And then I felt a memory, the sort that one senses physically in the body instead of envisioning in the mind. At that moment my body was a small boy's, and strong hands were reaching down to lift me up. I felt the grip of those hands in my armpits right at that moment, and the breeze at the nape of my neck as those hands hoisted me high in the air. I pushed the memory aside. 'I haven't seen him in years, sir,' I answered, still hoping to pass the test. 'My father's shipping company worked with him on occasion. He was a cotton dealer out of New Orleans.'

The brigadier-general chewed on his pipe as the three of them eyed me from what now seemed like a judges' bench. When he spoke again, his voice was slow and deliberate, enunciating each word. 'It seems that his professional aspirations have changed since you and he were last in contact,' he said, with a slight smirk. I was disturbed to notice that the two other officers smirked along with him. I began to suspect that this wasn't about a promotion at all. With deliberate, slow movements, the brigadier-general placed the pipe back in the holder, letting the smoke weave itself into a smooth veil before my eyes. Then he looked back at me and said, 'Henry Hyams is a Confederate spy.'

He might as well have told me that Henry Hyams was the emperor of Japan. 'A spy, sir?' It couldn't possibly be true. Was this another test? But no, the test was about to come.

'A very highly placed one, in fact,' the brigadier-general said, and tapped a finger on the table. 'With ties to Judah Benjamin.'

'What—what ties, sir?' I asked, barely able to choke out the words. The name itself had nauseated me: Judah P. Benjamin, the first Jew to serve in the United States Senate, and now the first Jewish cabinet member in history—but one who had chosen to devote his talents to, of all countries on earth, the Confederacy, where he served passionately as the Secretary of State and was the closest confidant of Jefferson Davis himself. Every Hebrew in the Union blanched at his name. As for me, I nearly vomited.

'It seems that Benjamin is his first cousin. But not yours, apparently, your being related through the wife, of course. We're quite pleased about that.' He smiled again.

For the rest of my life, I will be ashamed to remember that I smiled back. I mark that smile, now, as the beginning of the end, my first relinquishment of my own will, the moment when I began to succumb.

'Hyams has been in and out of the border states in the past few months,' the brigadier-general continued. 'As you know, he used to do frequent business in the North, before the war, and has many contacts there.' He paused, looked at me. Was it a reference to my parents? I couldn't help but look down, dodging his eye. 'He's also slipped over the border itself many times, and now we have managed to intercept his communications with Richmond. There is a dire plot afoot.' He paused, waiting for me, which I resented.

'What sort of plot, sir?' I asked, though I did not want to know.

'An assassination plot. Against President Lincoln.'

Lincoln?

'That's—that's not possible, sir,' I stammered.

'Why?' the major asked.

I saw that he and the others were genuinely interested, certain, it seemed, that I had something to say to them that they didn't already know. I wished I did. 'Mr Henry Hyams is—he's not that sort of man, sir,' I said. But even as I said the words, I knew they were irrelevant. It was impossible, I knew, but not because Henry wouldn't do it. It was impossible because no one would do it.

'We could show you rather convincing evidence to the contrary,' the major said. 'I hope that will not be necessary.'

'But—but it's impossible,' I insisted. I began babbling about the strength of the Union, the chivalry of the Confederate forces, the respect for the rule of law even in the South. It was impossible, I concluded, because he was Lincoln, because this was America, North or South, because no one had ever assassinated a president, because no one would ever dare.

'That is precisely what we propose that you ensure,' said the brigadier-general, still smiling, 'by assassinating Henry Hyams before the plot can progress.'

Surely this was some sort of mistake. The three men watched me, grinning. The blood in my body began draining into my shoes.

'Are—are you suggesting that I kill my cousin, sir,' I said slowly. It wasn't a question, of course. The three of them continued grinning at me. Perhaps it was still a test, I then thought. Perhaps I was being tested by God.

'Your actions would do honour to your race,' the major said.

I stared at him. My race?

'Do—do you mean my country, sir,' I stammered, this time trying to make it sound like a question, but without succeeding. I had not yet recovered from his proposition. *I will be a murderer*, I thought to myself. *I will be my own cousin's murderer*. I was theoretically aware, of course, that simply enlisting in the army had automatically enrolled me as a potential murderer—a role which the insufferable seventeen-year-old boy I was had been thrilled to embrace. But this was different. I wasn't merely cannon fodder; I was a bullet. And they were planning to fire me at will. At Henry Hyams. In my memory those hands held me under the armpits again, but now my body would not move.

'Both your country and your race, of course,' the brigadier-general said brightly, warming to his theme. 'Judah Benjamin and his kin have done your race a great disservice. Every Hebrew in the Union will reward you if you undo what he has done.'

The three officers looked me in the eye and, under their gaze, I realized what they saw. While I looked in the mirror and saw Jacob Rappaport, a tall, blond, seventeen-year-old American boy, the three men at this table looked at me and saw Judah Benjamin. And I suddenly knew that I would do anything not to be him.

The three of them continued speaking, their words buzzing through my brain in a blur. As I listened, numbed, to the cadences of their voices, it was like that evening years later, when I stood on stage before the hypnotist and played the violin. I smiled again. And then I felt, like the tug of sleep, the ebbing of my own will.

'It is dearly hoped that this is not a death mission for you.'

'Though if it should prove to be so, we are confident that you would not refuse the call of duty.'

'It is essential that it appear accidental.'

'Shooting is no good.'

'No one should discover that it was you.'

'You shall be pleased to know that a plan has been devised.'

'A dose of poison would be placed in his drink.'

'Subtlety is essential.'

'We would provide the lye.'

'If you were to be captured, you might consider using the lye yourself.'

'You would never consider disgracing yourself by returning without success.'

'If you succeed, the entire Union will immortalize you.'

'Lincoln himself shall thank you, on behalf of your entire race.'

'We know you are no Judas Benjamin.'

'Imagine yourself written up in the history books.'

'You would be another Hebrew spy, like in Scripture.'

'Cunning.'

'Inscrutable.'

'But don't bring us grapes. We prefer corpses.'

'It is essential that it appear accidental.'

'Shooting is no good.'

'Judas Benjamin has done your race a great disservice.'

'It can all be corrected with a little lye.'

'We would provide the lye.'

I don't recall saying yes. But it didn't matter. Their words enveloped me, became me. And then I disappeared.

The barrel was removed from the boat and hidden in what I later discovered was a stable near a dock in New Orleans around midnight on the second day, and I waited a long time before prying my way out. With my arms numb and my hands shaking, it took longer than I expected to force the barrel open. And then I emerged, standing on my crimped and shaking legs, and crept out of the stable, free at last in the empty southern night.

It was a warm and very humid, though of course I was already soaked with sweat. The breeze on that almost-full-mooned night was pure freedom. But my ecstasy at feeling my limbs unfold faded quickly as I remembered that now the real horror would begin. I hurried out on to the street and then past the end of the dock, where I climbed down on to the river bank. It was a few hours before daybreak, and despite this being cosmopolitan New Orleans, no one but me seemed to be out, not even any drunks. I stripped, buried the filthy rags from inside my trousers under a rock by the edge of the grass and then immersed myself in the water of the mighty Mississippi. I'm a city boy, of course. But never have I felt more pure than when I slipped beneath that murky river water on that moonlit night. I immersed myself again and again, unable to believe that I was still living, then floated on my back and admired the stars. I emerged from the water like a newborn baby. Then, after putting the uniform back on, I slept for an hour or two there on the river bank, knowing my own nerves would wake me before dawn, and they did. I watched as the first hints of sunlight greyed the sky above the mile-wide river, and I saw the sky seethe into full daylight as the first few people (smugglers, probably) stepped out on to the docks. I ate the last scraped bits of gruel from my tin and finished off the water I had been so carefully rationing out of my canteen. As the daylight broadened into morning, I reached further into my little bag and pulled out a paper sign which I hung around my neck. The sign had been my own brilliant plan. It read as follows:

Please excuse this HERO,
Who has been rendered
DEAF and DUMB
by YANKEE CANNON FIRE,
Tho' the Tune of 'DIXIE' rings in his Ears.

If you are wondering how cannon fire could render someone dumb, rest assured that such a suggestion merely renders those who read it even dumber. Once I had freed myself from bondage, this ingenious sign not only prevented me from becoming involved in awkward conversations with anyone thrilled to see a man in uniform on the street, but also allowed the Rebels themselves to reimburse a Union spy. By slackening my face into an idiotic smile, pointing to my sign, bowing grandly to the ladies and holding out my Rebel army cap (collected, I should mention, from a corpse who had been less than punctilious about the blood on the rest of his uniform, but very genteel when it came to his hat), I managed to amass a small fortune in alms. In this fashion I collected enough Confederate money to provide for whatever needs I might have during my time in the haunted ghost town that is New Orleans.

It was hot. I had never felt humidity like that. The whole city was dripping with sweat. I mean that literally. There were beaded droplets of sweat on every crooked porch railing of every house in town. And everything, everything drooped. The wooden porches of every house, even the newest ones, sagged in the centre, as if giving up on life. Low, heavy trees drooped their long, willowy branches almost down to the sidewalks. In the streets downtown, where I strolled for a bit before heading uptown towards the Garden District, the air was thick with pipe smoke, sweat and sloth. Even the people drooped.

After passing many drooping houses and many elderly men saluting me as I walked along my way, I came across the Hebrew cemetery. Cemeteries in New Orleans are like small cities of the dead. The ground is too soft and flood-prone for subterranean graves, so the departed are instead interred in above-ground stone mausoleums, some of which are rather grander than the homes of the living. But these necropolises are not the Hebrew custom; our forefathers insisted on our being buried in the ground. It has something to do with desert life, I suppose. But because they lived in a swamp, the Jews of New Orleans, as I discovered upon entering the Hebrew cemetery, had developed a unique custom. Forced to bury their dead in ground too soft for burial, the Hebrews had created a necropolis of their own, where each of the graves consisted of a small mound of earth covered in a layer of grass; raised mausoleums made to look like part of the earth. Each plot was like a grassy plateau, marked with a modest stone plaque, a city of small truncated mountains: small hopes, small fears, small triumphs and failures, all. I walked among the graves as the sun sank over the drooping trees, and it wasn't long before I came across the Hyams family plot, at the very edge of the cemetery, under a vine-draped tree. A generation's worth of Hyamses lay waiting for the messianic age beneath this small piece of soggy land. I paused above them, and began, out of force of habit and fear, to recite the memorial prayer. But then I saw the empty space to the side of one of the graves, blank sod, and I realized that I was the only person in the world who knew precisely who would occupy it.

I glanced up at the sky, where the sun was settting, the tops of the trees on fire. If I were a braver man, a wiser man, a man in full possession of his own will, I would have asked God what I was doing, why I was doing it, how I could possibly escape. But I wasn't brave or wise. Instead, I looked at that sun and merely realized that the hour was getting late, and that it was time to continue, to do as

I was told. And then, turning away from that disappearing sun, I hurried out of the cemetery and continued on to St Charles Avenue, remembering to remove my idiotic sign just before I reached the large and decrepit wooden mansion that was number forty-six.

A slave opened the door. I don't know whom I was expecting—Henry Hyams himself, perhaps, presenting me with a dagger to insert into his chest?—but this narrow-eyed Negro took me by surprise. He looked to be about forty years old, and he didn't smile. Most of the Negroes I had seen in my life had been in entertainments and the like, and of course they had all been quite jolly, or had acted that way, playing their imaginary violins onstage. But this man was clearly cross, levelling his narrow eyes at me. Looking down to avoid his stare, I saw that he was standing with one foot bent to the side; I had wondered at first why a slave his age wouldn't be working on a plantation somewhere, but a cripple must have been a discount as a house servant. He eyed my uniform, letting his gaze roll up and down my chest. Then he looked at me with an expression of astonishing contempt, sweat beading on his forehead. Here was a man who was done pretending to please. And I, just beginning to pretend, was already used to absorbing contempt. I narrowed my own eyes and grinned.

'Mrs Henry Hyams, please,' I said. I didn't know whether Henry Hyams would be home at that hour. And even if he were, I wasn't ready to look him in the eye.

Beyond the doorway, I could see an ornate foyer with carved, painted mouldings and pale, square patches on the walls between the sconces; I wondered if paintings had been sold.

The Negro looked at me again, his gaze crossing my chest, and for a moment I imagined that he could see the poison in my pocket. 'Who's callin'?' he growled. I saw that he was eyeing my uniform, and suddenly I imagined how my ancestors must have viewed their taskmasters at every moment until this very night, Passover eve, three thousand years ago. I'm a sentimentalist, really. Though I know how absurd it was even to think it, I wished I could whisper an '*amcha*' in his ear.

'Jacob Rappaport,' I said. After playing the deaf-and-dumb war hero, the sound of my own real name astonished me. The truth was like a gulp of cold water on a hot, hot day.

The Negro stared again, and for a moment I thought he might be about to spit at my feet. Then he turned his head. 'Miz' Hyams!' he shouted. 'They's a soldja heah! Mista Rappa!' He grunted, and then, as if dismissing me himself, turned and went into the house, letting the door drift closed behind him. I caught the swinging door with my foot and watched him progressing down the hall with an agonizing limp, until I could see an enormous blue dress moving into the foyer. As the dress approached, I saw a woman's head affixed to the top of it, hair piled in a tower adorned with shoddy-looking false pearls. Presumably there was also a face somewhere, though the place where it would be was obscured by an enormous fan made of turquoise peacock feathers.

The peacock feathers moved towards me as if the bird itself were strutting in my direction, waving its gaudy tail in a delicate mating dance. 'Rappa? Who is Rappa?' a voice behind them asked. The feathers slowly lowered, and I saw her face: the pale green eyes, the full-lipped mouth stretched into a society smile, the guarded greeting and the kindness lurking far beneath it. And then I almost wept, because in the face of Elizabeth Hyams, I saw my own mother standing before me.

It had been many years since we had seen each other and I know I looked quite different than I did when I was a boy. But I do look like my mother. People have always told me so, especially when I was seventeen and barely able to grow a beard. Elizabeth Hyams must have thought so too, because she didn't even say hello. Instead, she looked at my eyes and said, 'Dear God.' And then she fainted.

'Clearly I wasn't expecting you.'

Elizabeth had recovered quickly, with me raising her off the ground and the Negro man limping to the kitchen and back with the smelling salts. I was surprised by how frail her body felt in my arms. Her voice was my mother's, with a Southern accent. She looked me over. 'And in our uniform! But—but you're a Yankee!'

'There was no way to tell you,' I said, and tried not to sicken at the words. I then began reciting the story the officers had fed me— the long and tediously sentimental tale of how I had so courageously chosen not to betray my parents' relatives in the South, the name and number of my supposed Rebel regiment, the vague imaginary battle where I had lost my comrades-in-arms, how I had walked all the way to New Orleans, et cetera, et cetera. I had practised this monologue so many times, even in the barrel, that I could perform it without the slightest thought. What I hadn't prepared for, though, was giving this speech while being watched by my mother.

'So tell me all about everything—what you've seen, all of it,' she said, her eyes full of compassion. She had believed every word.

I tried to remember not to pity myself. But I thought of my mother and had to swallow a sob. Elizabeth mistook my muted sob for a sign of my own painful past, rather than her own painful future, and I had to swallow another sob as I saw tears gathering in her eyes.

'Oh, you don't have to speak of it,' she said, grasping my hands. 'It's so cruel of me to ask. It's just that I'm thinking of our boys. Please forgive me.'

The knot in my stomach tightened as her rings dug into my fingers. Again I told myself that it was nerves. And again I knew it wasn't. But then I remembered the mesmerizing words of those three men in the officers' tent, and I put myself into the act. 'We'll rout those Yankees yet, I assure you,' I announced, and swallowed bile.

'I'm delighted to hear it from you,' she said, with genuine joy. 'The newspapers have been so gloomy. Everyone is gloomy, I suppose. Even Henry.'

Henry! No, I wouldn't think of him now, I told myself. There was no point in thinking of him now. Luckily Elizabeth herself was able to distract me. 'How are your parents?' she asked.

It was a relief to tell the truth. 'Not ruined, which is saying quite a bit,' I replied, with my first genuine smile. Although I hadn't always succeeded in not thinking about Henry during the past few weeks, I had done an admirable job of not thinking about how this mission would affect my parents. In my mind, they were preserved innocently, seated around our Passover table in New York, opening the door with earnest eagerness to welcome me home. It did not once occur to me to think otherwise. 'They're doing more business with Canada now, but it has been difficult,' I told her. 'Of course, they have been so concerned about you.'

Elizabeth flapped her fan, and I saw her looking at the floor. 'Oh, we are all fine, really quite fine,' she said, and I heard her first false note. I glanced around the bare, shabby room, then back at her, and was astonished to notice a small hole in the toe of her shoe. 'Though we're always worried about our boys,' she continued. 'All three of them are away, of course. Everyone's boys are. For the first time in my life, I've envied those mothers with daughters, the ones who used to envy me.' She smiled. 'But how glorious to have you here, a fine substitute for our boys! Henry will be so pleased to see you,' she told me, fairly chirping. 'And in our uniform, too! He already has such admiration for you.'

One fancies oneself a real man for failing to show emotion, for succeeding in pretence. I stared down at the hole in her shoe with my lips pursed, in an attitude of what I hoped would come across as modestly hidden pride. I looked into her eyes, but I closed my ears and let my mind wander, trying to think of anyone or anything but her. My memory landed on the previous autumn and Mendoza, whom I now loathed all over again. What a traitor he was, to take a private conversation and hand it over to the command, and suddenly here I was about to murder someone in my own family, all because of Mendoza! But then I wondered if perhaps this mission really was a mission from God, if Mendoza had in fact been God's unwitting agent, if I really was about to save the life of the President of the United States, to save the entire Union, to be a second Moses, a young Moses, if Mendoza's petty betrayal was actually an essential step in the repair of the entire world. And wasn't Henry Hyams a small price to pay for the repair of the entire world? But I didn't see it that way, then. All I saw was my mother's cousin doubled over in grief, as she would be that very night, if I succeeded. I wasn't Moses. I was the angel of death.

'Judah shall be here, too, I'm sure you shall be pleased to know, though he said he may be late,' I heard Elizabeth say. Her words halted my dark thoughts in their tracks. 'I don't imagine you ever met him before. His sister is ill, so he shall come alone. His wife and daughter live in France.'

'Judah?' I asked. My face showed only gentle curiosity, but I couldn't believe my luck. Could it possibly be?

She looked at me as though my brains had spilled out on to my uniform. 'Why, Judah Benjamin, of course!' she announced. Her cheeks reddened with pride. 'He's Henry's first cousin. Oh, I see why you're confused,' she said with a laugh, though I was more astonished than confused, and then I worried about why I ought to be confused instead. 'He married a Catholic, of course,' she said, in the low voice that society women use to tell you that someone has had a disease, or an affair. As a Rappaport, I had heard that voice many times. 'But that was just for the show of it. Hardly even for the show of it, actually, since he barely shows it. He often comes back to New Orleans for Passover.' She beamed.

I found this nearly impossible to believe. What secretary of state abandons his president in the midst of conflagration, travelling for days on end, just to celebrate a holiday? Benjamin may not have become a Christian, but it was impossible to believe that as a Hebrew he had suddenly become devout. There was another reason for this visit. And I rallied as I realized what it must be. Then I had another thought: that the poison in my pocket might be given to Benjamin instead, surely a more worthy target. But I was too paralysed by my hypnotists, too horrified of doing something horribly wrong. Henry was expendable; Benjamin was practically a head of state. I had to maintain the plan. In the meantime, I waited for the sun to set, made small talk with Elizabeth about my mother and Elizabeth's sons, and dreaded the moment when Henry Hyams would come home and join us for the evening meal.

Just half an hour later, he did. To my great relief, he came in the door with ten other people in tow, which mitigated my need to speak with him more than was bearable. Of course, he nearly passed out himself when he saw me standing in his foyer. But I was the one holding my breath. 'My dear boy!' he exclaimed, doffing his hat in my direction. 'The young Rappaport scion—a real man now! And a Yankee turned Rebel! I never would have guessed it!' He was taller than me, over six feet high, and the top hat he tipped in my direction reminded me of my father.

'I would never have guessed it either,' I replied, and Elizabeth began rattling on about how I couldn't bear to betray the family and so forth. I must admit I was relieved not to have to repeat the story again. I had to work hard enough not to tremble. Henry absorbed the lies, and grinned.

'Tell me, son, do I look older?' he asked me with a laugh.

'Not a bit,' I told him. And when I dared to look more closely at his face, I was surprised to see that it was true. I suppose one always imagines that people are preserved precisely as they looked when one last saw them. But in Henry's case he actually was. The war, which had so clearly aged his wife and nearly everyone else I had crossed paths with in the past year, seemed to have had the opposite effect on Henry Hyams. Unlike everyone else in America, who had become haggard and ill, Henry Hyams appeared even younger than when I had last seen him. His arms and legs and even his stomach looked lean and muscular. But more than that, it was the look in his eyes. They gleamed, as though they saw more than they would let on, like a boy playing a prank. When I was a child, that look had intrigued me, making me think of him as a boy in man's clothing. But now, as I stood before him in my Rebel uniform stolen from a corpse, I saw that gleeful look of his and felt sickened, sensing, for the first time in my short life, what it means to be a boy in man's clothing.

'I must admit, Jacob, I never imagined that we would see each other again. Eight years, has it been? How life has changed. How the world has changed.'

I smiled at him as he kissed my cheeks, and wondered what on earth I could possibly say.

An old man standing beside him removed his hat. 'We're proud of you, son,' he said, shaking his head. 'This isn't the old kind of war. My father was a veteran of the Revolution, and always spoke of how war should be about principle. I know up north they think it's about principle, but it isn't, son. It's about land. Our boys are seeding this land with their blood.'

Never in my life—my city life, my life lived in carriages and on cobblestones, lived with my parents and their business partners and the rest of their merchant friends—had I heard anyone talk about land. No one in my family had owned land for the past twenty centuries. But now I realized that many of these men did, and they meant it. I had to stop listening, I realized. The more I listened, the worse everything would become.

Fortunately, that was when Elizabeth began ushering us into the dining room for the holiday meal. As I followed the other guests, I saw Henry turn to Elizabeth. I expected to hear a friendly greeting, or even see him kiss her hand, but he didn't. Instead, I heard him say, in a voice so harsh it shocked me, 'Where is Judah?'

'Late,' she whispered back. 'He told me he would be late.'

'He had better come,' he said.

Elizabeth smiled. 'Oh, he'll be here. Be patient, you old fool,' she told him.

Henry grumbled as Elizabeth hurried past him to the table. This astonished me. All of my memories of Henry were of a cheerful, boyish man who was impossible to annoy. But those were a child's memories. After so many weeks of trying not to think of Henry, I decided to watch him, to listen, to see what kind of man I was plotting to kill. I took a seat towards the end of the table, with a good view of Henry's place at the head. And then the service began.

I'm not sure if there's anything stranger than sitting down to a Passover Seder, the feast of freedom, with every part of the meal served by slaves. But that's exactly what happened at the home of Henry Hyams. It was a good thing a fair amount of the service was in Hebrew, I suppose, because it was a whole lot more comfortable without the slaves listening, though there were plenty of awkward passages about freedom that Henry read proudly in English from his seat at the table's head. The limping Negro who had answered the door, along with a Negro woman (the lame Negro's wife? Or—I forced myself to imagine—had his own wife been sold elsewhere, and this woman was a new household purchase, a stranger?), were the ones who carried the platters of matzo and bitter herbs in and out of the somewhat shabby dining room while we sang the Hebrew hymns thanking God for freeing us from bondage. I was the new Moses, I reminded myself— not the Moses of leading the people out of Egypt (that was the president whom I was about to save), but the young Moses, the Moses who murdered the Egyptian taskmaster and then fled, saving the future of the older Moses in the process. The others, I saw, avoided eye contact with the slaves who delivered their food and dishes. But I made sure to look at them each time. The woman avoided my gaze, but the man stared back at me, with a look of strange and vicious triumph. It frightened me even more than Henry did. I looked away.

Henry Hyams led the service, rising from his seat to raise his first glass of wine and recite the opening prayers. As he sat down and slaves began to pass around the basin and pitcher for the ritual washing of hands and then platters of green vegetables, Henry introduced every man at the table, each of whom seemed to be the owner of some large plantation or mercantile concern. And then he came to me. 'And this,' he said, raising his glass in my direction with a wink, 'is my cousin, Jacob Rappaport, the greatest turncoat of the century.' I had to force myself to laugh with the company, but luckily not for long, because a moment later Judah Benjamin entered the room. And then everyone stood.

Every Hebrew in the Republic was fascinated by Judah Benjamin. Southern Hebrews saw him as the messenger of the Messiah, the herald who would proclaim liberty throughout the land to anyone who had ever felt that Jewish fear of power. Northern Hebrews saw him as the horrifying beginning of a descent into an American Jewish hell, and whispered secretly at Friday night tables that if the Confederacy were to prevail, the rot of centuries would eat through even the freshness of America and the Jews would be blamed again. My parents had shared the Southern Hebrew smugness about him, proud as could be. But after spending the past few months reading everything the officers gave me to read about Benjamin, I found that my every thought about him put me ill at ease, and it was only at a length of many years later that I was able to understand why.

Judah Benjamin was a clear American genius, one who had achieved nothing through birth and everything through self-transformation. Born on some godforsaken Caribbean island before his family relocated to North Carolina, where they sold fruit on the docks, Mr Benjamin had been admitted to Yale Law School at the age of fourteen, despite his name, lineage and utter lack of funds. Leaving Yale after being accused (falsely, I am convinced) of stealing, and unwilling to return to his poverty-stricken parents, he decamped to New Orleans, where he quickly took advantage of being the cleverest man in town by opening a law practice, getting himself elected to the state legislature and then graduating to the United States Senate. Along the way he acquired a gorgeous wife from the city's French elite and later his very own plantation, a fine prelude to becoming the second most powerful man in the entire Confederacy. It was American genius, plain and simple. His entire life was an elaborate refusal to be the person he had been born to be. The problem was that it was all a sham. He was a lawyer without ever having finished law school, a planter who knew so little about farming that he travelled to France to learn about seeds, a patriarch of a Catholic family who would never dream of believing that Jesus was a god, a man married into the Southern aristocracy whose wife and child had permanently traded the South for Paris. And everyone who looked at him remarked that they had never seen such a Hebrew face.

He stood in the doorway for a moment without advancing towards his seat. He was short, not much more than five feet tall, with rounded, smooth cheeks like a boy's, dark skin and dark eyes. I had heard of his perpetual mysterious smile, but it was a shock to see it in person. His eyes roamed the room, pausing at each face, and the smile on his lips wasn't an invitation to friendship but a guard against it. It was impossible to guess what he was thinking and unnerving to try. 'It is a pleasure to be here, Henry,' he said slowly, as Henry hurried to show him to his seat. His voice was careful, articulate, with only a very slight drawl. 'It was so gracious of you to include me this evening.'

I watched as Henry drew out his chair for him, with a slight bow. The entire company, I saw, avoided his penetrating gaze. It was as though we were in the presence of a king. Benjamin took his seat, and it was only when Henry returned to his place and announced the next part of the service that everyone felt the freedom to smile. And Benjamin gave each person his haunting smile back, opened his book and followed as Henry continued leading the service, chanting along with the company that we had once been slaves in Egypt until God took us out with a mighty hand. It was extremely odd. My memories of Henry were of a grand presence, a man who filled a room. But here I saw a different Henry: timid, diffident, waiting for permission. As he continued reading the service aloud, he seemed under a spell.

Since it was my great ambition, at seventeen years old, to achieve the kind of victory that Benjamin had achieved at becoming an American hero, I observed him across the table for the rest of the evening, looking for clues from the master as to how to pretend. I watched very carefully. And what I saw was that there was something odd about him, though I couldn't quite place it. It was obvious that he was fiercely intelligent, for everything he said was a sort of aphorism, though I didn't know whether or not they were original. When one of the guests asked him, rather jovially, what new plans Richmond had in terms of strategy, I was disappointed and then frightened when he looked straight at me and said, as though quoting, 'Three can keep a secret if two of them are dead.' The company seemed to find this witty, and when everyone laughed, I joined in, hiding my fear. For the rest of the meal he seemed friendly enough, always smiling. But he had a certain awkwardness about him that made me even more uncomfortable than I already was. He answered questions put to him, but didn't inspire one to continue the conversation. It was as if every word he said were carefully parsed out in his mind beforehand, after he had decided whether it was worth saying. While he was silent, he would smile at you—a strange smile, as if he were laughing at you without your knowing why. The newspaper articles where I had read descriptions of him had always attributed his oddness to his race. But as a fellow member of that race, I found him odd as well. The more I thought about him, the more I wondered if he just might be the sort who was, well—well, a man's man, shall I say. I had been around enough soldiers to know how a lonely man talks about women (his own beloved back home, or just about anyone else's). Yet when the conversation turned to families, it was clear that this gentleman cared not at all that his own wife had lived in France for the previous twelve years, and that he had sought no substitute for her in her absence. When he was in New Orleans, it appeared, he lived with his sister, and when those around the table asked him about his social life—even when Henry insisted, 'Judah, let us put the war aside now, shall we?'—I heard him mention only one name: 'Mr Davis', 'Mr Davis' and 'Mr Davis'. At one point, to my astonishment, he even referred to him as 'Jeff'. A man's man, and I wondered if the Confederate president himself were the man.

But this train of thought was just a distraction for me, an indulgent escape from the riveting personage of Henry Hyams, imminent murder victim, seated before me. I trembled my way through the text of the service, with Henry Hyams reading aloud and then offering his own commentary, which made the knot in my stomach tighter. Instead, I tried to concentrate on the story being told as we chanted the liturgy around the table, describing the anguish of our ancestors, slaves in Egypt, and the vast vindications wrought to set them free. It is one of the few moments of Hebrew glory in all of history, perhaps even the only one. But I often imagine how terrible it must have been to live through: the tortures of slavery, and then the horrifying vindication of the angel of death, slaying the firstborn of Egypt so that the Israelites might be set free. And now I wondered: what did the Israelites feel as the great cry went up in

Egypt, when there was not a single household where there was not
one dead? Victory? Vengeance? Or horror at their sheer power,
through the will of their God, of determining life and death? Did
one of them feel, perhaps, that still, small fear that I felt as I listened
to Henry Hyams, with the poison in my pocket?

'In every generation,' Henry chanted from the book in his hands,
'each person is obligated to see himself as if he personally had come
out of Egypt.' Henry read with the alacrity and expression of
someone who didn't just recite the words, but felt and believed them.

'We ourselves shall come out of Egypt soon enough,' Benjamin
said cheerfully when Henry paused. 'I have good word of it from
Richmond.'

The company laughed aloud as the lame Negro—unnoticed by
the other guests, glaringly present to me—came to serve the small
dishes used for the bitter herbs.

'But I thought you said it was all a secret,' Elizabeth replied, with
a playful air. It was even more painful for me to look at her than it
was to look at Henry.

'Victory is no secret, but an inevitability,' Benjamin said. 'The
means may be hidden, but the ends are there for all to see.'

The people around the table cheered. There was something mad
about this, I saw, hypnotic. Every person in the company was in his
power. Soon the meal was served, and the conversation consisted
almost entirely of compliments to him, prodding questions about war
strategy, which he consistently refused to answer, and sad laughter
as the women shared stories about their sons who were away and,
though I was the only one at the table who could imagine it, quite
possibly dead. The delusion was grand, glorious, and they were all
part of it. But I was under suggestions of my own.

The service would continue after the meal, but for the time being
the company had retired to the rather shabby parlour, to relax
and circulate before returning to the table. By then it was quite dark
out; the crippled Negro had lit the lights. I tried to make small talk
with Elizabeth and some of the other guests, but positioned myself
with my back just in front of Henry when I saw him moving to a
corner to speak with Judah Benjamin. I kept the small man in the
corner of my eye as I stood beside Elizabeth, letting her babble on

about her army boys while I listened to the conversation behind me.

'Judah, I know you have abandoned your fathers' faith, but perhaps you would be willing to join me in the drawing room for a discussion about the meaning of freedom,' I heard Henry say, his voice low.

I could hear the grin in Benjamin's voice as he replied, 'in fact, a good pipe is what I'd prefer.'

Henry let out a puff of breath. 'Alas, I must report that my wife is a bit more traditional than I, and will not tolerate smoking in the home during the holiday.'

'It is only on the Hebrew festival of freedom that one feels more liberated after returning to everyday life,' Benjamin proclaimed. 'An oppressive tradition if ever there was one. I suppose we shall have to retreat out of doors.'

'A brilliant idea.'

'The idea is brilliant, but its execution must not be. Brilliance requires no subtlety; but if we are to succeed in our transgressions, we must take to the least brilliant corner of the property.' The man spoke like he was writing a book.

'Out past the house, then, by the latrine.'

'A less-than-brilliant idea, Henry, unless you mean upwind.'

'Indeed, I do.'

'Good, then.' Benjamin turned, and for a moment he stood staring me in the face. His expression was a blank; it seemed he hadn't thought he had been heard, or if he did, then that he thought nothing of it. He clapped a hand on my shoulder. 'We have great admiration for you, young man,' he said. 'It's a rare man who sees his kinsman's plight as you do, and comes to his aid. A true loyalty to one's own.'

It was a hard compliment to accept, especially coming from Judah Benjamin, Jewish prince of the Confederacy, but I thanked him heartily and shook his hand. It was easier than looking Henry in the eye. Then the two of them excused themselves and headed for the back of the house. I listened a bit more to Elizabeth's pining for her boys, then excused myself in turn, even indulging in a slight bow, leaving Elizabeth with three women who had been anxiously awaiting their turn to speak with her. And then I hurried through the halls to the back of the house, in pursuit of my prey.

The moon was bright and round, as it always is on Passover, like a coin resting on the moist black velvet of the spring night sky. I waited by the house until Henry and Benjamin had rounded the corner of the wooden shed, then proceeded, softly, to the open door of the latrine. It was easy to walk undetected on the ground. The drooping tree branches drifted in the wind. I entered the latrine soundlessly, securing the door behind me, then leaned over the cesspool against the shed's back wall. Their voices came through clearly, over the stink.

'So we've come to discuss the meaning of freedom, then?' Henry asked. I could hear his smile. 'I must admit, I find it hard to believe that I am the only reason you are here.'

'Don't flatter yourself,' Benjamin spat. 'Perhaps you haven't heard that the delta is surrounded? All of New Orleans could fall in less than two weeks. Trust me, you are a very minor part of my business here.'

I heard a match being struck, then struck again, then silence. In the fetid shadows of the latrine, I imagined Benjamin's dark face lit by the sudden flame, his black eyebrows illuminated from below like a Christian devil in hell.

'I've come to confirm that the log will be ready for the axe,' Benjamin added after a few breaths. 'In the manner we discussed.'

Log, I had been told, was the coded term that Confederate agents used when referring to President Lincoln. It had something to do with the President's log-cabin birth, or his height and posture, or perhaps both, I don't recall. I heard the word and held my breath.

'Oh, there's nothing to confirm,' Henry replied, almost breezily. 'The axe is in place.'

For the first time, I realized that it actually was true. The bare ground in the latrine was soft, like all the ground in New Orleans. Henry's entire house was built on a swamp. I listening, sinking in.

'You are certain that you are ready,' Benjamin said, more question than statement.

'I only regret that I have but one life to give for my country,' Henry quoted, with an unmistakably unctuous tone. At that moment, for the first time in my life, I hated him.

So did Benjamin, it seemed. 'You aren't the one who will be giving his life,' the Secretary snapped. 'You will give only a bullet. Two at most.'

'But if I should be caught,' Henry said, 'it is something to consider.'

'It is something to consider only if you do not follow the plan exactly,' Benjamin replied, and I could hear how his jaws were clenched. 'I hope you don't have any secret ideas about firing shots in the air, or shouting public proclamations about the death of tyrants, or any other such nonsense.'

Henry cleared his throat, and I could hear the regret in it. But Benjamin continued, and I heard his voice rise in what I imagined to be his attorney's tone. 'Glory isn't for the Jews, Henry,' he said. 'Just think of me. If I am to be remembered at all, even if we are to triumph, it will be only as one who designed the plans that were heroically executed by someone else. We can be slave owners, we can own whole plantations, but as far as everyone else is concerned, you and I will always be slaves.'

I was astonished to hear this from Benjamin, who, as much as I detested him, had certainly appeared to be in a position of glory. But now I knew that what he said was true. And what was worse, I knew that it also applied to me. I listened, sickened, as he continued.

'American honour,' he said, in his aphoristic way, 'the hard unseen labour that raises a country from dust—that can be yours, and you deserve it. But American glory, that belongs to someone else. And besides, Henry, you aren't suited for it. No one wanted you for this, but you wanted it yourself. And if I let them choose you, it was only because you didn't seem like the sort to have a death wish. My task tonight is to confirm that.'

A pause. 'You doubt me,' Henry said at last, his voice exacting and composed. 'You shouldn't. I've been supplying that camp over the Maryland border with all the rum they could dream of for the past six months. I'll be on my way back there again next week. The log visits once or twice a month, and they do a parade for him. They always warn me when he comes, to make sure I'm not intercepted with goods on hand. I've even gone to the parades before, to see where the log sits. It's a public parade; the people from town crowd right up to him. Even the officers know me by sight. They're thrilled to see me. They're only concerned about the rum.'

'And how will you do it?' Benjamin said, like an impatient father reviewing his son's schoolwork.

'I take my place alongside the seats they have for him. I wait for the part of the parade with the gun salute. I keep the revolver under my cloak even when I draw, and I time my shot to correspond with the salute,' Henry recited, like an obedient child. For a moment, I felt ashamed for him. And then, as I recognized how familiar that obedient voice sounded, I felt ashamed of myself. 'No one hears where the shot came from, and before anyone even sees him fall, I slip out of the crowd.'

Benjamin's voice was languid. 'You slip out of the crowd,' he repeated. 'Not, for instance, by jumping in front of the parade and waving your revolver in the air while draped in a Rebel flag.'

Henry sucked in his breath. 'You doubt me. But you know that no one can do it but me. There's a reason you need me to do this. I'm the only one who still goes there without anyone raising an eyebrow. I know every seventeen-year-old imbecile in that camp. No one will suspect me. For anyone else it would be a death mission.'

I was another seventeen-year-old imbecile, I knew, feeling light-headed. I barely breathed.

'I don't doubt your capacity to carry it off,' Benjamin replied. 'I doubt your capacity to carry it off without glorifying yourself in the process. Remember, glory will never be yours. Or mine either. Save your dreams of glory for the world to come.'

Someone knocked on the door of the latrine. Startled, I nearly tripped into the pit, catching myself on the side walls and turning around on the soft mud. I realized I had to make my escape back to the house. There was something I needed to do at the house, in the dining room, and now, for the very first time, I wanted to do it. Behind me, through the wall, I could hear Henry making some kind of reply; neither man paused when I creaked open the latrine door.

To my surprise, the person behind it was the Negro cripple. He stared at me with what I thought was again that look of contempt; it was difficult to see in the dark. But then I saw him waving one arm, almost frantically, gesturing at me to go back to the house. When I stepped forward, he took his other arm and pushed me, soundlessly, out the door, urging me on as he waved the other hand towards the house. I assumed he had a desperate need for the latrine, and wondered if slaves usually used the same latrine as everyone else. But as I hurried back to the house, I glanced over my shoulder and saw him flinging the latrine door open and closed, back and forth, then turning around and limping back to the house himself. Whatever he was doing, it certainly distracted the two pipe-smokers behind the latrine. As I closed the door of the house behind me, I saw Henry and Benjamin emerging from the other side, Henry yelling something at the slave. Both of them were too focused on the crippled Negro to notice that I had been there. I slipped back to the empty dining room, tore open the packet of poison and poured it into Henry's empty glass, which I then refilled from the decanter of wine, stirring it a bit with Henry's spoon. I was shocked by how easy it was, how little of anything I felt at all.

As I was replacing the glass, the crippled Negro entered the room. He looked at me with a strange expression that I couldn't quite decipher, as though, perhaps, he were laughing at me. Then he picked up the decanter and began filling the other glasses around the table, humming one of the Hebrew tunes that we had been singing. And then, horrified, I retreated to the parlour, just in time for Henry to call the company to return to the dining-room table.

The second half of the Passover Seder is either tedious or triumphal, depending on how much you drink compared with how much you eat. Most years, the feast is a feast in every sense, and people drag themselves back to the table tired, sluggish and ready for the whole evening to be done with. But in war-stricken New Orleans, that wasn't the case. Food wasn't yet scarce, but it had become harder to come by; liquor, on the other hand, had been laid up for years. Even at the shabby, genteel table of Henry Hyams, the food had not quite been balanced by the drink, and so the tone that night, after everyone made their way back to the table, was triumphal: most of the guests were more drunk than full, and it showed. The guests sang the grace after meals loudly, with gusto, the older ones even singing aloud the parts usually chanted to oneself. Afterwards, before Henry rose to read the next passage, some of the older guests began laughing about Elijah the Prophet, messenger of the Messiah, for whom one opens the door at the end of the evening—joking that perhaps Elijah might arrive this year in the form of a swarm of mosquitoes full of Yankee blood, or perhaps even General Lee himself. I would have expected to be nervous at this point, to be thinking about Henry, or even my father or my mother, but I wasn't. Instead, I was impatient. I stared at Henry's raised glass and tapped my foot on the dingy floor as I waited for him to bring it to his lips.

Henry pronounced the blessing over his glass of wine and I watched, riveted, as he drank it. When he put the glass down, he made a face and leaned back on his cushioned chair, turning to the side, where the Negro was waiting.

'Badly decanted, Jim,' he called. 'Bring another bottle, will you? There's something peculiar about this one.'

The Negro muttered and then wandered off, returning with another bottle that he began to serve into fresh glasses around the table. I watched Henry, ridiculously—hadn't the officers told me that results wouldn't be immediate? I began to feel as though I myself had been poisoned, but Henry showed no other signs. Instead, he rose to his feet, holding his half-empty glass before him. He was slightly drunk. Steadying himself on the table's edge with one hand and raising the glass with the other, he began to read aloud—in English, this time—the cry of vengeance from the very end of the Passover meal. He drawled out the words slowly, pronouncing them each with a firm and almost terrifying passion: 'Pour out Your wrath on the nations that do not know You, and upon the nations that do not call upon Your name. For they have devoured Jacob, and laid waste his habitation. Pour out Your indignation upon them, and let the wrath of Your anger overtake them. Pursue them with anger, and destroy them from beneath the heavens of the Lord.'

At all of the Passovers in my short life, I had heard those biblical words recited dutifully, by happy men with full stomachs who rushed through this passage so as to finally reach the evening's long-awaited end. But in Henry Hyams's voice, I suddenly heard an unexpected tone of real and horrifying rage. He looked up from his book and around at the company, and smiled a cruel smile. For an instant, I felt that I was the Jacob who had been devoured.

'I would like to dedicate this fourth glass of wine to the Union,' Henry said, in a loud and angry drawl. 'May it go the way of all tyrants. May our dear Judah Benjamin lead us as we pursue the Union hosts with anger, and may we destroy them from beneath the heavens of the Lord.'

The company broke into applause. Judah Benjamin applauded too, modestly at first. But then the applause began to escalate, becoming

181

louder and wilder than even he could bear. The room roared. Everyone stood, raised their glasses, banging them with their forks.

And then, to my astonishment, Benjamin's composed face changed, reddening with passion. 'Death to the Union!' he bellowed, his voice louder than I could ever imagine it. Soon everyone took up the chant. It was the drinking, I was sure—or so I believed, until Henry Hyams cried out, 'Death to Lincoln!'

The company echoed him, man to woman to man, cheering for the angel of death. I stood with them, of course, banged my glass like the rest of them, and in the wave of passion that circled the Passover table, I was washed clean of all remorse. When Henry turned to face me, I didn't even wince.

'My dear boy, Jacob,' he said, with the hardened edge still on his drawl as the company's chants died down, 'would you please do us the honour of opening the door for Elijah the Prophet, may he arrive speedily and in our time.'

I smiled, bowed to the ladies at the table and turned around to walk towards the door. But when I reached the hallway, I heard a horrid sound, a kind of rattled, muffled gasp. I turned in my tracks, a Yankee facing a table full of Rebels, with Henry at the head, looking straight at me. And at that moment, Henry Hyams poured out his wrath on to the dining-room table.

I never imagined it would happen so quickly, or that it would be so supremely terrible to witness. The commanders must have given me something other than ordinary lye. Henry's eyes rolled back in his head as he vomited black bile on to the silver trays in front of him. He vomited, and vomited, and vomited: his entire life poured out of his mouth before the heavens of the Lord. As the women at the table began to scream and the men rushed to his side, I turned back around and walked, slowly, towards the door. I opened it wide, for the Prophet Elijah. And then I ran out into the moonlit Southern night.

□

GRANTA

HARD CORE
Gabe Hudson

Gabe Hudson was born in 1971 and grew up in Austin, Texas. He served as a rifleman in the Marine Corps Reserve, and received an MFA from Brown University. His short story collection, 'Dear Mr President' (Knopf), has been translated into seven languages, was a Hemingway Foundation/PEN Award finalist, and has received the Sue Kaufman Prize for First Fiction from the American Academy of Arts and Letters. Hudson teaches in the creative writing programme at Princeton University, and is an editor-at-large for 'McSweeney's'. In recent years he has travelled extensively in Thailand and Vietnam, where he met his fiancée, Tu Tuyet Ha. 'Hard Core' is an excerpt from his novel-in-progress, 'American Buddha', which will be published by Knopf.

My buddy Meat's the one who showed me the true joy of handling the M203. I mean, yeah, the M16 was okay. You hear a lot of us Marines making a big hoo-ha about our M16s. 'This is my rifle, there are many like it, but this one is mine' and all that. But after rolling with Meat, I'd take my M203 over an M16 any day.

You hear all those Nam doggies bragging on their old-school Blooper Gun, the M79 grenade launcher. It could blow up NVC from a hundred feet away. My instructor at Survival Evasion Resistance Escape school, what we called SERE, was Sergeant Bloodworth, a Force Recon Nam doggy who used to brag on how he could fire a grenade with the Blooper Gun and blow up a running NVC in mid-stride. But the Blooper Gun was a pain in the ass, an extra weapon you had to tote around in the bush. So after Vietnam, they came up with the M203 grenade launcher, which clips on to your service rifle. The M203 is one size fits all—jack that puppy into the forward receiver of your M16A2, your M4A1 carbine, whatever you got, and let fly. If you timed it right, your grenade would blow up right in the Iraqi soldier's face. We called that a facial.

Because of my training in *muay thai* kickboxing, I'd been the punter for my high school football team down in Austin, Texas. Nobody in their right mind wants to be the punter. On Sundays you see all those other NFL guys doing what they've dreamed of doing since they could pee straight. And then there's the team's queer little punter, jumping up and down on the sidelines like he's begging someone to punch his lights out. But there in the desert, with the M203 in hand, I was the quarterback. It definitely put a new twist on the term 'long bomb'.

I scored my first facial back in February. I'd been in the desert for a month. We were in a firefight with a small pack of Iraqi soldiers— they'd ambushed our convoy as we crossed the bridge at Samarra— when I spotted a lone Iraqi perched on the berm. My guys were taking a lot of heat. I saw Meat pinned down in no-man's-land, behind our Jeep, which was up on its side and covered in flames. Every time Meat tried to scramble out, this Iraqi sprayed the area with his AK-47. *Tat-tat-tat-tat*. I scrambled for cover behind some brush along the Euphrates. I was gasping for air. By then I didn't have to use the M203's sights, so I just cocked back and squeezed the trigger and watched the grenade sail through the sky. Straight towards the end zone.

At the last second, I shouted, 'Yo!' The Iraqi stood up and turned around. Just in time to make it a facial.

Touchdown!

Meat galloped up. 'That's right, G! You rollin' tight! Hard core, baby! That's hard core!'

I pumped my knees in a crazy war dance, a little number Meat and me liked to call the Baghdad Boogie. Meat jumped in too, right then and there. Meat's version of the Baghdad Boogie was breakdancing, doing the robot. In his MOPP 4 gear, popping and locking with those AK-47 rounds whizzing by, Meat looked hilarious.

'Who's your monkey now?!' I shouted at the sky. 'Who's got the big monkey dick now, bitch?!'

Meat stopped dancing and looked at me.

A hailstorm of rounds buzzed by us.

'What?' I said, the smile sliding off my face.

'Anh Hung,' Meat said. 'Dude, why you gotta talk smack about Lam Binh? Talking about your big monkey dick like that? That shit's completely disrespectful.'

Lam Binh. Always back to Lam Binh. Even out there in the desert, there was no escaping Lam Binh.

My twin sister Lam Binh's the reason I became a Marine. Lam Binh or maybe Meat, though I never would have told Lam Binh that. Lam Binh has always hated Meat. Or at least since 1981. Me and Lam Binh were thirteen years old, living with our American dad in Austin. One day after school, before I knew what was happening, Lam Binh came streaking into my room naked, laughing her head off.

'Hey! Let's play a game!' She jumped up on my bed, squatted over me so that my face was just a few inches from her vagina. Then she said the name of the game was POW. She said that POW meant Prisoner of War, and that some of the older girls had been talking about POW in the girls' bathroom. Lam Binh said POW was like Truth or Dare, but way better. Lam Binh said she would tie me up and do things to me, and then I would tie her up and do things to her.

'But first you have to get naked! Hurry up!' she said.

'Get the heck out of my room, willya?' I shouted. But the truth is I couldn't take my eyes off of what was right in front of my face.

'Don't be that way! You'll like POW. But you have to get naked first.'

'Okay. Hold on,' I said. 'Lemme go to the bathroom first. I gotta pee. Be right back.'

And with that I ran out into the woods behind our house. It was as if my legs had a mind of their own, ferrying me out into the wilderness.

The next afternoon Lam Binh repeated her performance. I was inspecting the *shuriken* Japanese throwing stars that I'd bought at a head shop when she bolted into my room, laughing. 'POW! POW!' she shouted. Only this time she was wearing cammies and a pair of combat boots. She looked like a regular GI Jane.

Lam Binh chased after me when I fled out into the woods, clinging to my stars. 'Hold up!' she cried.

I ran in a zigzag. I threw one of my stars as far as I could, so that when it struck the ground it would distract Lam Binh. I hid in a tree for a while. I lay down in the creek and used a dirty straw to breathe underwater as Lam Binh ran by, shouting my name. That's how I first learned about Escape and Evasion.

And hunting, too. Because while my sister hunted me out in the woods that afternoon, I did some hunting of my own. I'd been practising with those throwing stars for a few weeks, nailing empty beer cans set up on the ground. But that afternoon I moved on to my first live target: I killed a field mouse from thirty feet away. Clean head shot. Then I nailed a couple of birds. Then a raccoon.

I wasn't sure what to aim for next—there were too many squirrels, they were too easy—when I saw a stray dog that must have wandered into the woods from my junior high grounds down the street. It was a Scottish terrier.

I could hear Lam Binh calling out my name. 'Anh Hung! Anh Hung!'

To be fair, I tried to give that Scottish terrier a head start before I began the hunt. But it just kept coming up to me with its tail wagging. Finally I got pissed and it ended up being me who had to run away from the dog—to get enough distance between us so that I could chuck my throwing star at it. But it kept running back to me! So I ended up having to take down that Scottish terrier from close range.

I hadn't heard Lam Binh calling for a while, so afterwards I just headed home.

The next day, at school, it turned out that the Scottish terrier belonged to this blonde girl named Zoe in my algebra class. Zoe was the girl who had gotten everyone calling me Chinky Dinky Poo Poo, which all the kids eventually shortened to just plain Chinky Dink. There were LOST signs posted all around the school about Zoe's missing dog that Friday morning. They said that Zoe had been walking her Scottish terrier, Tigger, around the school track, when a giant black man in a ski mask came running out of the woods and snatched the dog up and ran off. I knew that was a lie, but I couldn't say anything, because then everyone would know it was me. I was scared as hell of getting caught, and so I can't say I was too upset when I heard in the cafeteria that day that the police had already brought in a suspect for questioning, a semi-retarded black man I used to see playing Space Invaders up at the 7-Eleven.

Don't get me wrong. I'm not a racist—in fact I hate racists. But as a minority, there's only so much you can do for another minority before you have to think about what's best for you. Besides, the way I figured it, I'd be a lot more useful to black people in the free world than locked up behind bars.

To prove my point, that afternoon I went up to Tolesha, the black girl in my world geography class, and offered to let her copy my homework for the rest of the year. Free of charge. Tolesha got bussed in from the other side of town and I figured she probably had a job after school, something that helped her family make ends meet, and being able to copy my homework would free her up to work more hours at her job. Turned out I was right. Because Tolesha, with a big white smile, gratefully accepted my offer.

When the final bell rang that afternoon, I raced out to the woods and hid that dead Scottish terrier where no one could find it.

When I came back to my house, I saw my new neighbour, Timmy, sitting in his wheelchair out in his backyard. He had only just moved to town, but he was already captain of the Students for Christ club at school.

'Hey! Come here a sec!' he said.

I trotted over.

'Help me out, buddy. Fetch me that bird I just killed.' He pointed at the ground under the bird feeder. I found a dead cardinal there and handed it to Timmy. He held up his fancy slingshot. 'Pretty cool, huh?'

'I guess.' I held up one of my stars. 'But not as cool as this.'

Timmy eyeballed the star with admiration. 'You a soldier, too?' he said. 'What you been hunting, soldier?'

I stared at Timmy in his wheelchair. His legs looked weird, like pipe cleaners all twisted up below him. There was a red, white and blue sticker on his wheelchair that said: LET US COUNT OUR BLESSINGS. Something in his voice made Timmy seem hugely vulnerable, trustworthy.

The next thing I knew I heard myself confessing, telling Timmy what I'd done to the Scottish terrier. When I was done talking, Timmy practically bit my head off.

'You idiot! Your sister's always in those woods. She's definitely gonna find that dog!'

Timmy was right. If Lam Binh discovered the Scottish terrier, she'd surely put two and two together. After all, Lam Binh was a genius. The star of the Gifted and Talented programme. Perfect score on the CAT test. Straight As.

I grabbed Timmy's chair and wheeled him out into the woods. When we reached the little clearing, I said, 'Here it is.' Then, with Timmy barking instructions, I built a little fire.

Let me say this, though: the dogburgers were totally Timmy's idea. One thousand per cent. Timmy insisted we go back to his house to get his dad's hunting knife for skinning. Timmy brought the buns and ketchup from his kitchen. Timmy even brought paper plates in his backpack. And Timmy said if I didn't help him eat the burgers, then he'd rat me out himself.

He said, 'I'm on your side here. But I can't do everything.' He handed me a plate. 'Now eat your chow, soldier.'

Scared of getting caught, I scarfed my first burger as the late afternoon sun bled through the canopy of leaves overhead. About halfway through I heard Lam Binh calling out my name, way off in the woods.

'Anh Hung! Anh Hung! Come out, come out, wherever you are!'

Timmy said, 'She'll never find us. Hey, your sister's hot, though. Do you like to fuck her or what?'

I didn't know what to say, but I could tell Timmy would like me more if I said yes. So I said, 'Of course. Whaddya think I am, a homo?'

We'd erected a spit over the fire. Timmy said he'd learned this stuff in Boy Scouts, and that one day he would become a United States Marine. Timmy said, 'That's why I pray so much. God's gonna get me out of this here chair. Miracles happen.'

'Whatever.'

'It's true. Shoot. You should read the Bible. And you should come to one of our Students for Christ meetings. Free cake and juice. Sometimes pizza. Then you'd know all this stuff. I'm gonna get out of this wheelchair soon. I mean, all I have to do is find Jesus, and then nail Jesus to a cross. Then God'll get me out of this wheelchair, so I can become a Marine.'

'A Marine?' I said. 'Give me a break. I'm going to train in the black arts of *bushido*. One day I'm going to be a Samurai warrior.'

'What's that?' said Timmy.

'Something that could kick a Marine's ass with his eyes closed.'

'You Chinese or something?'

'Half Vietnamese. I was born in the tunnels of Cu Chi. My mother was a mighty NVC warrior. They called her Blue Dragon. My name means Hero in Vietnamese.'

'Talk about serious freaksville.'

'I thought you were my friend. If you're not my friend, just say the word.' I picked up one of my throwing stars.

'You a Commie bastard? My dad says he killed all the Commie bastards in Nam.'

'No, dickweed.' I raised the throwing star, poised to throw.

'Take it easy, dude. My dad says those Commie bastards could fight real good.'

'Not as good as a Samurai,' I said.

That's when Lam Binh burst into the clearing. Her cammies made it hard to see her against the trees but the sun was glinting all around her. Her eyes swelled when she took in the scene. 'What the hell are you guys doing?! What the frick is that?!' she said, pointing to what was left of the Scottish terrier on the spit. She pinched her nose. 'Whew. It stinks.'

'Wow,' said Timmy, his eyes suddenly filled with a weird light. 'Why didn't you tell me your sister was Jesus?'

I didn't say anything. Timmy said, 'Grab her! Get her before she runs away! Use the rope! It's miracle time!'

I stood up, dusting my palms off on my jeans. I saw Lam Binh's smile fade, replaced by a look of uncertainty. Then Lam Binh bolted back into the woods, and we chased after her.

I don't want to talk about what me and Timmy did to my sister that afternoon. How we created a whole new version of POW, and how it changed all our lives forever. But I will say that those dogburgers were rancid. I was sick that night, throwing up everywhere. That's how I came to be a vegetarian. And that's how I gave Timmy his nickname, the name I've known him by ever since: Meat.

You might know Lam Binh from her porn movies, but you'd only know her by her porn name: V.J., which stands for Vietnamese Jesus. The same Lam Binh that graduated from Yale *summa cum laude*, with a double major in Post-Feminist Theory and Asian-American Studies. The same Lam Binh that was approached by the FBI about possible employment, and the same Lam Binh that told the FBI that she'd rather shoot herself in the vagina than work for the same American government that raped and pillaged Vietnam.

Or maybe you know Lam Binh from her anti-war commercials. A few months ago, during the build-up to the Gulf War, an international human rights organization hired Lam Binh to do a graphic series of anti-war commercials called 'No Blood for Oil'.

Because of how graphic the commercials were, HBO was the only channel running the series. But when they became hot on college campuses, the media picked up on the whole phenomenon, and now they can't get enough of Lam Binh: her father a decorated Vietnam Vet, her mother a member of the VC resistance, her brother a Marine deployed in Iraq.

I saw Lam Binh's latest commercial before shipping out to Saudi Arabia. A bunch of us from 2nd Platoon were partying at Meat's pad. We were playing quarters and doing shots of Goldschlager with the tunes pumping—Public Enemy, I think it was. The TV was on in the background with the volume off. When 'No Blood for Oil III' came on, Corporal Danberger cried, 'Holy shit! Here we go!'

On the TV, a chimpanzee in a Marine Corps dress blue uniform was beating his meat. He was standing on top of an M1A1 Abrams tank in the desert and he had his trousers around his ankles. That chimpanzee was really going at it. Lam Binh was crouched below him with her mouth open. Suddenly the chimpanzee grimaced, like somebody had kicked him in the nuts. Then he came all over Lam Binh's face. But when Lam Binh looked at the camera, the chimpanzee's come was black. And shiny. Like oil. And it spelled the words NO BLOOD FOR OIL across her face. Then in bold yellow letters the words FIGHT THE WAR AGAINST WAR: BECOME A SOLDIER FOR PEACE flashed across the screen.

'Oooh-rah! Bomb's away!' Meat cried. Then he grinned at me and said, 'That monkey gave your sister there a facial! Like his dick was an M203 firing grenades, yo! Oooh-rah! Yo Monkey!' he said to me. 'Tell your sister I seriously dig "No Blood for Oil III"! Tell her that's my favourite.' He made a circle with his hand and moved it up and down like he was jerking off.

The next night, I drove over to Lam Binh's apartment in Oceanside for dinner. On the way I promised myself that I would never tell her what Meat had said. But of course I immediately spilled the beans. Lam Binh was in the kitchen, making *pho*—which our mom used to make for us when we lived in Saigon—and I was on the couch, cleaning my Beretta 9mm pistol.

'Meat said he loves "No Blood for Oil III". I mean, your *art*.' That's how Lam Binh told me to refer to her commercials. I didn't mention the thing Meat did with his hand. 'That's how Meat put it,' I said. 'He seemed real sincere.' I had my Beretta 9mm broken down into pieces, spread out on the coffee table. I ran a rag over the magazine catch assembly.

'What!' Lam Binh's eyes got big. 'Where does he get off? What an asshole!'

I knew I'd made a mistake by bringing it up. 'I thought you liked Meat. I thought you'd forgiven him. That was all a long time ago. We were just kids.'

This was classic *damashi*, which in *ninjutsu* is used to mean 'deception'. Shadowhand. I was trying to run some interference, to throw Lam Binh off the scent before she got any more pissed. Lam Binh is a worthy adversary, but I knew how to do this from SERE. In the POW part of the training cycle, Sergeant Bloodworth locked me up in this tiny wood box for a couple of days—you didn't eat—and then he dragged me out for repeated interrogations. Sit you in the chair, jack you for information. I learned how to outsmart my interrogator with covert misdirection. How to tell a truthful story by telling lies. Because if your captors get the whole truth they'll kill you—or kill your mates because you ratted them out. The trick is to tell your POW story without making your interrogator cut off one of your hands, or throw acid in your face. You've got to plot each word like your life depends on it, but give the impression that you don't fucking care if you live. Your delivery has to be a perfect mixture of fear and courage. You also have to be ready to die. That part's total Samurai.

Lam Binh said, 'Are you fucking kidding me, Anh Hung? You're gonna have to do a helluva lot better than this, with your Jedi mind tricks. Give me a break.'

By this point, I'd put the Beretta 9mm all the way back together again. The weapon was so clean you could wipe your ass with it. I chambered a round.

Then Lam Binh slammed a carrot down on the cutting board. She said, 'Listen. I'll. Tell. You. What.' Then Lam Binh said she'd cut Meat's dick off if he ever came near her. 'Just like this!' And brought the knife down right through the carrot.

The day after I scored that facial along the Euphrates, me and Meat were sent into Basra for a little Sneak and Peek under the cover of darkness. Intel had given the word that some Republican Guard were holed up in the local junior high school. A renegade band, using the school as a hide site, were terrorizing the locals and making hit and runs on our guys along Highway 10. We came flying over Basra in a Blackhawk and pulled into position above the school.

Hertz, the pilot, turned and shouted, 'Okay, gents! Time for me to drop a load. Go! Go! Go!'

Meat and me jumped out the hatch. We fast-roped down about halfway and then busted through a second-floor window in a shower of glass shards. There were old desks strewn around the room and a chalkboard on the wall. It reminded me of our old school. I half expected to see a Scottish terrier running around with a throwing star sticking out of its head. Then a giant, bearded Republican Guard leapt out from behind a desk and charged Meat. He was running at top speed, but his pistol was steady and I saw the red light dance across Meat's chest. And that's when I knew we were in big trouble. ☐

● soho theatre

free your imagination

The Verity Bargate Award 2007
Soho's hunt for the most daring, original new play.

Every two years Soho Theatre launches a national competition to find the best new play by an emerging writer. The winner will thrill London audiences with their imaginative, daring and relevant work.

Passion is more important than polish, so why not give it a go?

The winner will receive:
- £5000
- the chance to have their play produced at Soho Theatre

'Soho's Verity Bargate Award, named after the founder of the central London new writing powerhouse, is a litmus test for the success among the various awards for new writers.'
Screen International

Workshops
We are holding writing workshops on 20 February, 15, 22 March, 2, 19 April, 17 May, 7-9pm. Workshops are open to everyone and they will explore the process behind writing a script. Tickets: £15 (£10). To book, call 0870 429 6883 or visit www.sohotheatre.com
21 Dean Street, London W1D 3NE

The closing date for submissions is 20 July, 2007.
Please see www.sohotheatre.com for rules.

Registered Charity No: 267234   Image: Mike Slocombe, Urban75.com

GRANTA

DANCE CADAVEROUS

Uzodinma Iweala

Uzodinma Iweala was born to Nigerian parents in 1982 in Washington, DC, the second child of four. After attending St Albans School, he graduated from Harvard University in 2004 with a degree in English. His first novel, 'Beasts of No Nation' (John Murray/HarperCollins), has been translated into eleven languages. It won the Sue Kaufman Prize for First Fiction from the American Academy of Arts and Letters and the John Llewellyn Rhys Prize, among others. Interested in health and human rights issues, Iweala has worked on development projects in Nigeria and New York, and will attend Columbia University medical school in the fall of 2007. 'Dance Cadaverous' is a new story.

My parents wake me up, both of them together in the doorway of my room, their faces wrinkled by concern and slightly shiny because of the sunlight streaming through the windows.

My father says, 'Morning, Daven. Why don't you get up now? I think we should all go to church, don't you?' as if the softness of his voice hides the fact that this is not really an open question.

I roll over to the window and the sound of paper crinkles in the pillowcase. It means the letter is still there, the pictures are still there, and that I did actually meet Zhou's father early yesterday morning while I was stretching before my run. His eyes were bloated and still red behind his metal-rimmed glasses. He said nothing and didn't even attempt a smile. He just handed me the envelope with the letters and the pictures, and stood there for a moment trembling before he stepped away and back to his idling car. I didn't go for a run that morning. I went upstairs and looked at the pictures, read the letters, reread the letters and then looked at the pictures again. And then I slipped them into my pillowcase, buried my head in the pillow and began to cry.

Outside I can see the driveway shining black with the wetness of last night's rainstorm. The sun is bright and beautiful, but its reflection warps in the black shine of the smooth tar. It glows strongly in the pond of the roundabout that sits in the middle of our cul-de-sac. Green grass grows in a ring around the pond and the mature oak trees that line the streets drip into the white concrete gutters. It looks like it should be solidly spring, but it has been extremely cold and the tree leaves are still tiny rolls of green.

'Daven.' My father's voice gets much more authoritative, like when I've seen him in court, or when he appeared on the news after the Philson case. 'Daven, I said we're going to church. Now. So would you please get up and get ready?'

I pull the covers over my head, hear him say my name once more, hear my mother whisper to him and then hear him walk out. My mother walks to my bed and sits down next to me. I can feel her indentation in the mattress. She rubs my back through the covers and I want to tell her to stop, but you can't tell your mom not to comfort you. Moms wouldn't have anything else to do if you did.

She sighs softly like she used to when I was younger and she would hold me in her lap and read to me. It's funny that of all things from being small, I remember this most—her purple housecoat, the light glistening in her long light brown hair and the smell of rose-scented perfume and her leather-bound books lingering on her even after she had traded them for one of my fairy tales or adventure stories. It was her voice that made everything just fine—her voice and the fictional escapades, the fantasies that turned my day of babysitters and her day of academic politics into a night of magic. It was brilliant.

She doesn't say anything but I can tell she wants to and just doesn't know where to begin.

'What's his problem, Mom?' I ask.

She swallows deliberately. 'Daven,' she says, 'please don't be difficult today. He's just worried. I'm worried. I mean, after all, Zhou was a responsible kid. It's just so sudden—for all of us—you know. It's almost too much to comprehend. And it's too close to home, don't you think?'

'You're telling me,' I mumble into the pillow so she can't hear me. I press my cheek down into its softness and hear the paper crinkle again.

'Your father took last week and this week off to be with you, and you haven't even seemed to notice. He's just trying to be there—'

'I just don't see why I have to go to church. I'm not going to find anything there. It's just not for people like me.'

'Daven, don't say that.'

'I just don't believe in—'

'Don't start on that now. It's not the time. Just please get ready so we can go. Trust me, you'll feel better if you go. Even if you just get out of bed,' she whispers before standing up. 'I'll be downstairs.'

At the door she stops. The outside light frames her body and for a moment she is transfigured, like a divine messenger. 'I'm telling you as your mother,' she says. 'Of all the things you need, you need this most right now. Just trust me. I wouldn't ever lie.'

She leaves the room and I realize that she didn't kiss my forehead like she usually does, so I feel like she doesn't really mean what she says. I have trouble believing things now—simple things like the earth spins around the sun, or Jesus loves us all—now that Zhou is dead.

Zhou is dead, I say to myself. Zhou is dead. He died last month in a car crash. I imagine it happened just like this. His black BMW doing ninety down River Road—Ludacris or OutKast or maybe Coldplay blasting in his ears, with the bass so deep he can't feel his own heart beat. There's the smell of liquor on his breath. Then the car accelerates and, after the first wave of terror, he lets his fear go and sinks deeper into the seat. It's only a matter of seconds now. Perhaps he has second thoughts, but the police say there were no skid marks or the bits of rubber that sometimes flake off the tyres. And then it's too late. There's a tree—a massive maple just down River Road from Whitman High School. Now it's his tree. There's a shrine to him there.

His mother won't leave the house and his father still won't speak. My parents are sober and thoroughly convinced that no one under the age of twenty-five should ever drive at night. I don't know what to think about it. I can't really think, because if I think about it I'll cry.

I go to the bathroom to shower—in the dark with cold water, because I want to get sick. The water hits my skin and each drop feels like the prick of a pin. I try to feel my body succumb to some sort of virus and I rub the water into my skin and shiver. I feel like I'm standing in the midst of the Arctic, but it's Bethesda and it's April and outside it's supposed to be warm. Soon I feel satisfied that I've done myself some sort of damage. My skin cracks, my hands are numb and I can feel my throat constricting. I felt this way at his funeral, but I didn't cry. I managed to hold it all in.

Reverend Ericson talks about God. I sit on my hands in the wooden pew behind my parents to keep my ass from falling asleep in the midst of God's glory. My father is super attentive—his head follows Reverend Ericson as he moves across the blue carpet of the sacristy, his black face dripping with sweat as he talks about the beauty of heaven—'what them sinners and evildoers gonna miss real bad'. God is great, he intones. And my father affirms, yes, sir. Trust God. Yes, sir. God is in the little things. Mmhmm. God is in everything. Amen. God is for the righteous. He is. God is for the sinners. Yes, Lord. God will set you free.

The sanctuary smells of incense and perfumed candle wax, and light streams through the stained glass in different colours before it gets lost in the mahogany interior.

'Heaven,' Reverend Ericson says. 'It ain't for the weak of heart. It ain't for those who live in sin and revel in abominations. *Heaven!* I said, ah, *Heaven!*'

'It isn't for me,' I mumble to myself, and slip quietly out of my pew. My father breaks from his rapture and turns around to say something, but my mother places her hand on his arm. I leave and sit on the steps outside and watch the clouds lumber in low overhead. It's quite cold to be sitting outside in only a blazer. I wish I had a cigarette even though I don't smoke—it just seems like the right thing to have in this situation, the right warmth and scent for this solitude. It's Sunday and there are hardly any cars on the road. There's hardly any noise.

The world feels so weird when you're in dress shoes. I wish I were wearing sneakers—I wish I had tried to wake early and run. If I don't run today it will be three days that I've missed training. I'm out of sync and getting worried about the way I operate. I'm always remembering things now, remembering instead of imagining. I'm constantly remembering how Zhou and I met only because he kicked a ball into my backyard. How he came with us to France the summer after seventh grade, when we ate Italian ices on the beach. How he told me that my dad was much cooler than his dad because my dad had energy to do stuff, because he smiled, and because he treated my mom like they were still going out. Zhou's dad is a neurosurgeon and tired all the time. When we were younger he said he liked his mom better, because she was interesting—something other than white. At high school he started hanging out with his Asian friends because he wanted to know more about China. He started trying to learn Chinese and started dating Asian girls and criticizing me because I had never had a black girlfriend. We would watch the moon during the summer of sophomore year and think of all the parties we would go to if either of us could drive. We would sit by the window in my family room during thunderstorms and watch the lightning when the power went out and we couldn't play video games, and that's when he would tell me what really happened in his house.

'My mom doesn't love me,' he would say. 'She didn't want to have me.'

I never said anything when he spoke like this.

'You know my dad was in the military—right? Was one of those soldiers who went for R and R in Hong Kong to sleep with prostitutes. He never made it to the red-light district, but he found my mom, got her pregnant and then tried to leave, but somehow his parents found out. They made him marry her and bring her here to have the baby.'

Another time he said, 'My mother doesn't really speak to me—

she can't. And my father sleeps around a lot. Sometimes when he says he's on call, he's really just fucking around.'

We got our first cars. He totalled his brand-new Audi after two months. I still have my Volvo but I don't drive any more because he's dead.

My father is furious when he and my mother leave the church early, before the last hymn. When my father gets angry, his skin seems to darken, like he's one of those African tree frogs that change colour when they begin to secrete toxins. He's almost the colour of the black leather when we leave the parking lot and he isn't speaking to either of us any more. My mother flashes me a look of concern and disapproval that I can see in her sun-visor mirror that she pulls down to check her lipstick.

Dr Chavin is leaving his house when we pull up to our driveway, but he doesn't notice, or he pretends not to. My father shakes his head and my mother looks out of her window, away from the Range Rover that slides from their driveway. Nobody says anything and once inside I go upstairs to my room and take out the pictures and the letters Zhou wrote to me. I hold them and stare out of the window for a while, and then put the envelope back into hiding inside the pillowcase.

My mother drops me off at track practice the next morning and I go to join my teammates, who are already warming up. I suck at track today and the coach asks me what's wrong, but it's like I don't even see him or anyone else as we run the speed workout. When it's finished and I'm sweating and shivering at the same time because of the cold, I put on my sweats, change my shoes and head for the bus stop, still trying to catch my breath as I wait.

There is nobody home when I get there and I am a bit surprised because my father isn't supposed to be at work. I drink some water in the kitchen, head up to my room and flop down for a nap.

'Daven! Are you home?' I hear through my sleep.

And then I hear my mother say, 'Jackson, calm down. Just control yourself.'

'Daven! You get down here right now.'

It's only when I lift my head up and wipe my cheeks wet from my own drool that I realize that the colour of my sheets has changed from beige to blue. The house is silent and I can hear my heart beat.

The heating system whirrs and the walls creak and click. I feel scared like when I was younger and we first moved here. At night I would lie awake listening to the house shift and I would imagine the stone crumbling around me until nothing was left.

I go down to the kitchen, where my mother stands at the sink island. Sunlight streams through the skylights and gets tangled in her wispy white hair. She glows. Her skin is such a light brown that it seems to pick up whatever colours surround her. Now she's an amalgam of stainless steel, dark cherry wood and the shimmering red of the thick ceramic plates she washes. Her hands are pink and wet from the light and water.

She points to the table and says, 'Sit down,' before she turns and walks from the room. I hear her close the bathroom door. I hear the water running. I think she is crying. I hope not because I wouldn't know how to comfort her. I sit down at the table with my hands folded on the mat in front of me and I stare at the paintings I made in grade school, stick figures of Dad and Mom and me.

Then my father walks in, wearing a grey suit. I love my father's walk. It's such a subtle swagger, such an understated, 'you can kiss my ass if you don't like me' kind of step. At school they tell me that I walk like that also, with just enough hip that it looks confident and not sassy, cool and not contrived. But it frightens me today and I know what other lawyers must feel when he walks into the courtroom. My mother sits down next to me. We are all there, close to each other, waiting for the words, and I am reminded that the three of us have spent more time together in the last month than we have since I got my driver's licence. I haven't driven since Zhou died and I think my parents are secretly relieved, although they've had to revert to juggling their schedules to fetch me from school every day. We've had conversations and debates while listening to NPR—like we used to when they took me to school. We've talked about how to thank my teachers for their recommendations and how Harvard is going to be next year. They've both gushed about fantastic Harvard. You'll love it, they say. You'll just love it. My father has stressed the law school point of view. 'Those undergrads were lucky,' he's said when looking at my mother and smiling. 'They didn't have to do a damn thing.'

But he's not smiling now. He reaches into his suit jacket and pulls out the thick white envelope and waves it back and forth in front of me. I am not surprised. I've known something was coming since the moment I realized the bed had been changed.

'I knew there had to be a reason he's been acting like this,' he says, and glares at me. I look at my mother, who looks down at the floor. 'I knew it. I don't believe it. I don't believe this. My child's a—'

'Jackson!' my mother shouts. 'Don't you even dare. Don't you even start—you should be ashamed of yourself. A civil rights lawyer like you.' And then as quickly as she starts she finishes and is silent again, save for the click of her heels against the wood floors as her legs bounce up and down.

'Felicia, it's not that. It's just not... It's just not... Daven, what the hell have you been doing—carrying on like that? What the hell has gotten into your little head?'

'Jackson, you just sit down right now and control yourself.'

'Control myself! You think I'm the one who needs control. You and all your liberal academy bullshit. That's what needs control. That's what's got this boy's head all confused, so he can go around doing— Davenport! What is going on here? Just what are you going to tell me?'

'Sit down, Jackson!'

'Daven, what is your—only God knows the things I've done to get this family to where we are now. Only God. And you're here living a life that's lying to us up and down—' and then he scrunches up his face to prevent the tears from flowing out of the corners of his eyes and into the stubble darkening the contours of his cheeks. 'And I will not take such a thing from a boy who has never worked—not that I wanted you to—never really known what it means to suffer. No. I just won't stand for it. You understand me? Am I making myself clear?'

And then he slams his hand down on the kitchen counter. The toaster shakes and rattles, as do the glasses he has just set by the sink.

'You hearing me, Daven? You're going to stop all this foolishness. You're going to like women if it's the last thing I do for you.'

I know this is happening, but I'm not here any more. I'm remembering again. Remembering how we danced. I was alone at first. Just me under the parking-lot lamp, flailing my arms and pounding to the rhythm of my own heartbeat. My shadow danced also, but the limbs kept slipping out of the circle of light so that it looked like a wriggling worm. Zhou just stood there watching me, leaned up against his car. He stood there and absorbed the vibrations of his Harman Kardon speakers.

And he said, 'You're so good at having no rhythm. I've never actually seen a black person so rhythmically-challenged.'

'I can move,' I said, but only half-heartedly. I guess the real truth is I couldn't move. Zhou moved towards me.

My father tosses the envelope at me like it is evidence from one of his dossiers. It falls to the floor and its contents scatter—the letters to one side and the pictures to the other. I look down and I see Zhou and me kissing. Just kissing, that's all. And my father is asking, shouting, pleading *why!?* I want to tell him how, but I can't find the words. If I could, I would say to him, Dad, it's like this. I wasn't aware of anything happening. I mean, if I had been aware I'm sure it wouldn't have happened at all.

My mother composes herself and wipes her eyes, but her voice still shakes. 'What your father is trying to say is that we're just concerned about the way things—'

'I'm not gay,' I cut her off.

'Daven,' she says, 'will you just listen to me for a moment?'

'Mom, I'm not—'

'Isn't it hard enough being black?' she blurts out.

'But being black and gay?!' I am mocking my mother for the first time ever.

'Daven,' she says again, 'I've studied the rates of homosexual HIV transmission in gay black men in this area. I mean it's just not safe.'

'I won't date black men then,' I yell. The kitchen is so bright now because the sun shines through the bay windows as it moves closer to setting.

'Daven, how could you do this to me?' my father says. He leaves the kitchen with his head down and his jacket dragging on the floor.

Out of my mother's eyes the tears flow freely—soft and white in the sun's light. She stretches out a hand towards me, towards the tears on my face, but I lean back to avoid her touch. Then I get up and leave her there at the table, staring at the space where I once was.

At the track I am faster than before and the coach is happy. He is an older white man who insists on telling me that they won't have seen runners like me at Harvard—no, sir. His sweats flap in the wind and his voice is lost as we speed by on our intervals. We swish-swish by each other in our tracksuits, and as I pass the coach on my second loop he shouts, 'Quit looking behind you, Daven. S'only gonna slow you down. You ain't running from nothing.'

At home there is only silence. My mother has no lectures to give, but she's editing a book and won't leave her study. And my father and I? He leaves the rooms I enter without looking at me. Sometimes he hesitates, as if he is going to say something, but then he gathers in his words and seems to store them in the paunch that hangs just over his trouser line. I feel like it's getting bigger by the day. If I pass him on the stairs, then he kind of sucks in his breath and holds it, as if I give off a bad smell, like I'm surrounded by a perpetual cloud of fart. Because of this I stay in my room—I take the dinner my mother cooks to my room and eat staring out of the window at the growing dusk. I don't seem to taste any more, and what comes in rests in my stomach undigested.

They have arguments that they think I can't hear. But sound carries in this house.

I have heard my father say, 'Now I know why that boy's poor father won't even look at me.'

I have heard my mother say, 'Jackson, you're being so simple for a man so educated.'

I have heard my father say, 'It's what God wants, Felicia. Men are supposed to kiss women, to sleep with women, to lust after women. And women after men.'

And I have heard my mother ask, 'So you can represent a gay man that's been fired but you can't even look at your—'

'Philson wasn't my child, Felicia. Philson wasn't my own blood. You—you act like you're in support of his behaviour. Darling, what is going on here? Is there a conspiracy in my own house?'

'I don't support anything—especially not how you're handling this. There's a better way, Jackson. There's a better way.'

'Well, while you think of that—I'm gonna talk to him.'

'Jackson, you stay right there. You just stay right there. You understand me. You just sit and think about some things first. Let him have his space and you just cool off. You want what happened to Zhou to happen here? You wanna drive around the neighbourhood looking like Dr Chavin? Big family car and no family to show for it? I can't live like that.'

And then there is silence again save for the walls of the house shifting and settling—and the sometime sound of the rain outside.

My father wakes me up. He sits at the edge of my bed. I am still in my warm-ups and I feel like I smell of sweat. He wears a black golf shirt and khaki pants, but he doesn't have that 'I need to concentrate' look, where his brow is furrowed and his lips scrunch for a silent whistle, that he puts on before he goes to the golf range.

'Wanna go for a drive?' he asks softly.

I look at him, how his head is bowed to the floor and how his shoulder blades press out against the cotton of his shirt. And I nod my head yes. My father looks around the room, from the posters of rap and sports stars to my artwork, my watercolour landscapes and oil stills, my self-portraits and portraits of others. Then it's back to the posters. His lips part and he shakes his head. Before he leaves the room he says, 'You should change. I've got tickets to the Black Impressionists exhibit at the African American History Museum on the Mall.' He gets up. 'I'll be downstairs.'

We get in his silver Mercedes and he backs down the driveway. I still feel strange sitting in the passenger seat of his car. I feel like an impostor. My father has his own spaces which he is very particular about. His study is one. His wardrobe another. And then there is his car. It smells of him. I haven't quite decided what that smell is, but it's something like a mixture of stress and new-car scent. We hit River Road and then veer off on to the Beltway to take the George Washington Parkway directly downtown.

'Do you want to listen to anything?' he asks as he fiddles with his steering-wheel controls.

'What do you have?'

'Just scroll through and see.'

I put my fingers to the shimmering panel in the dash and point at changing coloured boxes until a menu of the different albums appears. I can't find anything I really like or want to listen to.

'Did you pick a song?' he asks.

I scroll through again and am surprised to find Beyoncé's CD listed among the options. 'Dad, you like Beyoncé?'

'She's quite the woman,' he says, and it hangs in the air between us. Then he adds, 'She can really sing too.'

The CD starts to play but I'm too tired to even bop my head like I normally would when listening to music. I can almost see my father's head moving to the beat as he reclines back into his seat and drops his right hand from the wheel on to the shifter between us.

'Yeah,' he says. 'She looks real good. Kind of like what your mom looked like back when I first saw her.' He smiles. 'Nothing like a woman with attitude.'

I stop listening to him and focus on the road ahead.

'Listen, Daven,' he says. 'The other day. In the kitchen. I didn't mean to create a scene. I was just shocked, you know. I mean, it's not an everyday thing that you find pictures of your son—'

'Dad.' I'm feeling very uncomfortable now. I clutch the hand rest on the door. 'Dad, I don't really want to talk about—'

'Daven, I'm trying to tell you something. I guess what it was that bothered me is that you didn't feel like you should tell me or that you could talk to me or we could—Look. It's perfectly okay to feel—'

'Dad, I'm not gay.'

He's beginning to get darker. 'What do you mean you aren't gay? What the hell do you think it means to kiss a guy?'

'Look. It wasn't like that. It wasn't just a guy. It was Zhou, Dad. It wouldn't have happened with any other guy. It was just a something.'

'Just a something! What? Just a something? You aren't making any sense. Look at me. Look at me! Turn this music off.' He decreases the volume from the steering wheel. 'I'm sitting here trying to be understanding and you're not even trying—'

'If you don't approve, you don't approve, Dad. But don't blanket me like I'm some sort of—I don't even know why I got in this car.'

'I'm trying to speak, Daven—'

'And I'm trying to speak.'

'Turn off the music and listen to me.'

I don't move.

'What's wrong with you? Okay, so you want to know what I think. I don't like it. I don't even understand how my child could turn out and do something like this. I don't freaking get it. And I'm not even going to hide that I think it's disgusting and sinful. But you're my child.'

'Dad, you're over the speed limit.'

He stares straight ahead and I can tell by the way that he keeps swallowing that he has a lump in his throat, that he wants to say more. He keeps looking in the rear-view mirror and then suddenly swerves into the fast lane. The car jumps forward and all the exit signs become blurs of green and the other cars streaks of colour. I look out of the window and I start to get sick. I look at the speedometer but that makes me feel worse. The yellow needle hovers around the white ninety miles per hour reading.

'What about the police?' I plead, and clutch the dashboard with all of my might. I push myself back into the leather seat that doesn't want to cradle me. 'You're going to—'

'I didn't drop a hundred grand on the sport package for nothing, did I?' he responds, with his eyes fixed on the asphalt ahead of him. 'Did I? Answer me. Just like I didn't spend all this time raising you for nothing, did I?'

'Please slow down. Please. You're scaring me.'

'Is this how he did it?' he shouts. 'Is this how he got rid of his trouble? Once you hit ninety it's almost like a plane crash. You get ejected. You burn. You're mangled. You die. Is this how he did it? Right into a wall. All that liquored-up blood spilling ungratefully all over the seat of the car his father bought for him with some hard-earned cash. You kids don't appreciate anything. Any damn—'

'Stop it. Please stop it.'

'Stop what?' he yells. His eyes are fully on me and not on the road. 'Stop remembering that I've seen pictures of my son kissing another man, read his love letters. Stop remembering the look on that boy's father's face. Looking at me like I'm Satan or something. Stop thinking about where your filthy hands have—'

'Are you insane? What are you—Dad. Just pay attention to the fucking road. Pay attention. Why are you doing this?' I'm trying my best to sound manly but my voice cracks. The imprint of the Mercedes logo is pressed firmly into my palm. 'Let me out. I don't want to be here any more.'

'You just stay where you are until we get where we're going.'

'*No!*' I yell and unbuckle my seat belt. He slaps my hand and the car swerves. There is a horrible screeching sound. I unlock my door and open it. 'Let me out,' I shout. I can feel the door quiver against the rushing air. The wind drowns out my yells, as does the sound of horns and the engines of the other cars left in our dust.

'Close the door!' he screams.

'Pull over. Pull the fuck over. I want to get out. Now!'

'Daven, be calm. Just *close the door*. You're acting crazy.' He reaches across me to try and pull it shut, but I stick my foot out of the door and hold it just above the ground, knowing full well that if I lose control it's lost. I don't care. Nothing can hurt me any more now.

My father slows down and signals to change lanes.

'Please close your door, Daven.' I can tell by the way his voice wavers that he is ready to cry like last time.

'Daven, trust me please.'

He slows and crosses over the white line into the shoulder lane. The car crunches to a stop on the loose gravel and my father slumps forward on the steering wheel, sobbing. 'Fucking fuck,' he chokes. 'I just wanted you to…'

I can smell the hot ground metal of the engine as it clicks furiously while its parts contract and cool. I get out.

'Wait, Daven. Please wait!'

I begin to run. It feels so strange in dress shoes, but I run away from him, towards the end of the concrete sound barrier to where the trees of people's backyards obscure their houses from the highway.

I walk for hours. My shirt is wrinkled and my khakis have a black streak from where they rubbed against the bottom edge of the door. I sweat profusely and I can feel the salt residue drying on my face as I walk through some neighbourhood I barely know. It's probably going to dry white on my face like it does after track practice. I'll look like black marble with white streaks in it. I am cold but I keep walking, following my feet and not my head. This city's suburbs are a maze of American perfection—the house, the car, the kids and toys tossed carelessly about in the yard. Perfect trees line each street, providing just the right amount of shade in the sun and in storms the right amount of danger. Moderation—Zhou's family never had that. Was Zhou's family even a family? And my family?

It's hours and dark before I recognize anything. I've made it back to Bethesda and I'm heading to the Potomac River, back along time to February before Zhou died. It's dark outside and it's started to drizzle. And I realize that it shouldn't be this way, that this isn't some sort of movie with all its melodrama. Things don't happen that fast or that slow in real life. Before this I was just a kid who drove a

Volvo, got good grades, got along with his parents. Now I'm gay. And wet, and standing at the entrance to the parking lot where February happened. The park closes after dark because the lot would be one of those places where psychotic men take little girls. There are trees on both sides, blocking the lot from the Clara Barton Parkway and the Potomac River. I can hear the water rushing by, but above it I can hear Zhou and me speaking as we sit in his car.

'Shit,' he says. 'I can't believe you're going to Harvard next year.'

He's fiddling with the bass and treble settings on the dashboard.

'You've known for the longest time what's going to happen to you,' he says softly without looking up. 'Sometimes I wonder if— well, I just wonder. I mean, I'll have to do another year 'cause my grades are shit. I mean, they'll have to send me to community college. My dad is going to die of anger.'

His thin lips quiver. He's a good-looking kid. Mixed people are always somehow beautiful. Zhou used this to his fullest advantage at his high school. Girls loved him.

'Zhou, it's all good. You've got to go the road that—'

'Shhh. Just listen,' he says, and moves my hand away from the stereo as I prepare to turn down the volume. His fingers are cold and spindly, thin like his mother's. He turns up the volume so the whole car speaks. Then he looks at me and for the first time in my life I realize that his eyes don't slant in either direction. I had just assumed. 'I'm already finished, Daven,' he says.

I feel fluttery and disconcerted. He grabs my hand strongly and we move towards each other to touch shoulders the way handshakes are done. Then his head is in my shoulder and he's crying and I don't know about what.

'Zhou, it's all good.' I repeat over and over again as I look at how the BMW dials glow orange-red in the darkness. I open my door. 'Let's get some air.' And I step out, leaving him with his chin propped against his elbow and his head vibrating with each subwoofer pulse. It's February but it's not that cold. The car is parked just at the tip of a parking space with the headlights off so that we won't attract attention. We started coming here two summers ago—on bikes first—just to chill and shoot the shit. It became a hang-out. We brought our friends here and sat and talked. We brought our girlfriends here together and made out in front of each other because it was all comfortable like that. I walk towards the single parking-lot lamp and stand in its light.

Zhou moved towards me and I didn't move away because it seemed so natural. I hugged him. We swayed. We did a dance so sensual, so private and yet—framed in the streetlamp—so public. All the while I could feel his arms around me, begging for comfort, and me struggling to hold him and myself apart. And that should have been the line, but things always move too fast or too slow and somewhere in the middle something happens that you don't realize. I felt his lips brush mine, but it was too fast to feel shame, too fast to feel indecent.

Then a full kiss. We only kissed—nothing more—and I felt my whole body stiffening and melting at the same time. I wanted to say stop, but I wanted to taste his salty lips and feel his tongue. It just seemed like the right thing to want, the right thing to do.

I don't know why we took pictures. It wasn't my suggestion but I agreed. I think I knew what he was going to do with his car and that I wouldn't see him again, that I wouldn't feel this again. And I think he wanted me to remember him as more than just a feeling. He had a Kodak disposable in the car that he'd been using to take shots of the party we had just come from. And we took shots, normal shots, and then shots of us kissing. And that was it. That's all. Nothing more.

I want to tell him I hate him. I taste the drizzle on my tongue, feel it on my face and mutter to myself, 'I love you with all my heart.'

I want to tell him that I want my heterosexuality back, but I don't know if I ever lost it. And if I did, I don't know that I miss it so much. I want to tell him that he didn't have to go like that. I want to ask him what I should do now.

A car slides into the parking lot and flashes its lights at me. I see the Mercedes sign glistening with drops of rain. It slows down as it approaches and the windows slide away. My mother is in the driver's seat. Her make-up has run. My father slouches beside her. 'How did you know?' he mutters to her without looking at me.

'I could tell by the picture,' she responds, still staring at me. 'You used to take him here when he was younger. All the time.'

I open the back door and a tinge of rose softens the inside of my nostrils. This isn't quite how I expected the answer to my prayers, but it's a start. ☐

GRANTA

MY PAINTER
Nicole Krauss

Nicole Krauss is the author of the novels 'Man Walks into a Room' (Hamish Hamilton/Anchor) and 'The History of Love' (Hamish Hamilton/W. W. Norton), which won France's Prix du Meilleur Livre Étranger, and was shortlisted for the Orange, Médicis and Femina prizes. She was born in New York City, where she still lives, though from time to time she imagines and even makes overtures towards living elsewhere. Her books have been translated into more than thirty languages. 'My Painter' is a new story.

When I first met the painter of this picture I'd just lost my job
and, if I remember correctly, I was reading the poems of the
Japanese writer, Shiraishi. I got the book cheaply in a used bookstore
and so felt a certain responsibility to it, but the more I read the more
I liked it, and sometimes I even went around reciting bits of the
poems in my head. Things weren't going well. I was sleeping on the
floor of a friend's apartment, a photographer from Berlin who used
to take pictures of the plants on his windowsill, a few potted greens
that seemed to share a certain wistfulness, as if they had once lived
in the great glass and cast-iron hothouses of Europe and didn't know
how they'd got to that homely window ledge. They were nothing
special, those plants, but I didn't say anything because after all the
photographer was letting me sleep on his floor and use the soap in
his shower. At that point I didn't know he was also the one who
would introduce me to my painter, but if I had it would have been
yet another reason to have practised silence as a form of gratitude.

In those days I was spending a lot of time in the little park on
Second Avenue outside Beth Israel Hospital. During the day I didn't
have much to do. I'd walk the streets with a book in my pocket,
revelling in the winter sunlight and taking in the window displays
designed to make you want to change your life, or at least rub the one
you have until it starts to shine. That park was a strange and maybe
even beautiful place, although you had to spend a fair bit of time there
to begin to see its beauty. People who'd come to visit the patients in
the hospital would go to the park to get a breath of fresh air and make
calls on their cell phones. They were pale and exhausted, and you could
see how their whole world had been honed to a single point. It was
the ones who were waiting, who were hunched against the cold and
didn't know the outcome, who stood out most sharply. There was
one couple whose baby was in the ICU, and every time I saw them
it took my breath away. You could tell they were sleeping in the
hospital because they always wore the same clothes, and sometimes
I heard them explaining to someone on the phone how the doctors
were going to try this or that treatment. The baby was sick, he
couldn't breathe. Is it possible that sadness can make people graceful?
Usually I saw the man and the woman each on their own, I suppose
so that one could stay behind with the baby. But once they came out
together. The sky was tamped down heavy and grey, and it had just

started to snow. The two of them were walking away from me, so I couldn't see their faces. But they looked too small for their enormous coats. I don't know who was staying with the baby, maybe the woman's mother, or maybe they left him with the nurses. After that I never saw them again, but sometimes I think about that child and wonder what happened to him. Not long afterwards I met the painter of this picture.

The story she likes to tell is that she saw me across the dance floor, but as I remember it we were introduced by the photographer at a friend of a friend's apartment. The apartment was about to be gutted, and everyone was allowed to draw something on the walls. I don't know why this was so exciting, but it was. I was given a piece of white wall in the hallway near the kitchen. It didn't get much light, but otherwise I was happy with it. I didn't know anyone at the party, and so the photographer looked around for someone to introduce me to. Just then my painter walked by. The photographer called her over and handed out our names. Then he went off shaking a can of spray paint.

During that time in my life I had a lot of elaborate ideas for jobs that I didn't know how to get, but which I believed in my heart I was meant for. I can't remember all of them now, but one involved operating a pleasure boat for tourists on the Gowanus Canal. I knew a girl who lived in Brooklyn, and I think the idea had something to do with my affection for her, and the way it brought me closer to her. In her bedroom she had a plastic model of a human brain, and many times I took the F train and ended up sitting in the sunshine on her floor, playing with it and trying to scrape together the courage. My mother used to say that I was my own worst enemy, and though I never thought she was right about that, the situation with the girl would certainly have fitted neatly into her argument. In the end it was always the girl who did most of the talking—she was, in so many ways, exemplary—while I sat Indian-style with the pieces of brain scattered around me. I don't know why I thought of the girl just now, or my plans for the Gowanus, except that it was around the time that I met my painter that my longing for her had reached its pinnacle. Since then I've thought about her less and less, and now I hardly think of her at all.

As I was saying, we were all given a little piece of white wall and the chance to draw on it however we saw fit. Unlike my painter, I am not an artist, nor have I ever wanted to be one. But I'd gotten it into my head to paint a jungle on fire, and wild pigs running out of it, sparks on their feet. The idea came from one of Shiraishi's poems. In it the wild pigs are afraid of humans and always run away from them, until one day a fire breaks out in the virgin forest and they come crashing out of it towards the human beings who they have always been right to fear. I started by drawing the jungle licked by flames which looked fine, more or less, but when it came time to draw the pigs they had none of the speed or terror I'd pictured in my head, and could have passed for dogs or even rats as easily as pigs. What had begun in excitement ended in disappointment, as has been the case with so many things in my life, and because the wall was quite large, and I could do nothing to hide the pigs, I felt embarrassed, then humiliated. I decided to abandon it and wander around the rest of the apartment to see what other people were doing, and simply hope that the fiery jungle and the wild pigs or dogs wouldn't continue, in the minds of the others, to be associated with me.

As I remember it, it was then that my painter and I first began to talk, and I realized, at some underpass in the conversation, that we would be seeing each other again after that day. Maybe I already knew then that she was going to paint me, or maybe I hoped that she would, or maybe I didn't care either way, was just glad to be free of the jungle on fire, and those poor and terrible pigs. My painter was busy painting a landscape of a tree, and what impressed me was how small it was, how she'd chosen to leave so much of the space allotted to her blank, the way the little landscape drew your attention to the wall itself, not letting you forget that it was a wall, and that it was something special to be painting on it.

It was also around this time that I acquired, by chance, the shirt that I am wearing in this picture. Someone left it behind in the photographer's apartment, and one day I put it on and went out for a walk with a book, I've forgotten which one, in my pocket. The shirt had an unfamiliar smell, but I felt immediately at home in it, and even took a liking to it. It was red, like the birds of Kalimantan that Shiraishi describes in his poem. Wearing it became something of a habit until I, too, left it behind somewhere, and now I suppose someone else is going around making a life in it. I'd forgotten it until just now when I saw this picture, in which, as you can see, my painter caught me in a moment that is somehow rare and yet not uncharacteristic. □

GRANTA

VALETS
Rattawut Lapcharoensap

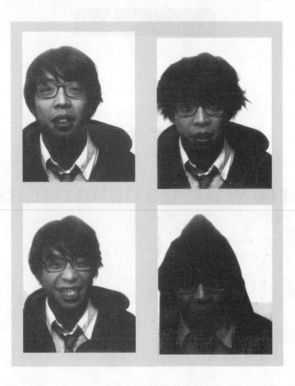

Rattawut Lapcharoensap was born in Chicago in 1979 and raised in Bangkok. He currently lives in Brooklyn and teaches high school English. He misses his family in Thailand and hopes they won't have to live under martial law for long. 'Farangs', his first published story, appeared in Granta 84. Since then, his work has been published in several literary magazines, as well as in 'Best New American Voices 2005' (Harvest Books) and 'Best American Nonrequired Reading 2005' (Houghton Mifflin). 'Sightseeing', a short story collection, is published by Atlantic Books in the UK and Grove Press in the US. It was selected for the National Book Foundation's '5 Under 35' programme, won the Asian American Literary Award and was also shortlisted for the Guardian First Book Award. 'Valets' is a new story.

It's a slow night again. The other valets are out back playing pétanque with the kitchen staff. I'm sitting with Dang and Uncle Judo, watching the tour buses unload at Fai Mangkon on the other side of the Bangna–Trat Highway, when Uncle Judo says what we've all been thinking for many months now. He says it's over. He says it's time to find a new job.

'Just look at that,' Uncle Judo says, pointing at a group of Chinese tourists. The Chinese wear matching green hats, pose for a picture in front of Fai Mangkon's mascot: a six-metre animatronic dragon that tilts its head, flaps its wings, emits actual flames from its mouth.

'Look at how happy they are. You know it's all over when the competition's got the Chinese.'

'It's not the Chinese they've got,' Dang says. 'It's that fucking dragon.'

'How is that a restaurant?' I say. 'How is that authentic Thai cuisine?'

'Don't be so naive.' Uncle Judo flicks his cigarette into the gutter. 'Don't think for a minute that we're selling them food.'

I just blink at Uncle Judo, watch the Chinese disappear through Fai Mangkon's replica Sukhothai-era gate.

Dang points to our wooden marquee.

'Last I checked,' he says in my defence, 'that sign still said restaurant.'

'That's our problem, you see,' Uncle Judo says. 'We persist in the illusion that these people are here to eat. We've grossly misinterpreted our demographic's demands.'

Ever since he started taking weekend classes in business and economics at Ramkhamhaeng University, Uncle Judo's been full of this talk. Supply and demand. Fordism and Taylorism. Management tactics and human resources. Adam Smith and the invisible hand.

'Here we go,' Dang says. 'Go ahead. Enlighten us, Professor.'

'It's not the food they want,' Uncle Judo says. 'What they put in their mouths is entirely incidental. It's not the dinner that matters— it's the dining experience. That's what the Fai Mangkon people understand. They understand the dynamism of the free market. They understand that those tourists aren't going to remember the food— they're going to remember the dragon. And now we're going to lose our jobs.'

'Fuck the free market,' Dang says. 'And fuck Fai Mangkon.'

'You've got to admire them,' Uncle Judo continues, ignoring Dang. 'They've taken our model and innovated. We, on the other hand, refuse to adjust to the market's demands. It's like we're Sony, but a stupid Sony. We've invented a portable cassette-player but keep producing them long after cassettes have become obsolete.'

'I still own a Walkman,' Dang responds. 'Don't call me obsolete.'

A white van turns into our parking lot then, pulls up to the valet area. Uncle Judo approaches the driver's side for the keys. Dang slides open the van door to reveal a half-dozen farangs laughing inside. I bow at them, give the customary farang greeting in English: 'Welcome to Thailand. Welcome to Ban Kluaimai.'

The farangs stop their laughing, eye me curiously.

'Is this Fai Mangkon?' the Thai driver asks, rolling down his window.

Dang shuts the sliding door on the farangs. We resume our places in our chairs.

'You see that dragon?' Uncle Judo says to the driver, pointing across the highway. 'The one that breathes fire? That's where you want to be.'

Ban Kluaimai was the first restaurant of its kind in the city, a testament to the General's entrepreneurial foresight and ingenuity. In the early 1980s, armed with insider knowledge about the construction of an eight-lane highway through the city's south-east, the General purchased forty rai of seemingly worthless flood fields from a group of local rice farmers. Within three months, the General's men had converted the bog into a pristine lagoon. They erected thirty traditional *salas*—open-air pavilions on stilts, all connected by an intricate maze of boardwalks. A floating stage was built in the centre of the lagoon. Every hour—as soon as the sun set over the green fields of Samutprakan behind the stage—traditional dances were performed while, in English, a narrator told diners about each number through a state-of-the-art sound system. Men with caged sparrows offered customers the opportunity to release the birds from captivity: good karma, they said. Women paddled in small canoes from *sala* to *sala* selling desserts, local fruits, jasmine wreaths, commemorative T-shirts and buttons. Thousands of carp and catfish were bred in the lagoon so diners could feed them scraps from their meals, watch the still water turn into a busy sheet of gaping fish-maws.

But, above all, Ban Kluaimai was notable for its size. It was—until the advent of Fai Mangkon—one of the largest restaurants in the world. Petitions were made to the *Guinness Book of World Records*. Ban Kluaimai could accommodate up to 1,500 customers and in its heyday it had a hundred-strong wait staff that roller-skated the long distances between the restaurant's sixty-burner kitchen and its 400-odd tables.

Royalty attended the opening ceremony. So, too, did the prime minister, retired generals, various actors, singers and television personalities. A short film was screened about the General's life: his humble provincial beginnings, his illustrious military career, his philanthropy and visionary business ideas. The prime minister made a speech about Ban Kluaimai's role in the tourism industry, its importance to the economic livelihood of the city. He called Ban Kluaimai a world-class dining facility. He said it made him proud to be Thai.

So older employees like Uncle Judo remember a better time. They remember bright and profitable years when every table was occupied, every performance was applauded, every fish was fed, every caged sparrow was released, every Singha- and Mekong-filled customer—farangs and wealthy locals alike—parted freely and easily with tips. They remember sleeping like exhausted children, their pockets filled with the day's meagre though tenable earnings, instead of laying awake each night worrying about their jobs.

For there were things the General did not anticipate. He did not anticipate the green fields of Samutprakan becoming pink condominiums towering over the floating stage. He did not anticipate the city's brownouts, plunging the restaurant into darkness every time it rained. He did not anticipate the carp and the catfish's decimation by disease, their bloated carcasses occasionally bobbing on the lagoon's surface for all to see. He did not anticipate the hyperactive farang child who climbed over the boardwalk's railing and fell into the lagoon, breaking his arm and nearly drowning. He did not anticipate the child's parents filing a lawsuit that—though unsuccessful—would blemish Ban Kluaimai's increasingly spotty reputation. And, finally, he did not anticipate Fai Mangkon. He did not anticipate its fire-breathing dragon flapping its wings across the highway. And he certainly did not anticipate the headlines announcing the competition's arrival that week: FAI MANGKON, one of the business papers declared, BIGGER AND BETTER THAN BAN KLUAIMAI.

We get a van now and again but the larger tour buses have deserted us for good. Traffic these days consists of farangs with outdated guidebooks, middle-class provincials vacationing in the city and—every night without fail—the General's son Thanet and Thanet's ridiculous friends. Ever since the General retired to the south last year, Thanet has been responsible for running the restaurant. He and his friends arrive now, a Mercedes-Benz and a BMW swerving into the parking lot, competing bass speakers vibrating the night air.

We all check our uniforms, bolt from our seats to receive them. Uncle Judo opens Thanet's door, bows to him, while Dang opens the passenger side. A lithe, skinny woman gets out with Thanet, her face and her hair fastidiously arranged. She's not a woman we've seen before. They rarely ever are.

'Good evening, sir,' we all exclaim, bowing again.

'Okay,' Thanet says, hooking the woman's arm in his own, running a few fingers through his thick and shiny hair. 'Enough already. Go take care of my friends.'

Uncle Judo drives Thanet's Benz to its place in the lot while Dang and I tend to the BMW. Three young men emerge from the sedan: buffed leather shoes, neatly pressed pants, sunglasses, watches, amulets on gold chains. They're a little like their car—sleek surfaces, glinting corners, gilded edges.

'Oh, boy,' one says to Dang. 'It's you.'

'Watch this one,' says another.

'Listen,' says the driver seriously, handing Dang the keys. 'Be careful this time.'

'Of course—'

'Don't speak. Just do your job. Be careful with my car.'

I worry the hem of my uniform. I can sense Thanet watching from behind, smell his cologne souring the air. I turn briefly and see his pale face smiling wryly under the lights, his thin lips pulled back from his perfect teeth.

Yes, I'd like to take advantage of this special subscriptions offer:

UK/USA £6.99 Save 30% ☐ Euro/S. America £7.99 Save 20% ☐ Canada/ROW £8.99 Save 10% ☐

Payments will be collected every three months following the despatch of each issue of Granta

PLEASE SELECT YOUR PREFERRED PAYMENT METHOD:

All prices include delivery!

[1] Direct Debit:

Instruction to your Bank or building society to pay by direct Debit

Bank / Building Society account number

☐☐☐☐☐☐☐☐

Branch Sort Code

☐☐ ☐☐ ☐☐

Originator's identification number

9 1 3 1 3 3

To the manager (bank or building society name)

Address

Post code

Account in the name(s) of)

Signed

Date

Instructions to your Bank or Building Society
Please pay Granta Publications Direct Debits from the account detailed on this instruction subject to the safeguards assured by the Direct Debit Guarantee. I understand that this instruction may remain with Granta, and, if so, details will be passed electronically to my bank or building society.

Banks and Building Societies may not accept Direct Debit instructions from some types of accounts

Granta ref no. (for office use only)

[2] Continuous credit card: I authorise Granta Publications to charge my credit card until further notice for the sum and at the intervals stated overleaf. I understand that I may cancel this authorisation at any time in writing and that I will be notified in writing in advance of any changes.

☐ Mastercard ☐ Visa ☐ Amex Expiry date: ☐☐ / ☐☐

Card number: ☐☐☐☐ ☐☐☐☐ ☐☐☐☐ ☐☐☐☐

Signed _____ Date _____ 07ABGNS0

THE DIRECT DEBIT GUARANTEE

- This Guarantee is offered by all Banks and Building Societies that take part in the Direct Debit Scheme. The efficiency and security of the Scheme is monitored by your own Bank or Building society.
- If the amounts to be paid or the payment dates change, Granta Publications will notify you 10 working days in advance of your account being debited or as otherwise agreed.
- If an error is made by Granta Publications or your Bank or Building society, you are guaranteed a full and immediate refund from your branch of the amount paid.
- You can cancel a Direct Debit at any time by writing to your Bank or Building Society. Please also send a copy of your letter to Granta.

Please complete the address section on the front of this card, detach and return to Granta Subscriptions at:
PO Box 6712, Brunel Road,
Basingstoke, RG24 4FP, United Kingdom
Or telephone +44 (0)1256 802 873

Your details will be processed by Granta and our suppliers, who may or may not be located within the European Union, in full accordance with the UK data protection legislation. Granta may occasionally contact you with information about other products and services. Granta occasionally shares data, on a secure basis, with other reputable companies who wish to contact you with information about their products and services.
Please tick if you prefer not to receive such information by post ☐ by phone ☐
Please indicate here if you would like to receive this information by email ☐

'You hear me?' the BMW's driver continues, gesturing with his chin at Dang. 'Do your job properly for once.'

'Yeah,' says one of the others. 'Don't dent the car this time.'

'But I didn't dent it,' Dang says, looking bewildered. 'I never dented your car.'

'Hey,' Thanet interjects, pointing at Dang. He walks towards his friends, the woman still on his arm, her high heels stabbing the asphalt. 'Is there a problem here? Are you arguing with the customers?'

Dang shakes his head. He looks at the ground, grips the BMW's keys in his hand.

'You idiot,' says the driver before suddenly, inexplicably, shoving Dang in the chest with both hands. Dang stumbles backwards. One of the men catches him before he falls, holds him up by his armpits, and the look on Dang's face as he's held there—surprised, panicked, helpless—makes my stomach lurch.

The driver leans over Dang. Their faces nearly touch.

'I was joking,' he whispers, smiling. 'I know you never dented my car.'

They all laugh and guffaw then, even the woman on Thanet's arm. Dang collects himself, smooths his shirtfront with both hands, smiles weakly along with the men.

Thanet takes a twenty-baht bill from his wallet.

'You're a good sport,' he says, offering Dang the money.

Dang shakes his head. He won't take it. He refuses again and again. In the end, Thanet simply shrugs, puts his money away, and Dang disappears to park the BMW, leaving me with Thanet and his friends.

Thanet puts a hand on my back. 'Tell those guys to come by our table later. Tell them I want to buy them a drink.'

I nod. I pretend to busy myself with the arrangement of our chairs. It's all I can do not to look at Thanet's alabaster face, at his hair gleaming under the lights, at his friends still laughing and patting each other on the back.

'And you should come too,' he adds, before they all climb the gangplank into the restaurant. 'You look like you could use one.'

Uncle Judo's not really our uncle. We call him that because he's worked here so long: he's one of Ban Kluaimai's original staff. A few other 'uncles' and 'aunts' remain from that first generation—

Uncle Chiap in the kitchen, Aunt Bua from the dance troupe, Uncle Wirot from the wait staff—but their numbers have dwindled significantly since cutbacks began a few months ago. Uncles and aunts were often the first to go then. Judo's the only uncle left among the valets. 'We're like an endangered species,' he said one night. 'We're like pandas and manatees. I'm like the last dodo.'

Judo's not his real name. Nobody knows what it is. We call him Judo because he used to be a nationally ranked judo master. At least once a week, when conversation's slow, he'll produce a small black-and-white photo from his wallet. The photo shows his younger self in a white judo outfit, the national flag embroidered on its lapels. He'll tell us then about the Olympics, how he almost made it to the '76 Games in Montreal. He'll tell us how he was ranked second in the country that year, how everybody considered him an automatic selection. He'll tell us how, during qualifiers—which were only supposed to be a formality—a clumsy seventeen-year-old amateur sent a strong heel ploughing through his right knee, shattering the kneecap, tearing every cartilage, ending his judo career. He'll roll up his pants and show us the surgery scars and he'll tell us about the long years after the injury, how all he could think about was that boy's heel hitting his knee—its blunt, surprising force—its crushing, sickening sounds— and the way his balance had fled him like air from a deflating balloon. He'll say that for years it seemed he never got up from that judo mat. All he could think about was the past. The future no longer existed.

But things are different these days, he'll say. After fifteen years of parking people's cars at Ban Kluaimai, there's finally been a change. The future's back again. And as soon as he finishes his business degree he plans to find out what it's like.

Though we've heard it many times before, Uncle Judo tells his story again. It's his way of consoling Dang. 'The lesson here,' he concludes, 'is forget about the past. Stop dwelling on your injuries. Focus on the future.'

'I'm not dwelling on my injuries,' Dang says. 'I'm dwelling on theirs. You know, if he wasn't the General's son—'

'But he is. So there you are.'

It's nearly ten-thirty. Traffic on the Bangna–Trat Highway has thinned. We watch a few more tour buses turn into Fai Mangkon, the animatronic dragon tilting its head, flapping its wings, spewing its ribbons of propane flames. Floodlights send Fai Mangkon's logo twirling across the night sky. According to their promotional materials, Fai Mangkon diners will soon be treated to a laser-light show chronicling the country's history. There will also be a modern jazz interpretation of the *Ramakien*, a fireworks display and—at the end of the night—a restaurant-wide singalong of 'We are the World'. Then they will go home satisfied.

Over here, meanwhile, we're staring at a vast ocean of cracked asphalt. There aren't even a hundred customers inside.

I tell Uncle Judo and Dang about Thanet. I tell them he wants to buy us a drink. Dang shakes his head, mutters under his breath, says it's another trick. But Uncle Judo wants to go.

'Don't be senile,' Dang scoffs.

Uncle Judo doesn't say anything. He simply grabs one of his business textbooks from under his chair, pulls out several sheets of handwritten notes from its pages, and hands the papers to Dang.

'I don't need your study notes.'

'They're not study notes,' Uncle Judo says. 'They're a business proposal.'

Dang and I just stare at him.

'A business proposal for Ban Kluaimai,' Uncle Judo explains. 'A proposal for our future. I want to give this to Thanet. I want to tell him my ideas for renovating the restaurant.'

Dang thumbs through the papers for a while. 'This is crazy.' He hands them to me. 'Please tell him this is crazy.'

Uncle Judo peers at me brightly while I look at his papers.

'We're being mismanaged,' he declares, gesticulating with his hands now. 'We're going to lose our jobs. If implemented correctly, however, my proposal might save us all.'

'You might feel mismanaged,' Dang says. 'I just feel abused.'

I try to read Uncle Judo's proposal. I can't make sense of any of it. There are eight pages written in his cramped, meticulous hand. The writing's been organized under a series of general headings— INNOVATION AND INGENUITY; MARKET-SHARE ANALYSIS; DEMOGRAPHIC RESEARCH; FISCAL RESTRUCTURING; MAXIMIZATION OF HUMAN RESOURCES. There are tables and charts, drawings and diagrams. There's even a bibliography: Adam Smith's *Wealth of Nations*, Karl

Rattawut Lapcharoensap

Marx's *Capital* and John Maynard Keynes's *General Theory of Employment, Interest and Money* are all listed as sources.

'Uncle,' I say, handing back his papers. 'This is very impressive. But Thanet's not going to read it. He's not going to listen to you.'

'He'll listen. That boy may be cruel, and that boy may be a petulant drunk, but above all that boy's a businessman. Any self-respecting businessman would see the sense in my proposal. Remember that he's the General's son. Remember that business is in his blood.'

'That's not business in his blood,' Dang says. 'That's spite. That's cruelty. Egomania. Whisky.'

Uncle Judo dismisses Dang with a wave of a hand. 'And besides,' he says to me, 'he's seen me around since he was a child. Surely that has to count for something.'

The other valets—Samak, Worachai and Piak—return from playing pétanque with the kitchen staff. They've pocketed thirty baht tonight—a good haul—but there's little joy when they tell us about their victory.

'I didn't sign up for this,' Samak says, settling into his chair. 'I didn't sign up to gamble and play pétanque. I didn't sign up to sit around and chat with you monkeys. I signed up to work, damnit. I signed up to fetch people's cars.'

Nobody says anything for a long time. We just sit there smoking, fidgeting in our seats, watching freight trucks motor down the Bangna–Trat Highway. A pack of stray dogs ambles across our parking lot, pausing here and there to sniff the asphalt before moving on to scavenge elsewhere. Fai Mangkon's fireworks start blooming in the sky then, throwing their lurid lights on to our faces, filling the air with their syncopated reports.

'Okay, killjoy,' Piak mutters, producing a pack of playing cards. We quickly rearrange our chairs into a semicircle.

'Rummy. Five baht a hand.'

After a few rounds, Uncle Judo, Dang and I leave to see Thanet.

'Let's go get humiliated,' Dang says, sighing, while we're walking up the gangplank.

'Don't come then.' Uncle Judo tucks his business proposal into his back pocket. 'Go back. Disobey Thanet if you want.'

'No thanks,' Dang says. 'I've already been personally humiliated tonight. From now on, I prefer team humiliation.'

'Nobody is going to be humiliated,' I say. Uncle Judo smiles at me gratefully. 'We're just going to have a drink. We're just going to give him the proposal.'

Dang looks at me sideways, shakes his head. I share his reservations, of course, but the old man's enthusiasm prohibits us from saying anything more. We're going for Uncle Judo.

Inside, it's another night at Ban Kluaimai. The customers sit scattered all over the thirty *salas*. Wait staff stand sentinel over them, leaning against the rails, shuffling in their roller skates. Onstage, the band and the dance troupe perform a traditional north-eastern dance number—the men on one side, the women on the other, a member of each intermittently flirting in the middle—all of them bored beneath their make-up and their bright silk outfits. The English narrator's voice crackles the sound system. No one is really watching.

A few women paddle their boats listlessly, drift around the lagoon with their racks of unsold wares. We see a young farang boy releasing a cage of sparrows. He slides open the cage door but the birds only fly a short distance to twitter on the roofs of the restaurant. 'Go!' the boy screams at them in English. His parents urge for calm. The other customers turn to look. 'Be free!' he continues, flapping his arms. 'Fly away, stupid birds!'

Thanet and his friends are sitting in the southernmost *sala*. During the silence between dance numbers, their gruff voices echo around the lagoon. As always, an all-female wait staff tend to their needs—bringing them their food, clearing their dishes, replenishing their drinks. There's a feast of half-eaten entrées on the table: fish curry, crab fried rice, stewed pork leg, oysters simmered in egg whites.

'Look who it is,' one of Thanet's friends says, pointing at Dang when we arrive.

'What do you need?' Thanet asks us, frowning. He has a thick arm slung around the woman's shoulders. He's flushed from the liquor, the mottling on his neck and his cheeks a pink frame around his pale face.

'I'm very sorry, sir,' I say, bowing to them all. 'But you said you wanted to see us. You said you wanted to buy us a drink.'

Thanet's friends chuckle, twirl the ice in their whisky tumblers. Dang and Uncle Judo shift from foot to foot. I realize then how ridiculous I must sound, how ridiculous the three of us must seem. Thanet eyes us silently for a long time, tucks a stray hair behind an ear. It's all I can do not to flee from the General's son. But then he says, 'Of course. I almost forgot. Take a seat, gentlemen.'

He gestures to the waitresses to bring us chairs. As we're sitting down, Thanet's friends tease Dang some more. 'I never dented the car!' one of them squeals, cowering theatrically, but Dang just stares abstractedly over the *sala* railing.

Thanet silences his friends with a look. He leans towards the three of us, his hands clasped before him.

'As you all know—' His voice is serious. He takes a few deep and insincere breaths. 'As you all know, there have been some cutbacks around here lately—'

I feel light-headed, nauseated, stupid; my body seems to constrict into a small, hard knot. But Uncle Judo interrupts the General's son before he can finish his sentence.

'Sir.' He holds his proposal aloft. 'I have something for you, sir.'

Thanet stares at the document hovering between them, the pages rustling from Uncle Judo's shaking hand. The mottling on Thanet's cheeks spreads across his features, his face a fruit ripening before our eyes.

'It's a business proposal, sir,' Uncle Judo says. He deposits the papers on the table, shoves his hands inside his trouser pockets. 'A proposal for Ban Kluaimai. My colleagues and I—' he gestures at Dang and me—'we wrote the proposal together, sir, after many long months of study. I think you'll find it of interest.'

'You think I'll find it of interest.'

'Yes, sir,' Uncle Judo says. 'Yes, I do.'

Thanet purses his lips, squints at Uncle Judo. He picks up the proposal. The woman peers over his shoulder while he glances quickly through the document. Every now and again, Thanet's face twitches with disgust.

'This,' he says, 'is fucking ridiculous.' He tosses the papers on to the table. A corner lands in the fish curry. 'Don't tell me how to run my business.'

Uncle Judo blanches.

'Oh, don't be so mean,' the woman says to Thanet. She picks up the papers, tries to clean the curry-stained corner with her slender, manicured fingers. 'I don't think it's ridiculous.' She smiles at Uncle Judo, offers back his proposal. 'I think it's very cute.'

Thanet grunts. The woman immediately leaves the proposal on the table again. For a long time, Uncle Judo just sits there staring at the papers, his face vacant, ashen, crestfallen. Beneath the table, I see him clenching and unclenching his hands. Dang, meanwhile, plays with his nails, shakes both his legs, keeps staring over the railing. The waitresses pretend to busy themselves with the ice, the spare ashtrays, the arrangement of condiments and spices.

'Wait,' one of Thanet's friends suddenly declares. 'I have a business proposal too. I propose we go across the highway and destroy that fucking dragon. See if business doesn't pick up then.'

'Now that,' says another, 'is a business proposal.'

They all erupt with laughter then, raise their whisky tumblers, their voices high and excited. Thanet smiles for the first time since our arrival. He leans back in his chair, puts his arm around the woman's shoulders again, seeming to relax, though still squinting at Uncle Judo the entire time.

'You should thank my friends,' he says finally. 'I was going to fire you all tonight, but now I've changed my mind.'

'Thank you,' Uncle Judo says, his voice barely audible. 'Thank you so much, sir.'

'Oh no. Don't thank me yet, old man.'

The General's son rises from his seat. He gestures for everybody to do the same.

'Let's go and destroy that dragon,' he says, grinning. 'Let's go and do that first. Then I'll let you keep your jobs.'

The other valets pause when they see us approach with Thanet and his friends. We stand there trying not to meet their bewildered gazes before they go to retrieve the cars.

'Don't look so worried,' the BMW's driver says, ushering us into his leather back seat. Thanet and the others get into the Mercedes-Benz. 'This will be fun.'

Across the Bangna–Trat Highway, Fai Mangkon has closed. Their floodlights are off. The tour buses have finally gone. For once, their parking lot is as dark and as empty as ours.

During the two-kilometre drive north to make our U-turn, I

consider tossing myself out of the speeding car. I think that I might actually do it, but then I notice Uncle Judo gripping my hand. His grip is strong, hot and slick with sweat. He's gripping Dang's hand as well, staring at the empty highway ahead, moving his mouth silently all the while, and for a moment I wonder if he's praying or if Uncle Judo has simply lost his mind.

Dang produces Uncle Judo's business proposal from his shirt pocket. He must have picked it up before we left Thanet's table. He offers it to Uncle Judo now in the air-conditioned darkness of the BMW. Uncle Judo lets go of our hands, stops moving his mouth, blinks at the proposal for a while.

'We'll be okay,' he finally responds, smiling sheepishly. He takes the proposal from Dang, pats us both on the knees. We nod. For some reason, it's nice to hear his voice again.

'You're good boys,' he says. 'Wonderful people.'

'What's that, old man?' the driver interjects through the rear-view mirror.

'I wasn't talking to you,' Uncle Judo responds. 'I was talking to my friends. So keep driving. Follow your orders. Get us where we should be.'

At Fai Mangkon, Thanet and his friends emerge from the Mercedes-Benz. The woman stays in the car. When we get out of the BMW, the driver retrieves a golf bag from the trunk.

'Go ahead,' he says, handing us each a club. 'Get to work.'

We stand there staring at the dragon for a while, the clubs heavy in our hands. The polymer grip feels snug in my palm. I've never held a golf club before. Its weight is strange—natural, even, like a metal extension for my arm. There's a tuft of sod clinging to the sleek, knobby club head like a toupee over a bald spot.

The dragon looks much smaller than it did across the highway. Its wings are folded, its mechanical head slumped against its breast. It looks like a sleeping chicken, in a way, and briefly I think that the dragon might be real, that if we rouse it from its slumber it might incinerate us with its breaths of flame.

'Come on,' one of Thanet's friends yells.

'Get going,' says another.

Somebody shoves Dang in the back. He careens forward, totters on his feet, nearly falls to the ground. Somebody shoves Uncle Judo and me as well. When we regain our balance somebody shoves us again. Soon, it seems a thousand hands are at our backs, pushing us towards the dragon, and it's all we can do to remain on our feet, keep the world correct, while the young men's lunatic laughter peals across the Fai Mangkon parking lot.

I hear Uncle Judo yelling. I hear his golf club clattering the concrete. I see him grab one of the offending hands and with a quick quarter-turn of his body tossing the hand's owner to the ground. They cease their shoving and their jabbing then. The men fall silent. It's Thanet on the ground—his body writhing, his pale face contorted, his shiny hair splayed across the gravel.

'You're fired,' he croaks, pointing at Uncle Judo. 'You're all fired.'

It's only then that Uncle Judo picks up his golf club and heads for the dragon. He moves slowly, deliberately, weighing the club in his hand. When he finally arrives at the dragon, he cocks back the club and smashes it into one of the dragon's wings. Sparks fly. The clanging sound echoes across the Bangna–Trat Highway. Uncle Judo hits it again and again, each time with more force, and the racket is so loud that it wouldn't surprise me if he's woken up people far down the highway in Pattaya. The wing starts to loosen at its joints, exposing cables and wires, and Uncle Judo's not only hitting it with the club any more, he's also kicking and tearing at it with his one free hand.

Dang and I run over to join him. Dang takes the other wing while I climb up the dragon's back, thinking I might try its fire-breathing head. As I make my ascent, hooking my fingers into the dragon's iron scales for leverage, I can feel my compatriots' fury jangling my spine, vibrating the monster beneath me, the air thick with their cacophony.

I'm at the head now, sitting astride that dragon's neck. Thanet and his friends have disappeared. I see policemen's lights rolling down the highway. So I lift up my club and give that dragon everything I've got. I hit that dragon until my arms burn, until my back aches, until I'm dizzy from the pain. We've lost our jobs. We're going to be arrested. But at the station later tonight we're going to learn Uncle Judo's name. □

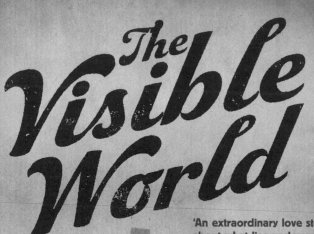

The Visible World

'An extraordinary love story
about what lies underneath.
This is a book that will last.'
Colum McCann

'A moving novel'
Richard Ford

'An atmospheric mix of adventure, mystery
and romance, as well as a nuanced tale of one
family coping with the nightmare of history.
The sheer beauty of Mark Slouka's prose will
draw comparisons to *The English Patient*.'
Gary Shteyngart

MARK SLOUKA

GRANTA

HOUSE FIRE

Yiyun Li

Yiyun Li was born in Beijing, China, in 1972. In 1996, she came to the US to pursue a PhD in immunology, and three years later she gave it up to become a writer. She worked in a hospital for three years and then attended the Iowa Writers' Workshop. Her collection of short stories, 'A Thousand Years of Good Prayers' (Fourth Estate/Random House), has won the Frank O'Connor International Short Story Award, the Hemingway Foundation/PEN Award and the Guardian First Book Award. She lives in California with her husband and two sons. 'House Fire' is a new story.

They called themselves saviours of burning houses, though none of the six women, their ages ranging from mid-fifties to early seventies, had had much experience outside the worlds of their employment before they retired: small cubicles behind barred windows for the two bank tellers; large offices shared by too many people for the three secretaries; and a front room in a six-storey university building, where for many years Mrs Lu had guarded the door to a girls' dorm.

The six women, friends and comrades for about two years now, had first met at a local park, where mothers, keen for their children's marriages to happen met other equally anxious mothers. Between them the six women had four sons and four daughters, all of them unhurried by the ticking of the clock that kept their mothers sleepless at night. Hitting it off from the beginning, the women made ingenious plans in the hope that some of them would become connected by marriages and then by shared grandchildren. Meetings of their children were arranged, coerced in some cases. In the end, none of the matches produced any fruitful results. Still, the six women remained close, and when Mrs Fan, the youngest among them, realized that her husband was having an affair with a woman whose identity he refused to reveal, the other five women, enraged by the audacity of the husband who was approaching sixty yet behaving like a foolish boy without a heart or brain, appointed themselves detectives to find out the truth.

Their success in uncovering the mistress' name, address and place of work did little to save Mrs Fan's marriage. 'An old man in love is like a house on fire', went a popular joke, that circulated for a while as a text message from one cell phone to another around the city. The joke must have been made up by some young, carefree soul, but how sadly true it was. Mrs Fan was taken aback by the intensity of the fire that engulfed her marriage: three decades of trivial arguments and unimportant disagreements all turned out to be flammable material. More appalling was the simple procedure for divorce. In the old days the employers of both parties, the neighbourhood association, the local workers' union and the women's union would all be involved in the mediation, and the court, as the last resort, would not grant the divorce without making a lengthy effort of its own to save the marriage. After all, any assistance in breaking up a marriage was more sinful than destroying seven temples, but such a belief no longer held in the new era: an application speedily granted by the district courthouse soon left Mrs Fan a single woman and released her husband to become the bridegroom of an immoral intruder.

The six friends declared war against love outside marriage. They did not need to look far before they found another woman suspecting a cheating husband, and with their previous experience, and a talent that seemed to come naturally to them, they identified the mistress within two weeks. It dawned upon Mrs Guan, whose son was a recent graduate from a top MBA programme in America, that they could turn their skills into a business, and soon, through word of mouth, their clientele expanded. As agreed by the six friends, they would work for the principle of cleansing society and fighting against deteriorating morals, so they charged less than other firms and only accepted cases in which wives were endangered by disloyal husbands and conniving mistresses. Saviours of burning houses, they called themselves, their belief being that, discovered early enough, a fire could be put out before more harm was done.

The story of six older women working as successful private investigators was, against their will and without their consent, reported by a local newspaper in a gossipy column called 'Odd People at This Unique Time'. What transgressor would have thought that an old granny in the street had a mini walkie-talkie hidden in her palm, or that her most innocent conversation with your acquaintances would reveal your secrets to your enemy? The story was soon picked up by a woman's magazine, and when the city TV channel proposed a short documentary on them as part of a month-long series on family values in the new era, the six friends decided to welcome the opportunity.

The anxiously awaited filming took place on a blustery day in early spring. Their complexions, Mrs Tang explained to the woman in charge of make-up, ranged from raisins to months-old apples, so she might just as well save her powder and rouge for other women with better reasons for looking desirable. Such self-mockery amused the TV people. Even more surprising to them was how relaxed and natural the six women acted in front of the cameras, but when complimented, several of the friends looked confused. She had no idea what the director was talking about, said Mrs Cheng, the oldest and the loudest. If they were expected to be themselves, why the comment on their acting?

The documentary aired on a Saturday night and the six women became instant celebrities to their neighbours, relatives and acquaintances. Soon it became a routine for the six friends to watch a tape of the programme in Mrs Mo's flat, which also served as the headquarters of their sleuthing business. Mrs Mo had been widowed for twenty years, losing her husband in a traffic accident in a snowstorm, and at sixty-five she played tennis, belonged to a ballroom dancing club and had a full collection of Agatha Christie novels on her shelf. With the looks of a Hong Kong film star from the 1940s, Mrs Mo seemed not to belong to the group, yet it was she who had organized the friends, inviting the other women to her flat whenever she had a day off from tennis and dancing, and later offering her home phone number as the contact for their business.

Sherlock Holmes was more to her husband's taste, commented Mrs Tang, who was married to a retired army officer. Mrs Mo smiled tolerantly. She was aware that some of her friends envied her freedom. Now and then Mrs Cheng and Mrs Lu discussed Mrs Mo's long-widowed situation with her, asking why she had not thought of remarrying, expressing admiration at her bringing up a daughter all by herself. Mrs Tang, the least tactful of the six women, never missed the opportunity in these conversations to mention her own healthy and well-pensioned husband. Such petty competition, which also occurred when the women brought up their children's incomes, usually amounted to nothing more than harmless bantering. They were not about to give up the friendship that had made them famous late in their lives.

After the programme was broadcast, however, their business slowed down. Perhaps prospective clients feared that the women's covers had been broken and it was unwise to hire them now, Mrs Guan wondered aloud; or else they thought they could not afford the celebrity price, Mrs Lu added. There was no real pressure for them to make money in any case, said Mrs Tang, and Mrs Fan agreed, adding that their main goal was to raise the awareness of out-of-wedlock immorality, and that their TV documentary had made their stand known to more people than their fieldwork ever could. Such rounds of talk to ease any worry and doubt were repeated every day, though none of the six friends would admit that she was upset or disappointed by the fact that they were not sought out as they had been. While the talk went on, Mrs Mo would brew tea and come round with a plate of nuts: green tea and pistachios on some days, red tea and cashews on others, since the tastes of the group were divided on many small things. The nuts were ground and taken in small spoonfuls, as several of the members had dentures, and when all was settled, Mrs Mo would put the tape into the VCR player and turn on the TV.

After days and now weeks of watching, rewinding, and watching again, Mrs Guan still felt a thrill the moment the blue screen flickered and the theme music started. Such a joy was shared by all six friends, and every viewing was accompanied by new comments and laughter. Familiar by now with every shot, they watched the programme more for random glimpses of themselves. See Mrs Cheng chat up two guards at an upscale apartment complex, her cheerful nosiness not eliciting any suspicion on the young men's part. See Mrs Lu hovering patiently over a pot of watered-down tea on a bench outside a Starbucks where the cheating husband is holding an intimate conversation with a chic young woman. Thirty years of guarding the girls' dorm had taught Mrs Lu a few things about shameless females, and every time she saw the young actress's hand covered by the middle-aged actor's hand, Mrs Lu would relate yet another story about one of the girls from the past who had come back to the dorm after lights-out, lips too wet and cheeks flushed unnaturally. The girls would knock on her window and beg her to let them in, and often she yelled at them and said any day now she would report them to the university and they had better be prepared to move into the street with the rest of the whores.

The discussion of the degenerating morals of the younger generation was then replaced by laughter over Mrs Fan's secretive phone call to a wife about the cheating husband's whereabouts. Their little hen had some visitor in her nest, Mrs Fan said over her cell phone, a cheap, bulky model that few people used any more, her coat flapping in the wind, while in the background could be seen a blurred image of a man entering his mistress' building. Where on earth had the TV people got that hen line from the friends laughed, as they had never used such codes in their work, and had been given a script to follow. Amid the laughter, Mrs Fan sighed. No wonder her ex-husband wanted a younger woman, she said, pointing at the fine lines in her face magnified by the close-up shot, which she had paused for the friends to see. The other women stopped laughing, and Mrs Mo, the one who dealt with any uneasiness with a perfect gesture, broke the silence and said that husband or not, it was more important to have a fun life of one's own than to serve a king at home. Mrs Fan nodded, and then reported that she had heard from her children that their father had just lost his new wife to a younger man and they wondered if she would be willing to go back to him for everybody's sake. But why would she want to have anything to do with that man twice divorced by now, Mrs Fan said. It was not totally untrue, though her children's suggestion of a reunion had been rejected not by Mrs Fan but by her ex-husband.

The five women studied Mrs Fan, who smiled back and reassured them that she had long passed the heartbroken stage; she might have to go out and find a younger man so that her husband would stop daydreaming about a reunion. The joke was hesitantly received and then Mrs Mo hit the play button, and more of their glorious moments lulled them back into happy oblivion.

When they got a phone call from a man who called himself Dao, the six women hadn't had any cases for a while. Not that they minded the chance to relax, the friends had been reminding one another, though after the phone call even Mrs Mo, the calmest of the six, showed unusual animation. They had never accepted a case from a man before, but in his call he mentioned their TV documentary, and that alone was enough for them to make an exception.

The women invited Dao to the teashop where they met all their clients, in a room separated from the main hall by a bamboo curtain, and by now the young girls who served their tea regarded them with awe and studied the newcomer across the big table with open curiosity. Start your own business to satisfy your nosiness, Mrs Cheng whispered, but it came out loud and unfriendly. Mrs Mo nudged Mrs Cheng to keep her voice down, though the man, who looked deeply distressed, seemed to detect nothing out of the ordinary, nor did he seem to find the seating arrangement bizarre, positioned as he was across the table from the six interrogators. Dao thanked the women for their kindness in seeing him, and then he did something odd that annoyed Mrs Tang: he drank up the tea in a gulp and lifted the translucent cup to the window as if to check the quality of the china. Mrs Tang coughed dryly; she wished she was the man's mother so she could give him a talking to about manners, as she often did with her own children, despite their being established in their own companies.

For a long time Dao seemed preoccupied, placing his teacup on the green checked tablecloth, then moving it a few squares down as if trying to position a chess piece, never looking up at the six women. Mrs Cheng and Mrs Tang shifted in their chairs and Mrs Lu exchanged a look with Mrs Guan. Many of their female clients had sounded hesitant when they had first called, but once they had made up their minds to come to see the women, their stories had gushed out before an invitation had even been issued.

'If you feel it easier to answer questions than just talk, we will certainly help,' Mrs Mo offered, her voice gentle and soothing. There was a girlish excitement in Mrs Mo that Mrs Tang was sure only she had detected. She thought of reporting this to her husband, as had been her habit for the past forty years, but more and more now the old soldier immersed himself in conversations with Sherlock Holmes, as if senility had turned him into a close friend of the famous detective. Her husband's obsession had been a major motive for Mrs Tang to become a detective herself, hoping for more attention and respect, but the doctors warned her that her husband's condition might worsen; that memory loss and personality change were to be expected. She might as well enjoy her days with her friends instead of gathering topics diligently to discuss later with a husband who had always been too stingy to participate in conversations and who had, by now, stopped listening.

Dao looked up at Mrs Mo and then at Mrs Fan, who was talking about a painful experience of her own with an encouraging smile. It was natural to be angry with the cheating spouse as well as the perpetrator, Mrs Fan said, using the words of the marriage expert her children had paid for her to visit—something she would never have admitted to her friends, as they congratulated themselves as the sole agents of her recovery. Natural, too, to be confused and ashamed, Mrs Fan continued, yet he should know that such emotions were unhealthy in the long run.

'Thanks, aunties,' Dao finally said, and Mrs Mo thought that despite his vagueness, he respected their ages and addressed them properly; such old-fashioned manners were less common in his generation. 'My problem is, I don't know where to start.'

'Start with your wife,' Mrs Lu said. 'Does she still live with you or has she left for someone else?'

The man thought about the question for an excruciatingly long time. Mrs Cheng, already losing patience, picked peanuts from the plate and lined them up in front of her in formations.

'There must have been something in your mind that we could do for you when you called us,' Mrs Mo ventured.

'We specialize in marriage crises, as you may or may not know,' Mrs Tang said. 'And trust me, we've seen all sorts of marriage problems in our business.'

'And we keep secrets well,' Mrs Guan added, and sent away the girls from the shop who had come in with newly boiled water. 'And there are things we can do better than younger people. You've seen the documentary. We're successful for good reasons.'

'Look at it this way, young man,' Mrs Cheng said with a grin. 'How old are you, by the way?'

'Thirty-four.'

'In the old days I would be your grandmother's age,' Mrs Cheng said. It had been a lifelong regret of hers that she had married late— she had been dazzled by all the possibilities and had forgotten that time acted against a woman. At seventy-two, all she wanted was to see a grandchild, though neither of her two sons was in a hurry to marry and produce a baby for her to dote on; in the old days women her age would be holding a great-grandchild by now. 'Look at it this way. You can tell us your problem as you would tell your grandmother. We've seen so much that nothing surprises us.'

Dao nodded in gratitude. He opened his mouth but a deep sigh came before the words. 'My wife, she still lives in our house,' he said.

'A positive sign, no? Do you have children? Still share a bed?' Mrs Cheng said. 'Well, don't let me interrupt you. Go on, go on.'

Mrs Lu and Mrs Guan exchanged a smile, but they did not stop Mrs Cheng. The same words would have come out wrong from a different mouth, yet Mrs Cheng, the most harmlessly nosy person one would meet in life, seemed to have a talent for turning even the most offensive question into an invitation.

'We have a son,' the man said. 'He just turned one.'

'How is your bedroom business after your son's birth?' Mrs Cheng said.

'Sometimes she says she is tired when I ask, but once in a while it is good.'

Men were creatures ignorant of women's pains, Mrs Fan thought. In her mind she was ready to dismiss the case as an inconsiderate husband unable to share a new mother's burden and casting unfounded blame on her. Mrs Fan's husband had complained about her lack of enthusiasm in bedroom business after both her children's births, and she wondered why she had never seen through his cold-hearted selfishness back then.

'Sometimes it takes a while for the new mother to return to her old self,' Mrs Mo said.

'But isn't a year too long?' Mrs Tang asked. 'Young women these days are pampered and way too delicate, if you ask my opinion. I don't know about you, but I served as a good wife once my baby was a month old.'

'Let's not distract our guest here with an irrelevant discussion,' Mrs Guan said, and then turned to the man. 'Please forgive us, young man. You must have heard that three women are enough to make a theatre troupe, and among us we have two troupes. But don't let us distract you.'

Dao looked from one woman to the other and returned to his study of the tablecloth. He seemed unable to grasp what had been said to him, and the thought occurred simultaneously to several of the six women that perhaps he had a problem with his brain, but before anyone said a word, he looked up again, this time with a tear-streaked face. He did not mean to be rude or waste their precious time, he said, but his problem was more than unsuccessful bedroom business between husband and wife—there was another man between him and his wife, and he did not know what to do about the situation.

'So you know the man?' Mrs Cheng asked. It came as a pang of disappointment that there might not be any puzzle for her to solve.

'My father,' Dao said. 'He's lived with us for two years now.'

'Your father?' the women exclaimed at the same time, all sitting up and leaning forward.

'You mean, your father and your wife?' Mrs Tang said. 'If your claim is baseless I'm ready to spank you.'

'Let him finish,' Mrs Guan said.

Dao looked down at his hands folded on the tablecloth and said it was only a feeling. The reason that he had come to them, he said, was to ask the women's help to determine if his wife and his father had in fact maintained an improper relationship.

'Your father, how old is he?' Mrs Tang said.

'And why do you suspect him and your wife of having any improper relationship?' Mrs Cheng said.

'Do you have siblings?' Mrs Lu said. 'Where's your mother?'

Dao winced as if each question were a bullet he was unable to dodge. Mrs Mo sighed and with a gesture she begged her friends to keep quiet, even though her own hands shook from excitement as she poured a new cup of tea for Dao and told him to take his time. The story came out haltingly: the man had been born the youngest of five siblings, the only boy of the family. His parents had been the traditional husband and wife of the older generation, he the king of the household and governing his wife and children with unquestionable authority, she serving him wholeheartedly. The four older sisters had been married off when they had reached marriageable ages, three to men picked out by the father, but the youngest sister, a few years older than the little brother, had chosen her own husband against the father's will. She had become an outcast from all family affairs, a punishment from their father and a precaution from the rest of the family, as they would not risk the father's anger to remain in touch with the estranged sister. A few years ago, the mother had been diagnosed with liver cancer. By then Dao was over thirty and, shy person as he was, he had not had a date. The mother, in her sickbed, begged the father to help their son secure a bride so that she could take a look at her future daughter-in-law before she exited the world. An arrangement was made and he was introduced to his wife, a pretty woman though not a virgin, as she had been widowed once and had left her only son for her in-laws to raise.

'Did your father know your wife before you met her?' Mrs Cheng said, thinking fast and sensing shadiness in the arrangements. What kind of father would foist a second-hand woman on his own son as a wife?

He did not know, Dao said. He had been nervous when he was introduced to his wife, and in any case he had not thought to question the woman and his father back then.

'Did you love her when you married her?' Mrs Cheng said.

Dao said that he supposed he loved her, or else he would not have agreed to marry her. Mrs Tang thought that he sounded uncertain, and what a despicable thing it was for a man to be so passive.

Dao continued, calmer now, as if he had got over the initial shock of hearing his own voice. The six friends listened, all bursting with questions they tried hard to hold back so the easily intimidated man would not drown in their curiosity. Life after the wedding was quiet and eventless, he continued, until six months later his mother passed away, and as was common practice, the newly-weds invited the father to come and live with them; Dao was the only son and it was a son's duty to support the father, even though at sixty he was still strong and healthy as a bull. For more than a year now Dao had been plagued by the fear that his father had cuckolded him. Such a thought he could not share with his sisters, and the birth of the baby, a boy who looked just like himself when he had been a bald baby, did not release him from the grip of suspicion.

'You mean the baby could be your half-brother?' Mrs Lu said.

Had he known the answer, Dao replied, he would not have approached the six friends. There was little evidence, but his wife worked odd shifts as a nurse, and there were always stretches of time when she and his father were at home together without him.

'But that doesn't mean they would cuckold you,' Mrs Cheng said.

It was a nagging fear, Dao said apologetically and hung his head low.

'How does she treat you?' Mrs Fan asked.

His wife treated him like a good wife should, Dao said. She cooked good meals, cleaned the house and did not ask for expensive clothes. She put her earnings in their joint account and let him control the finances of the household. What else could a man expect from a wife, Dao asked unconvincingly.

Mrs Cheng cleared her throat. 'Back to my original question,' she said, deciding by now that Dao must have some hidden illness he was too ashamed to share. 'How is your bedroom business? Do you satisfy each other?'

Dao blushed and mumbled a yes. Mrs Mo looked at him with sympathy and poured fresh tea to distract him from his own embarrassment. The world was intolerant of men with sensitive hearts, but how many people would bother to look deeper into their souls, lonely for unspeakable reasons? Her own husband, dead for twenty years now, had been nicknamed 'Soft Yam' by his colleagues; he was a regular target for bullying; the first to be taken advantage of in promotions. When she married him, her family and friends had thought her crazy; she had been an attractive girl, with better options than the man she had chosen for herself. He was a kind man was the reason she had given, but it was his sadness that had moved her. She had made herself an ally to his parents when she had courted him, and she had thought herself capable of liberating him from the sadness she could not understand. Such an innocent criminal she had made herself into, she thought, when she discovered his love affair of two decades with another man. She had always assumed that the traffic accident in the snow was a cover for a long-planned suicide, but their only daughter, then eight, adored her father, and Mrs Mo had taken it upon herself to uphold the image of the idol in her daughter's heart and to reject all offers for another marriage. People admired her virtue and loyalty, but people are easily deceived by all kinds of facades.

'I don't understand now,' Mrs Tang said. 'You do all right in bed and she treats you well. Then why do you suspect her of anything? If I were you, I would be celebrating my good fortune to have found such a wife.'

'And why on earth your father?' Mrs Cheng added. 'Just because the baby looks like your father's grandson?'

'Let's not intrude with our own opinions,' Mrs Guan said, trying to save Dao from further embarrassment. Mrs Guan was finding some of her companions annoying today, their attitude unbusinesslike; but on second thoughts, these women had always been like this and she had enjoyed them well enough. Perhaps she was the one running out of patience. Mr and Mrs Guan were well maintained by their pensions from their civil servants' jobs and an annual remittance from their son in America. Still, they were witnessing a historic economic boom in the country, and it hurt Mrs Guan not to be part of it. She had previously sold cosmetics and tonics to neighbours and friends, and perhaps it was time to invent another business now.

'But we need to understand his situation,' Mrs Cheng said. 'I, for one, don't see a problem unless the young man here is hiding something from us.'

It was how his father had changed, Dao said. A tyrant all his life, the older man had handed over his rule to his daughter-in-law ever since he had moved in with them. And how happy she was, Dao added. There was little reason for her, a widow who had given up her son to be remarried to a shy and quiet man, to be contented. They had never overstepped any limits in front of him, but he felt there was a secret from which he was excluded. 'Like they built a house within my house, and they live in it,' Dao said, shamelessly weeping now.

What sadness, Mrs Mo thought, and wondered if Dao would ever be able to reclaim his life. It had taken her years, but it might be different for him. Men were less resilient than women, and in any case, some sons never escaped their fathers' shadows.

'Aunties, I saw your programme. You're all experienced with men and women. Could you go meet them and find out for me?'

'But how?' Mrs Cheng said. 'It's different from locating a mistress. Shall we move into your house and make a nest for ourselves underneath your father's bed? Would you divorce your wife? Would you give up the baby to your father? Tell me, young man, what would you do if everything is true as you imagine?'

As if Dao had never thought about that possibility, he looked down at his hands in agony and did not reply.

'You want us to find out for you that they're innocent so you can live in peace, no?' Mrs Lu said. 'Let me tell you, if you suspect a ghost is sitting next to your pillow, the ghost will always be there; if you imagine a god, a god will look after you from above.'

The vehemence of Mrs Lu's words shocked not only Dao but also the five women. Mrs Lu bit the inside of her cheek and told herself to shut up. Peace came from within, she often said to herself, and she had taken up the detective work with her friends in the hope that by saving other people's marriages she would finally dispel the phantom of a long dead girl, but such hope had turned out to be in vain. She had done nothing wrong in reporting the girl, Mrs Lu repeatedly reminded herself over the years—she had found the girl naked in bed with a male classmate and both had been expelled from the university by the end of the week. The girl had snuck into the dorm building a month later when Mrs Lu had been busy with the mail and had jumped from the top floor. The thud, ten years later, still made Mrs Lu shiver at night.

'Mrs Lu has a point,' Mrs Fan said. 'We could work for you but you have to make up your mind first. What we find out could make you more miserable than you are now, you see?'

Dao looked down at his hands, folding and unfolding on the table. 'I wouldn't do anything,' he said finally. 'There's nothing for me to do. After all, he is my father. All I want to know is if they've cheated on me.'

Such a spineless man, Mrs Tang thought. Her husband would have picked up an axe and demanded the truth from the wife and the father instead of crying to some strangers. Her husband had always been the quickest to react, and how unfair it was that he, the most virile among his friends, was the first to be defeated by age.

The only truth for Dao to know, Mrs Fan thought, was that he would be locked in his unhappiness forever, as she herself would be. It did not matter any more if he was cuckolded, as it did not matter to her that her husband had been deserted by the second wife. For some people punishment came as a consequence of their mistakes; for others, punishment came before anything wrong had been done. Welcome to the land of the unfortunate and the deserted, Mrs Fan said, almost relishing the unfairness of her fate, and Dao's.

Mrs Guan looked at her friends. Already she could tell that they would not be able to take the case as a group, as they showed little of the sympathy towards Dao that they had shown to the other wronged women. She would find an excuse to speak to him after this meeting, she thought, about the possibility of working on the case by herself. A similar plan took shape in Mrs Cheng's mind, too, though it was not money she was after but to satisfy her own curiosity—Dao's description of his wife and his father intrigued Mrs Cheng: what kind of love had they fallen into that caused the father to scheme against his own son, and the wife to entertain her lover's son out of necessity? As much as she had seen in her life, Mrs Cheng still worried that she would miss something interesting before she left this world.

Mrs Mo observed her companions. She knew that it was her responsibility now to reject Dao gently and, despite her curiosity, she would not let his case break the friendship she had created for the lonely days she would otherwise have to pass by herself. Even as she was thinking up excuses to dismiss him, her mind wandered to the bi-weekly session of the dancing club that afternoon. She had discovered dancing late in her life, and had been addicted to it ever since, whirling in her partner's arm, their bodies touching each other in the most innocently erotic way. It was not a simple task to maintain an intimacy with another human being by the mere touch of bodies, and to accomplish it she needed her total concentration to keep her soul beyond the reach of the large and small flames of all the passions in this treacherous world. □

GRANTA

O TANNENBAUM

Maile Meloy

Maile Meloy was born in Helena, Montana in 1972 and has lived in southern California for the past ten years. She received an MFA from the University of California, Irvine, and is the author of a short story collection, 'Half in Love', and of the novels 'Liars and Saints' and 'A Family Daughter', all published by John Murray in the UK and by Scribner in the US. Her stories have appeared in 'The New Yorker' and the 'Paris Review', and she has received the Aga Khan Prize for Fiction, the PEN/Malamud Award for Short Fiction, a Guggenheim Fellowship and other awards. 'Liars and Saints' was shortlisted for the Orange Prize. 'O Tannenbaum' is a new story.

It was a fine tree, Everett's daughter agreed. His wife said it was lopsided and looked like a bush. But that was part of its fineness— it was a tall, lopsided Douglas fir, bare on one side where it had crowded out its neighbour. The branchless side could go against the living-room wall, the bushy side was for decorations, and now the crowded tree in the woods had room to grow. Everett dragged their quarry through the snow by the trunk, and Anne Marie, who was four, clung to the upper branches and rode on her stomach, shouting, 'Faster, Daddy!'

Pam, his wife, followed with an armload of pine boughs and juniper branches. She seemed to have decided not to say anything more about the tree, which was fine with Everett.

The Jimmy was parked where the trail split off from the logging road, and Everett opened the back to throw the tools and boughs in, then roped the tree to the roof with nylon cords. Pam brushed off Anne Marie's snowsuit and buckled her in the front so she wouldn't get carsick. The smell of pine and juniper filled the car as they drove down the mountain.

'Chest*nuts* roasting on an open fire,' Everett sang, in his best lounge-singer croon. 'Jack *Frost* nipping at your nose.' Here he reached over and nipped at Anne Marie's, and she squealed. He stopped, forgetting the words.

Pam prompted, 'Yuletide carols,' half-singing, shy about her voice.

'Being sung by a *choir*...' He reached for the high note.

That was when they saw the couple at the side of the road. Folks dressed up like Eskimos: Everett thought for a second that he had conjured them up with his song. The two of them stood in the snow, under the branches of a big lodgepole pine. The man wore a blue parka and held up a broken cross-country ski. The woman wore red gaiters over wool trousers, a man's pea coat and a fur hat. They waved, and Everett slowed to a stop and rolled down the window.

'Nice day for a ski,' he said.

'It was,' the man said bitterly. He was about Everett's height and age, not yet pushing forty, with a day or two of bristle on his chin.

'I broke a ski and we're lost—' the woman began.

'We're not lost,' the man said.

'We are *completely* lost,' the woman said.

She was younger than the man, with high, pink cheekbones in the cold. Everett felt friendly and warm from the tree and the singing.

'Your car must be close,' he said. 'You're on the road.'

'The car is on a different road,' the woman said.

'Well, we'll find it,' Everett said.

In the rear-view mirror, he saw Pam's eyes widen at him from the back seat. She was slight and dark-haired, and accused him of favouring the kind of blonde who held sorority car washes. It was a joke, but it was partly true. With a bucket and sponge, this girl would fit right in. But arguing over giving them a ride would make everyone uncomfortable, and Pam would agree in the end. Everett got out of the car and untied a nylon cord to open the back hatch. His wife had sleds and jackets in the back seat with her, and he thought she would want some separation of family and hitchhikers. She wouldn't look at him now.

'You'll have to sit with the juniper boughs,' he told the couple.

'Better than freezing in a snowbank,' the blonde said, climbing into the way back. Even in the wool pants, she had a sweet figure, of the car-soaping type.

'We really appreciate this,' the man said.

Everett shut them all in, lashed on the skis and tied the tree down. It made no sense for Pam to be angry. This wasn't country where you left people in the snow. The man looked strong but not too strong; Everett could take him, if he needed to. Back in the driver's seat, Everett pulled on to the road, as snow fell in clumps off the big pine the couple had stood under.

His daughter turned around in her seat, as well as she could with her seat belt on, and announced to the new passengers, 'We have a CB radio.'

The warning tone in her voice came straight from Pam. It was identical in some technical, musical way to Pam's *We're going to be late* and her *I'm not going to tell you again.*

'What's your handle?' the man in the parka asked.

Anne Marie looked confused.

'Your name,' Everett explained. 'On the radio.'

'Batgirl,' Anne Marie told the strangers, her cheeks flushing. Oh, he loved Anne Marie! Loved it when she blushed. There had been a rocky time when Pam was pregnant, when he had felt panicked and young and trapped, and slept with the wife of a friend. It had only been once, in 1974, after many beers at a co-ed softball game, but the girl had gone and told Pam. She said she needed to clear her conscience, which didn't make any sense to Everett. He'd ended up driving Pam to the emergency room after a screaming fight, when she threw a shoe at him and started to have shooting pains in her abdomen. The doctors were worried: Pam was anaemic, and if she lost the baby she might bleed to death. Everett spent the night in her hospital room, frozen with grief. The baby decided to stay put, and came along fine two months later, but the night in the hospital had scared him. He would never put his wife and child in danger again. He hadn't put them in danger now, and he resented Pam's eye-widened implication that he had.

'You got a handle?' he asked the hitchhikers in back.

'I'm Clyde,' the man said.

'Bonnie,' the woman said.

Everyone was silent for a moment.

'That's really funny,' Everett finally said—though between his shoulder blades he felt a prick of worry. 'You must have a CB, too.'

'No, those are our names,' the man said.

The CB crackled on. 'What's this continental divide?' a man's voice asked.

Everett picked up the handset, still thinking about Bonnie and Clyde. 'You mean what is it?'

'Yeah,' the voice said.

So Everett said that the snow and rain on the west side of the mountains ran to the Pacific, and the water on the east side ran to the Gulf of Mexico.

'I never heard of such a thing,' the voice said.

'That's what it is,' Everett said. He thought of something, the recruiting of a witness. 'We just picked up some hitchhikers named Bonnie and Clyde,' he said. 'How about that?'

A wheezing laugh came over the radio. 'No kidding?' the voice asked. 'You watch your back, then. So long.'

Everett hung up the handset. 'So,' he said to his passengers, as if he hadn't just acted out of fear of them, 'where's your stolen jalopy?'

'We parked by Fire Creek.'

'You didn't get far.'

'No,' Bonnie said.

'How'd you break the ski?'

Bonnie and Clyde both fell silent.

Everett drove. The windows were iced from everyone's breathing and he turned up the defroster. The fan seemed very loud. He took the road to Fire Creek, which was unpaved under the packed snow.

'This is it,' Everett said, stopping the Jimmy.

There was a place at the trailhead to park cars, but there were no cars. Just snow and trees, and the creek running under the ice. Everett didn't look back at his wife. He scanned the empty turnout and hoped this was not one of those times you look back on and wish you had done one thing different, though it had seemed perfectly natural to do what you did at the time.

'Where's the car?' Bonnie asked.

'This is where we parked,' Clyde said.

They were genuinely surprised, and Everett almost laughed with relief. There was no con, no ambush. He untied the rope, and the couple climbed out and walked to where their car had been. The girl's arm brushed against Everett's when she passed, but he didn't think she meant it. She was thinking about the missing car. He got in the Jimmy to let them discuss it. Pam reached into the way back to pull the saw and the axe from under the boughs Clyde and Bonnie had been sitting on, and she tucked the tools under her feet.

'What are we doing with these people in our car?' she asked.

'Can't leave people in the snow.'

'We have a child, Everett.'

'And,' he said, with the confidence he had just now recovered, 'we're showing her that you don't leave people in the snow. Right, Anne Marie?'

'Right,' Anne Marie said, but she watched them both.

Pam gave Everett a dark, unforgiving stare. He turned back in his seat and looked out at the hitchhikers. The girl, Bonnie, stamped her foot on the ground, her bare hands in fists. He liked the pea coat and fur hat combination a lot. He guessed Pam knew that. But he didn't like to be glowered at.

'I just worry,' he said, trying to adopt a musing tone, 'that someday I could roll all your things into a ditch, or take up with your sister, and you wouldn't have any looks left to give me. You'd have used them all up.'

Pam said nothing, but looked out the window.

Everett had once argued that his affair—if one drunken night could be called that—had saved their marriage. He had been restless and thought he wanted out, but he had seen that he was wrong, and had come back for good. Pam had not been convinced by that argument. The girl he'd slept with still gave him looks at parties, looks that suggested things might start up again. Even in her confessional fit, she hadn't felt compelled to tell her husband what had happened, but Everett avoided him anyway, and the friendship had died.

Outside in the snow, Bonnie and Clyde's voices rose a notch.

'You said we could leave the keys in it!' Bonnie said. 'You said this was Montana, and that's what people do!'

'That *is* what they do,' Clyde said.

'Then who the *fuck* stole our car?'

Snow off the trees drifted around them, and the two stood staring at each other for a minute, then Bonnie started to laugh. She had a throaty, movie-star laugh that rose into a series of uncontrolled giggles. Her husband shook his head at her in exasperation. Everett felt the opposite; he liked her even more. A woman who could laugh at her own stolen car, and who looked like that when she did it. She was still laughing when they started back to the car.

'*You* ask for a ride,' she told her husband, her voice not lowered enough.

Everett looked to Pam in the back seat; Pam frowned, then nodded. He got out of the Jimmy, and this time the girl did brush his arm on purpose, he was sure of it. When she and Clyde were bundled in the way back again, with the tree tied down, Everett called in the theft of the car on the CB.

'Do you think we should wait for the cops?' Clyde asked.

'*I'm* not waiting in the cold any more,' Bonnie said. 'Jesus, who steals a car at Christmas?'

'People do all kinds of things at Christmas,' Clyde said.

No one had any response to that.

The road was empty and the sky was clear. Barbed-wire fences ran evenly beside the road, and the wooden posts ticked past as they drove. In the snowy fields beyond, yellow winter grass showed through in patches. Everett peered up at the tip of the tree, which seemed stable on the roof. He wondered if Pam could ever laugh off a stolen car. He wondered if he could. Years ago, when Pam was still in school and they were broke, they had been evicted from an attic apartment near the train yard, with nowhere to go. They had gone out for burgers to celebrate their escape from the noisy, smelly trains. He couldn't see them doing that now.

'Let's sing a song,' Anne Marie said.

'*Dash*ing through the snow,' Everett began, and Bonnie joined in from the way back. But then Everett caught Pam's look in the mirror and stopped singing, and Anne Marie trailed out in shyness. Bonnie gamely finished, '*laugh*ing all the way,' in a clear voice, and then she stopped, too. Everett looked for antelope in the snow. The fence posts ticked past.

After a while, Bonnie asked, 'What will you do with the boughs?'

'Make wreaths,' Pam said.

'I hope we're not crushing them.'

'No.'

The two women settled back into a silence just hostile enough that Everett could feel it. There didn't seem to be any antelope. There were hundreds in summer. The white-capped mountains in the east, beyond the low yellow hills, were lit up by the late sun through the clouds, and he was about to point them out to Anne Marie.

'I broke the ski,' Bonnie said, out of the blue.

Everett had forgotten he had asked.

'I was cold,' she said, 'so we tried to take a shortcut through some fallen trees with snow on them. Clyde took his skis off, but the snow was deep and I tried to go over the logs. And the ski snapped right in half. Clyde, I'm so fucking sorry.'

'Bonnie, the kid,' he said.

'Sorry,' she said. 'But Clyde, I am.'

'I know.'

The sunlight had faded on the mountains again and Everett watched the road.

'He came up here to find himself,' Bonnie said. 'From Arizona, where we live, and he met this woman. She reminds me of you, actually.'

Pam glanced at the woman in surprise.

'You're totally his type,' Bonnie said.

'Bonnie,' Clyde said.

There was a long pause, and Everett wondered what Pam was thinking, if she was at all stirred by that.

'Anyway,' Bonnie went on, 'she skis, and dives into glacial lakes, and canoes through rapids and what doesn't she do. And he writes me and says the air is so high and clear up here that he understands everything, and he's met his soulmate.'

'Bonnie, shut up,' Clyde said.

'But we're married,' Bonnie said, like she was telling a funny joke. 'And have a child. So I have this crazy feeling that *I'm* supposed to be his soulmate. So I leave our son with my parents and come up here, too. And we go to a party where people get naked in a hot tub and roll around in the snow. And I meet the woman, his perfect woman, and the first thing she does is proposition me.'

Everett glanced at his daughter, to see what she understood. He couldn't tell. She was looking straight out the windshield. She'd seen people naked in hot tubs, so she'd understand that. He looked back at the road.

'So I told Clyde about it,' Bonnie said, 'thinking he'd defend my honour. And he said it was a good idea. He thought we might just move into his soulmate's cabin and get along.' She seemed to think about this for a second, about the right way to sum it up. 'So we tried to go for a mind-clearing ski,' she said finally, 'and the karmic gods stole our fucking car.' She started to laugh again, the throaty start and then the giggle.

No one answered her; the only sound was her trying to stop laughing. Everett pulled quickly to the centre of the road to miss a strip of black rubber truck tyre.

The CB crackled on. 'Continental Divide?' a voice asked.

Everett answered that he was there.

'You been shot full of bullet holes?' the man asked.

'Nope,' Everett said.

'That you reporting a stolen car?'

'Have you seen it?'

'Yeah,' the voice said. 'I just seen Baby Face Nelson drivin' it down the road. Ha. No, I ain't seen it. I'll keep a eye out.'

Everett thanked him and replaced the receiver.

'Why did he say Baby Face?' Anne Marie asked.

'There was a Bonnie and Clyde,' Everett told her, 'not these ones,

who were bank robbers. And Baby Face Nelson was a bank robber.
But he didn't like to be called Baby Face.'

In the back, Bonnie said, 'My first mistake was marrying someone
named Clyde.'

'I don't recall you being real reluctant,' Clyde said.

'Do you have to talk about this *here*?' Pam burst out, and Everett
was surprised. It wasn't like Pam to burst out, especially in front of
strangers.

'We have to talk about it sometime,' the woman said. 'We were
supposed to be talking up here. Then we got lost and I broke the
ski and Clyde goes apeshit—'

'I did not go apeshit.'

'You did,' Bonnie said. 'Because I'm not good at things like that,
I'm not your soulmate. And we're ruining our son's life. These are
the years that matter, he's three.'

'I'm four,' Anne Marie said.

Everett rumpled his daughter's hair. His wife was glaring out the
window, with her arms crossed over her chest. He turned back to
the road. Pam wouldn't speak again, he could tell. Whatever she was
thinking would bubble and ferment and grow, but it wouldn't come
out. Or it would come out where he least expected it, where it least
made sense.

They were nearing the outskirts of town, the first houses. A few
had decorations out: Santas and snowmen. Windows were already
lit with red and green outlines, in the dim afternoon.

'Should I take you to the police station?' Everett asked, because
he didn't know what else to say.

'That would be great,' Clyde said.

'I'm sorry,' Bonnie said. 'This has been a hard time.'

There was a long silence.

'What's the little girl's name?' Bonnie asked.

His daughter turned in her seat belt. 'Anne Marie.'

'Do you have ornaments for the tree?' Bonnie asked her.

'Yes,' Anne Marie said.

'What kind?'

'Angels, and two mice sleeping in a nutshell,' she said. 'And some
fish. And a baby Jesus in a crib.'

'Those sound nice,' Bonnie said, her voice wistful. 'We've never had a tree. Clyde thinks you shouldn't cut down trees to put in your house.'

'Bonnie,' Clyde said.

Anne Marie said, 'Our tree was crowding up another tree. So we made the other tree have room.'

'Would that meet your standards, Clyde?' Bonnie asked.

Clyde said nothing.

Anne Marie looked out the windshield again, trained in the prevention of carsickness. 'They could help decorate *our* tree,' she said.

'I think they want to find their car,' Everett said.

Anne Marie turned back in her seat. 'Do you want to help with our tree?'

'Honey, they're busy,' Pam said.

'I would love that more than anything in the world,' Bonnie said.

'No,' her husband said.

'Baby, please,' Bonnie said. 'We've never had a tree.'

'Leave these people alone,' Clyde said.

Everett turned on Broadway and stopped at the police station. He untied the rope and opened the back of the Jimmy for his passengers. Clyde didn't get out right away. He said, in a low voice to Pam, 'Look, I'm really sorry about this. Thank you for the ride.' Then he climbed out, past Everett, and walked with what seemed like dignity into the station.

Bonnie sat on the boughs with her legs straight out and gave Everett a forlorn look. In her fur hat, she looked like a Russian doll. She didn't say anything, as if she knew that silence was better, that it was what he was used to. Pam had leaned forward and was talking quietly to Anne Marie in the front seat.

'Why don't you go make your report,' Everett told Bonnie. 'See what they can do. I'll go home and unload, and then come back and get you both.'

Two things happened at once, as in a movie, one close up and one in deep focus. Bonnie broke into a brilliant, tear-sparkled smile, and Pam's leaning form stiffened and she half turned her head. Then she looked away again and occupied herself more fiercely with Anne Marie. Bonnie clambered out of the back and kissed the side of Everett's mouth, her wool-bundled breasts pressing against him for a long second. 'Thank you,' she said.

Embarrassed, Everett stepped back and unlashed the skis and poles from the roof. He gave them to Bonnie, and she stood with the spiky bundle in her arms as Everett pulled away.

Pam said nothing as they drove. Their daughter must have felt the tension in the air. Everett whistled 'Chest*nuts* roasting on an open fire' for lack of anything more sensible to do.

At the house, he parked the Jimmy and started untying the tree. Pam pulled the boughs out of the back, dumped them on the front deck and took Anne Marie inside. Everett carried the tree around to the sliding glass door and tugged on the handle. The door didn't open. He thought it might be frozen and he tugged again. They never locked the doors. He went around the corner of the deck and pulled on the other sliding glass door, the one to the kitchen. It was locked, too. He rapped on the glass and Pam came to it.

'The door's locked,' he said, pointing to the handle.

'Say you're not going back for them,' she said, her voice muffled by the glass.

The tree was heavy on his shoulder and he stood it up on the deck, holding the slender trunk through the branches. He studied it. It was a fine tree. He turned back to his wife. 'It's Christmas,' he said.

'I don't want them here,' she said through the glass. 'Say you won't go.'

'Did you lock all the doors?'

'Say it,' she said.

He sighed. The temperature had dropped when the sun went down and it was cold outside. 'I won't go back for them,' he said. 'I'll leave them stranded and unhappy, without a tree, at Christmastime. Are you happy?'

'They're crazy,' she said.

'Of course they are. Now let me in.'

She unlocked the door. He carried the tree through the kitchen, set it up in the corner of the living room and turned it until the bare side faced the wall. It looked like a lopsided bush. Anne Marie clapped her hands in approval. He showed her how to fill the reservoir in the stand with water. Then he crumpled newspaper in the fireplace, built a hut of kindling, and set it alight.

Pam called the police station to renege on the hospitality, asking them to deliver the message to the people whose car was stolen.

Everett strung the lights on the tree, and lifted Anne Marie to put the angel on top. There wasn't really a single top to the tree, but he helped her pick one. Pam moved around the kitchen, making dinner.

A stranger watching would have thought it a perfectly ordinary December night, and it was true that they talked no more than they often did. Anne Marie gamely kept up an almost professional patter, like a hostess who knows her party has gone wrong and her guests are miserable. She hung the ornaments: the two mice sleeping in the nutshell, the fish, the baby Jesus in the crib. Everett sat in the big chair between the fireplace and the kitchen, feeling the soreness from chopping and hauling set in. He wasn't twenty-five any more. Anne Marie sang Christmas carols to herself: 'It Came Upon a Midnight Clear' and 'Good King Wenceslas'.

Leaving a pot of soup on the stove, Pam made a juniper swag for the mantelpiece, her slimness in jeans set off by the firelight. She cut and arranged the boughs as she had every year they had been in the house, and as her mother had every year before that. She nestled three white candles among the branches, evenly spaced, and lit them. Everett watched her, thinking about the fact that she was Clyde's type, wondering why he still wanted to go get the outlaws and put himself in the way of temptation.

Pam turned from the mantel—there was sometimes a funny, ironic smile that came over her face when she caught him looking at her, a grown-up smile, at once confident and self-deprecating. But now she looked defiant and young. It was the look Anne Marie got at bedtime, when made to choose how to spend her dwindling time: this book or that book? Staying up by the fire or having ten minutes more with her dolls? Anne Marie always delayed and evaded, and chose the longest book, the most involved game.

Pam said, 'Look, if you want to go get them, just go.'

'They'll have gone by now,' he said, with a catch in his voice.

Pam threw the burnt matches into the fire. In the kitchen she put the matchbook in the kitchen drawer. Then she picked up and dialled the phone, watching Everett, as if waiting for him to stop her.

'I called earlier about the couple with the stolen car,' she said, in her businesslike phone voice. 'Are they still there?' She waited, looking out the dark glass door she had locked against him.

'Hi, Bonnie,' she said into the phone. 'It's Pam—from the car. We picked you up. Hi.' Her laugh sounded social, but Everett could hear the nervousness in it. 'No, I don't think I introduced myself. Do you still want to help with the tree? Everett could run down and get you.'

She paused, listening.

'Put Clyde on,' she said, and she turned away from Everett. He watched the curve of his wife's ass as she leaned on the kitchen counter, lifting her right foot and nervously tapping the toe on the floor. 'Clyde,' she said. 'Please come up for dinner. Anne Marie would love to show off the tree.' The pause again. 'Really, we'd love it,' she said. Then, 'Good. He'll be right down.'

She hung up the phone and turned to Everett. 'Merry Christmas,' she said.

He was not sure how to behave. Anne Marie was still decorating the lower branches of the tree, singing 'We three kings, of orien*tare*.' There were plenty of branches left for Bonnie.

'So,' Pam said. She stirred the pot on the stove with a wooden spoon, tapped the spoon against the rim and set it on the counter. 'Do you want to go get them?'

Everett pushed himself out of the chair. 'Want to come along, Anne Marie?' he asked.

His daughter looked up at him. 'Are you going to get those people?'

'Yes,' he said. 'To help with the tree.'

Anne Marie nodded, untangling the loop of string on a tiny ukulele. 'I'll stay here,' she said.

He kissed Pam goodbye on the top of her head. Was she attracted to Clyde? He wanted to take off her clothes right now and see. He was conscious of his own breathing, and he could tell she was unsteady.

'It's Christmastime,' he said. 'I'll be right back.'

He went out into the cold air. The Jimmy started up easily and he headed in low gear down the hill towards town.

He wanted to decide, as he drove, what they were doing. He wanted to separate his impulse to be a good Samaritan from the kiss on the corner of his mouth. Bonnie did not, he was fairly sure, just want to hang angels on a tree. Clyde's asking her to move in with his mistress had put her in a giddy, reckless mood, and Everett was the beneficiary. He wasn't going to think about Clyde's low, sincere apology to Pam. Or about Pam turning away on the phone to ask

Clyde to come to the house. Although he found he wanted very much to think about that.

He thought instead about Anne Marie, and how the evening might work out for her. The lesson about not abandoning people was a good one. The silent, submerged unhappiness of the evening couldn't be good for a kid, and now it was gone, dissolved by Pam's call into the buzz of unsettled excitement.

The streets were dark and empty, the houses warm with light. He wanted to keep thinking, but he was at the station before he had sorted things out, and Bonnie was waiting on the kerb. She climbed into the front seat and kicked the snow off her boots.

'Hi,' she said, and she clutched her hands in her lap. She shuddered once, from nervousness or cold. 'Clyde'll be here in a second,' she said. 'He's signing something about the car.'

'Okay,' he said.

She looked at Everett and seemed about to say something, and then she was in his arms. He gathered her up as well as he could, given her thick coat and the awkward position, and kissed her sweet face. Her cheeks were cold but her lips were warm, and she was trembling. The pea coat was unbuttoned and he reached inside to feel the curve of her breast through her sweater.

A second later they pulled apart—the time required to sign papers measured somewhere in both their minds—and Bonnie smoothed her hair. The lighted glass door of the police station opened, and Clyde walked with his long stride towards them and got in the back seat.

Everett thought there must be a smell in the car from the kiss, an electricity. But the husband said nothing, and Everett drove the outlaws back to his house. They talked about the stolen car, and the cold, and the tree. All the while, Everett felt both the threat of disorder and the steady, thrumming promise of having everything he wanted, all at once. □

Debut Novels. Debut Brilliance.

A Cabinet of Wonders by Renee Dodd

To the rubes that pay to see them, they are Freaks. To the carnies, they are a source of income, and sometimes, friends. To Dugan—scholar, romantic, dwarf—they are more than business, they are family, and he'll do everything he can to keep them together...

"A rare treat: a diverting and insightful piece of quirky fiction."
KIRKUS, STARRED REVIEW

"Dodd's prose is graceful, smooth, and intelligent."
LIBRARY JOURNAL, STARRED REVIEW

ISBN 15926416411

ISBN 1592641393

Our Holocaust by Amir Gutfreund

Shortlisted for the Rohr Prize, A B&N Discover Winner

Growing up among survivors, Amir is deemed too young to know what happened Over There. Undeterred, his quest for truth has alarming—and strangely funny—results. His obsession continues until, finally Old Enough, his unforgettable family open their hearts, souls, and pasts to him...

"Gutfreund's writing is brilliant, his teasing narrative mesmerizing, and the thought behind it subtle and extraordinarily limber. This is no beginner's effort, but a powerhouse accomplishment rivaling Günter Grass or Gabriel García Márquez." *CHICAGO TRIBUNE*

The Genizah at the House of Shepher by Tamar Yellin

Winner of the Ribalow Prize, Shortlisted for the Rohr Prize

Set against the backdrop of a changing Jerusalem over a hundred and thirty years, this is a large-canvas novel of exile and belonging, displacement, and the quest for both love and a true promised land.

"A writer of rare distinction." *THE GUARDIAN*

"...impossible to put down... Beauty, deep love, and a timelessness will likely make it a classic." *BOOKLIST STARRED REVIEW*

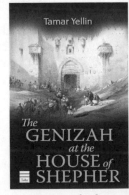

ISBN 1592640850

Toby   www.tobypress.com

GRANTA

BUFFALO SOLDIERS

ZZ Packer

ZZ Packer has been a high-school teacher and barmaid (though not at the same time). A graduate of Yale University, she received Masters degrees from Johns Hopkins and the Iowa Writers' Workshop and was a Wallace Stegner Fellow and Jones Lecturer at Stanford University. Her collection of short stories, 'Drinking Coffee Elsewhere' (Canongate/Riverhead Books), was a New York Times Notable Book, winner of a Commonwealth Club Fiction Award and an Alex Award and a PEN/Faulkner Award finalist. Her fiction has appeared in 'The New Yorker', 'Harper's' and 'Zoetrope', while her non-fiction has been featured in the 'New York Times Magazine', the 'New York Times Book Review' and 'Salon'. She has received a Whiting Writers' Award, a Rona Jaffe Foundation Writers' Award and a Guggenheim Fellowship. She lives in the San Francisco Bay Area with her husband, son, and her naughty miniature Pinscher, Punky. 'Buffalo Soldiers' is taken from her novel-in-progress, 'The Thousands'.

It had seemed that just riding at a walk was difficult enough, but heading into the mountains meant slight drifts of fear at every incline, every pass. It was enough to make Lazarus realize that whatever little hillocks they'd encountered on their march from San Antonio to their headquarters at Fort Stockton were nothing. They tried to file two by two, but there were some places the scouts had led them where the men had to go through one at a time, and it was then that Lazarus feared that the horse in front of him would lose its footing and fall, smacking him with the might of an avalanche of horseflesh, or that Grey Bat, his own horse—who was a little too fond of leaping up or rushing down a slope—would miscalculate, and that would be the end of them both.

No one spoke. All that could be heard were the horses negotiating the passes with grunts and whinnies and the razor sharp zips of passing mosquitoes and horseflies, locusts bouncing at crazy angles as the horses crushed their hiding places. Lazarus had never heard the men so quiet, and still the scout Liege seemed quieter than the rest, separate from the other scouts, looking around occasionally as if he were the colonel himself, surveying his men.

They stood at the next pass, waiting—for what, Lazarus did not know. All he could think upon seeing the land was that it was somehow ugly and strangely beautiful at the same time. Then without so much as a word from Lieutenant Heyl, they were ascending again, and with each ascent, a shoulder of rock on his near side or far side would bring blessed shade and calm, so different from anything he'd seen in Mississippi or Louisiana that he sometimes forgot that it was home he wanted to be going towards. He could not make out the expressions on the faces of the scouts up ahead, but they were pacing back on forth on their horses, as if in confusion, and when he went to look at Liege, Liege looked worried.

'I think they want you to get on up there, Mr Indian,' Redbone said, but Liege didn't pay Redbone any mind. He just started sniffing and rolling his eyes up to the ceiling of the sky, figuring.

Then came the sound of shots, and the horses started, and the men up front along with Lieutenant Heyl fought to keep them under control. Along with shots came Indian whoops and cries, sounding like they were calling for the end of the world to commence.

'This is it, Niggers!' Heyl called out, 'This is it!'

The men in front bounded forward, while Lazarus and the rest of the advance party manoeuvred behind. He could hear the front men returning fire but a blizzard of dust from the pounding of horse hooves made it impossible to see.

'Spread out you fucking niggers!' Heyl yelled, as if unaware that the men had already surged forward. Lazarus was deep in the middle of the men, and saw men in the very front line falling to an invisible enemy—all he saw were clouds of dust, and when the dust cleared just the sheer facing of rocks. He had to push his way against other men coming forward, the horses jostling each other, their flanks briefly caroming off one another while Lazarus sought partial protection by lying flush against Grey Bat's bristly mane.

The bullets came in little pings. One man was down already, his horse hit, whinnying and rearing before it fell on to the ground in a crash of meat, pinning his rider while everyone still upright sidestepped fallen horse and rider as if they were prickly cactus.

Heyl yelled out another command, and once again, the men shuffled into a loose formation—not nearly as tight as before. He didn't know if the formation had loosened because all was just complete chaos and men simply couldn't hear, but he knew there would be hell to pay from Heyl later. Lazarus wanted to shoehorn everyone into place just so he wouldn't have to hear Heyl yelling everyday for the next week, and he even tried lining up behind the horse in front of him, but Liege reined his horse sideways so that his flanks pushed at Grey Bat's. 'Don't fall into no formation!' Liege yelled at him, then yelled it again, his toad's voice shouting.

'We got to follow orders!' Lazarus shouted to him over the din. Insubordination. The word he'd heard Hatch hissing over and over again to his officers, and the officers to any of the soldiers who dared complain.

'Don't fall into no goddamned formation,' Liege said again, and though he didn't yell it, it had more force somehow, and all the men around him seemed to understand. His horse kept skittering sideways into Grey Bat, trying poor Grey Bat's patience. 'I been fighting with Indians my whole life. Ain't no way to fight 'em by standing in line, clear and plain for them to see, waiting for them to kill us off. That ain't no Indian way of fighting.'

Lazarus didn't know what Liege had in mind, but Liege kept his arm braced just inches in front of Lazarus, as if in ready to knock the carbine out of his hand if need be. It was as if Liege knew that it would take these few but vital moments before Lazarus understood what was happening. Lazarus now saw the limited use of the formation: point, advance party, support and reserve, if only because the Kickapoos were not coming from some designated place the Ninth could see, but from all around, and there was no way of knowing how many were in front of back of them, due to their stealth. Instead of one army meeting another, Lazarus now saw their situation was more like a spider lured into an anthill, and he had no way of knowing how Liege proposed to get them out, if retreat had already been struck as an option.

Heyl was busy yelling again, but this time, only a few scampered into formation while the rest were all scattered and shooting, advancing towards the rocks whichever way they could get there while the Indians kept up fire, and in the few beats it took Lazarus to understand what was happening—that Liege was taking over and giving the commands instead of Heyl—Lazarus and the wave of men who'd listened to Liege were swept up into the advance from behind. Suddenly, all was clear to see, and Heyl came crashing down in the volley of fire coming from the rocks.

'Man down!' came the call, and though all was chaos at first, with Heyl screaming for his life in one moment, and then in another— Lazarus charging forwards towards the rocks, and for the first time, sighting Indians. Not the roadside stumps he'd seen coming through San Antonio, drowsily biding their time with corn husks while their lethargic children wove baskets—and putted their leather balls about, but blurs of brown, a flash of some sort animal pelt covering their loins, and streaming hair, straight as a horse's mane.

He had finally managed to unleash his carbine and cock it, but hadn't the chance to use it for fear of shooting one of his own in the back while they had still been prisoners to the dust cloud.

For a time, he hid his face behind Grey Bat's mane. Then, as the wave of men cleared and without the least bit of pressure on the reigns, Grey Bat took off with even greater speed straight towards the whoops and ululations of Indians. He could not believe it; he was heading into fire, headed straight towards the of bullets, and so he aimed his carbine where the dust cloud had cleared before him—a straight shot with none of his own impeding the way—but when he went to shoot, there was nothing, nothing at all.

No bullet, no recoil, no shot.

They'd never used bullets for target practice, as the Army rationed out its ammunition with the coloured regiments. They'd all gotten their share of ammunition before heading out, and Lazarus had dutifully loaded his carbine as demonstrated, and yet, it did not fire.

He pumped his carbine furiously, and found to his surprise that this was the first time since the skirmish began that he began to fear for his life. 'Lord Jesus,' he said, or thought he said, and looked round for Liege, but could not find him. The fear that pulsed through his body kept him moving and dodging, but he had no gun that worked, and he could not turn Grey Bat around lest he be stampeded, and even if no one blocked his path, he knew he could never retreat, or he'd get branded as yellow, and furthermore, a traitor, and would have proven all the East Texas papers right: the Negro was not ready for battle. □

GRANTA

THE ANSWER
Jess Row

Jess Row was born in 1974 in Washington, DC. After graduating from Yale, he taught English for two years at the Chinese University of Hong Kong and in 2001 received an MFA from the University of Michigan. 'The Train to Lo Wu', his first collection of stories, is published by Dial Press. The recipient of a Whiting Writers' Award, a Pushcart Prize and an NEA fiction fellowship, he is currently at work on a novel and a new short story collection, of which the piece in this issue is the title story. Row lives in Princeton, New Jersey, with his wife, Sonya Posmentier, and is a professor in the English department at the College of New Jersey. A long-time student of Zen Buddhism, he was ordained a dharma teacher by the Kwan Um School of Zen in 2004.

It's a Thursday afternoon in late August. The year—I should mention this, shouldn't I? The year is 1993. I'm sitting in the grass on Old Campus with my roommates Michael and Jake, waiting for First Year Orientation to begin. A cloudless day, painfully bright, smelling of mowed lawns and sweat; the sun burning the backs of our necks like an angry eye.

In the middle of one of those strange conversations freshmen have when they first meet—breathless confessions punctuated by abrupt, uncomfortable silences—I cast about for somewhere else to look and see a tall Hispanic boy standing a little distance from us, arms folded, scowling at Connecticut Hall through thick square glasses.

I'm not a gregarious person. I've never been especially social. But it's the first week of freshman year and already I'm a little lonely, sensing that Michael and Jake will stop speaking to one another, and me, in a month. Hey, man, I say, leaning towards him on one elbow, trying to look relaxed. Are you in Trumbull? What's your name?

He sits awkwardly, as if he doesn't have much experience lowering himself to the ground. Despite the heat he has on a pair of stiff new jeans rolled up at the ankles and an untucked, long-sleeved dress shirt. Dark patches of sweat like Rorschach blots stand out against his collarbones. Rafael, he says, once he's arranged himself with legs folded. His voice is nearly drowned out by the faint music blaring from a window on the other side of the quadrangle. I'm from Delaware, he says. Wilmington, Delaware.

Baltimore. Just down the road from you.

He doesn't smile, or nod, or change his expression at all; his mouth hangs slightly open, waiting to see what I will do next. In the corner of my eye I can see Michael and Jake giving one another significant looks.

So what room are you in?

He turns and points to the window just above mine.

213. But there is a problem. I have to change.

What's wrong with it?

We have only one bathroom.

There's something strange about his way of speaking: he hesitates an instant too long after each phrase, as if mentally translating from another language. Not a Spanish accent—it seems Eastern European.

There are girls across the hall, he says. I have to share with them.

So what? Jake speaks this time. So do we. So does everyone. It's Yale policy.

He folds his hands in his lap and stares down at the grass between us. I'm a Muslim, he says. It's not proper.

Jake bites his lip, *chews* his lip, trying not to laugh.

Well, there must be something they can do, I say. They can find you a different room somewhere. Did you tell them that when you sent in your roommate forms?

His eyelids dip slowly and he fixes me with a sour look, an old man's tired frown. *Yes,* he says impatiently.

Shouldn't that be the end of the story? *I'm here,* his face says. *Isn't that enough for you? Do I have to explain myself again, every step of the way?* Across the lawn a whistle shrieks and eight hundred of us stand all at once, trying not to appear too eager, tugging out the legs of our sweaty shorts. Rafael stays seated, and I next to him, in a half-crouch, a helper's pose.

And then he stands up and dusts himself off and twists away.

We spend the next few days shuttling from one meeting and training session to another. We learn to recognize the signs of eating disorders and the signs of depression; to avoid sexual assault by travelling in groups; to understand that *no means no*; to squeeze the tip of the condom before rolling it on; to avoid muggings by travelling in groups; to give homeless people vouchers for food instead of money; to speak to our RAs if we feel angry, hurt, lost, anorexic, depressed or sexually assaulted; to avoid unpleasant encounters with roving townies by travelling in groups. Rafael isn't anywhere to be seen, and his name never comes up in any conversation, not even the ones you might expect: This guy, across the hall? You wouldn't believe it, he's some kind of super-orthodox Muslim.

A week later, when I come upon him staring into a plate of green beans and baked fish in the Trumbull dining hall, I've forgotten him altogether. He raises his head just as I'm scanning the tables, looking for a familiar face, and our eyes meet. By accident. He's sitting alone, and instantly I know—we both know—it would be unforgivably rude for me not to join him, though I'm in a hurry and the last thing I want is to get involved.

I know you, he says, when I introduce myself again. We met the first day. On the grass. He doesn't smile, but gives me a tiny nod, a slight inclining of the head. Isaac is a very interesting name, he says. Not everyone would choose that name.

Yeah. A little too Biblical. I went through a stage of trying to get people to call me Zack, but there were two other Zacks in my class.

A slight tightening at the corners of his eyes, as if I've slipped out of focus.

And the funny thing, I say, is that my town is mostly Jewish, and my high school was mostly Jewish, but *I'm* the one named Isaac.

He cuts a chunk of scrod with his fork and lifts it up, picking away the bones carefully. I assume you know the story of Ibrahim and the sacrifice, he says. The Jewish-Christian version. He unfolds his napkin carefully, as if it were an old document, a tattered map from the glove box, and uses one corner of it to wipe his mouth. But you haven't heard the Muslim version.

No.

Pushing his plate aside, he makes a V with his hands on the tabletop. Ibrahim has two sons, he says. Isaac and Ismail. So God— Allah—asks him to make this sacrifice, and when Ibrahim agrees, Allah says, This son, who you were willing to sacrifice, he will be the father of the chosen people.

And the sons of the other are the outcasts. The sons of Ishmael.

Right. A broad smile. Only Ismail is the chosen one, and Isaac is the outcast.

Well, that's only one way of looking at it, right? It doesn't necessarily have to be about winners and losers.

Let me guess, he says, expressionless, spearing beans with his fork. Your parents must be Episcopalians.

Unitarians.

And one of them is a doctor. At least.

I follow his eyes to my backpack, sitting in the chair next to me, printed with a lime-green logo: *zocor™ philotelenol hydrozolate*.

My mother's a dermatologist. And?

As if satisfied, in some obscure way, he looks up at the rafters of the dining hall, at the shields with heraldic crests and Latin mottoes underneath the leaded-glass windows, and nods distractedly. Give me a straight answer, I want to say to him. I've already picked my way through my own plate of overcooked fettuccine and too-sweet tomato sauce; and it's time for me to consider the other options: the salad bar, the bagel bar, another peanut-butter-and-jelly sandwich, a merciful quick escape to the library.

So you see, he says, the winners have many options. They can choose to feel about themselves however they want. They can even choose not to be winners any more.

Isn't it a little too implausible that I would hear a knock at my door two days later, at an hour when Jake and Michael happen to be out, and find Rafael standing there? Or that I would invite him in? I myself find it hard to believe. He looks helpless and bewildered, clutching a textbook and a ragged notebook under his arm, in a long white T-shirt and the same jeans as before. The outfit reminds me, uncomfortably, of a movie I've seen about Mexican-American gangsters in prison.

I'm sorry to bother you, he says. You're in my psychology class. Are you studying for the test tomorrow? I'm having a hard time with it.

You're in Salovey's class? I've never seen you there.

Yeah. I sit up in the balcony.

In our common room—a futon, a halogen lamp, a stack of milk crates for bookshelves, a Dinosaur Jr poster, a Rothko print, a stereo sitting precariously on its own box—he looks awkwardly from side to side, unsure of where to sit, twitching with discomfort. Finally I point him to the futon and move my desk chair to face him.

It's this influence stuff, he says, opening the textbook across his knees. This part:

> The human mind has an overwhelming craving for stability and symmetry, particularly in social relationships with strangers. Schloss (1967) demonstrated that adult subjects who feel an obligation imposed on them (even one they did not choose themselves) will make every effort to fulfill it, and report feeling unsettled and anxious if prevented from doing so. The same logic applies to all free-giveaway programs and one-on-one selling techniques.

Okay, I say. This is easy. Think of the example he gave in lecture. The Hare Krishna guy comes up to you in the airport and gives you a sticker that says 'Smile!' without asking you for permission first. Even if you don't want the sticker, he won't take it back, and you can't throw it away in front of him—that would be rude. So you have to talk to him for thirty seconds. That gives him time to make the pitch for his children's charity, or whatever he's trying to collect money for. Again, because he initiated the relationship with a gift, you still feel indebted, so you might wind up giving him a dollar or two or five—even though you know better.

He takes off his glasses and wipes them on the long hem of his T-shirt. It's a warm night, still now in mid-September, and the creases in his forehead are shiny with sweat. Without his glasses, and slightly flushed by the heat, he looks naked, defenceless as an overgrown newborn. Except, I notice now, he has a small white scar at the left corner of his mouth, a cut badly healed.

Only an idiot would act that way, he says. Doesn't it just seem like nonsense to you? All this manipulation, all these tricks?

I shrug. These are unconscious tendencies, I say. Some people are more strongly influenced by them than others.

That assumes that everybody has the same unconscious. And why should that be? Think about it. Why should some professor know what *my* unconscious is like?

Well, you know, the studies are all supposed to be multi-ethnic, so they factor that part in.

He laughs, the one and only time I will ever hear him laugh, a deep guffaw out of the belly that is also like a suppressed groan. Bullshit they do, he says. All these studies are done on college campuses, so who do you expect they're going to find?

Then why take psychology? If you've already decided you don't believe in it, why take it?

Leaning back, he tilts his head up to stare at the ceiling, and lets his hands fall uselessly on the textbook's open page, fingers curling skyward. The futon creaks underneath him. Everyone has to learn a skill, he says tonelessly, as if repeating a line learned in childhood. The Movement doesn't need illiterates. It needs doctors, lawyers, engineers. People with degrees. The new nation depends on those people.

Without looking at me, he digs into the pocket of his jeans and thrusts a battered yellow pamphlet in my direction: 'Jihad in the

Cause of God, Young Muslims United, Toronto, CANADA, for free distribution'. The paper is tissue-thin, the type a reprint of an older edition, printed on an inferior press, hardly legible in places. In my hands it falls open to a paragraph highlighted in orange:

> This religion is really a universal declaration of the freedom of man from servitude to other men and from servitude to his own desires, which is also a form of human servitude; it is a declaration that sovereignty belongs to God alone and that He is the Lord of all the worlds. It means a challenge to all kinds and forms of systems which are based on the concept of the sovereignty of man; in other words, where man has usurped the Divine attribute.

Each page contains more of the same—long paragraphs in tiny print, studded with quotations:

> There are many practical obstacles in establishing God's rule on earth, such as the power of the state, the social system and traditions and, in general, the whole human environment. Islam uses force only to remove these obstacles so that there may not remain any wall between Islam and individual human beings, so that it may address their hearts and minds after releasing them from these material obstacles, and then leave them free to choose to accept or reject it.

What does this part mean? *The whole human environment?*
He lifts his head and looks at me curiously.
Why? What do you *think* it is?
Well, what else is there? *God's* environment?
Exactly.
That's a circular argument. If you define God as everything *not* human and yet say that we're supposed to destroy our own environment and accept God's—
Shut up and listen for a second. Tiny drops of sweat trickle down his forehead, and he wipes them away with the back of his hand. This isn't just philosophy, he says. It's a *programme.* The first people going down are the governments of Egypt, Jordan and Saudi Arabia. It's all about reclaiming the Islamic world and making it real. Not just

a copy of the West. Those countries have their laws, and we have *shari'a*. We don't want to force anybody to become Muslims, but we want Muslims to be allowed to *be* Muslims.

As he speaks he squares his shoulders and leans forward, elbows on his knees, watching me, watching the room. Projecting. Did he learn that in theatre class, I'm wondering, and if so, can he tell I have a trick of my own, pressing my tongue against the roof of my mouth to keep from smiling?

I know what you're thinking. He flicks his fingers dismissively. Yeah, I was a Catholic. I went to Catholic school through eighth grade. Does that make you happy? You want to hear about how my mother waded across the Rio Grande with only her shoes in a plastic bag?

Look, you have to admit it's a little incongruous. Who's to say you won't decide to give it up in another year?

And who's to say you won't be a Muslim yourself in another year?

He stands and walks over to my desk, arms crossed, peering at the CDs piled along the windowsill, reading the posters and postcards I've taped to the wall above.

Cat Stevens is a Muslim. You like Cat Stevens, don't you?

I turn around in my chair to face him, as he bends over my desk, scanning the papers and open books curiously, dispassionately, as if looking at a museum display under glass.

Is that how you recruit new members? *Cat Stevens?*

He closes his eyes.

Islam has nothing to do with violence, he says. If you try it—if you pray, if you read the Qur'an, if you come to the *masjid*, you'll understand. And I really think you should, Isaac. Because I can tell that you're not happy. You may think you belong here, but you don't. Not really. No more than I do.

I have a curious tickling feeling at the back of my throat, as if I've swallowed something dry and scratchy by accident; I cough, once, twice, but it doesn't change.

What makes you so sure of that?

His smile lifts up only one corner of his mouth, at once wistful and patronizing. Why else would you be sitting here talking to me for so long? he says. Shouldn't you have somewhere else to be? He picks up his textbook and the pamphlet, tucks them under his arm, and pauses for a moment, his head lifted, reading another poster I've tacked to my closet door. A sepia-toned picture of Rilke, and a quotation from *Letters to a Young Poet*:

> The point is to live everything. Live the questions now. Perhaps then, some day far in the future, you will gradually, without even noticing it, live your way into the answer.

Have you read Rilke? I'll lend you his books if you want.

He shakes his head in a kind of spasm, as if coming out of a momentary trance.

It's not so hard, he says, giving me a sly, sideways smile. Why should you have to wait so long?

The next day, Thursday, I wake up late, having missed my nine o'clock English class, with a headache and a mouth that feels stuffed with cotton batting. The sky is the colour of wet cement and the air has a faint metallic chill, a fall feeling, for the first time. All day, following familiar paths across campus, I have a slight sense of drift, of not quite following a straight path from point A to point B. The cries of the woman who stands at the corner of York and Elm—*A flower for a dollar! Please, sir, a flower for a dollar!*—follow me down the block. In my philosophy class, describing Socrates' final words in the *Phaedo*, the professor, who walks with a limp and seems nearly eighty, turns his face to the blackboard for a full minute, as if looking over his shoulder at someone, and then returns to his lecture.

That night, at dinner, I strike up a conversation with two guys I've never met before, sophomores, and afterwards we go up to their room to listen to a live Coltrane date from 1966, and smoke pot, three bowls, until the lights in the room take on a bluish tinge and the music thickens into a single vibrating pulse. After midnight, walking back alone across Old Campus, I see a light still on in a second-floor window, just above mine.

Sovereignty is God's alone, and he is the ruler of all the worlds.

Without having quite meant to, I've veered off the stone walkway and come to a halt on the grass. A faint breeze ruffles the leaves of an oak tree off to the right. No one else is around; a long uninterrupted row of discs of light stretches underneath the security lamps, like a line of white coins. Inside these buildings there are 1,000-odd seventeen- and eighteen-year-olds, sleeping, smoking, fucking, leaning out of windows, mastering Russian grammar and particle physics, writing first novels, playing erotic games of Scrabble. But how many of them *know*, and know they know, the truth?

Is truth what we're paying for?

Sovereignty is God's alone, and he is the ruler of all the worlds.

He doesn't look surprised when he opens the door. Come in, he says. His accent thicker than the day before. I was just cleaning up. Have a seat.

The room has no furniture to speak of. A mattress in one corner, a plastic milk crate upended for a desk, a line of books against the wall, white T-shirts and dark jeans piled on top of a suitcase. Even the glass ceiling lamp has been removed, and the bare bulb gives off a yellowish glare. On the wall above the bed a calendar with a picture of a sunrise and Arabic writing across it. He's not staying long, I tell myself immediately, involuntarily. This is an encampment.

I talked to one of the maintenance guys, he says. I told him if he took away everything he could sell it if he wanted to.

I sit down on the edge of the mattress, clasping my knees together. My mouth has gone dry and the harsh light makes my eyes ache. I've forgotten whatever it was I planned to say.

It's cool. You've got a lot more space this way. It's very monastic.

All that shit is unnecessary, he says. It glorifies the body. Allah wants us to make palaces in his name and live in tents outside them. On tiptoe, he stretches out his arm and almost touches the ceiling. All this construction, he says, all this money. I mean, Okay, it's a cold climate, you can't live outside all the time, the way they do in Arabia. But they could have had some humility, you know what I mean? This is a student dormitory, not a fucking castle. You went on the tour, didn't you? All these buildings were put up in the 1930s, but they wanted to make them look old. So they poured acid on the roof tiles and broke the glass in the windows so it'd look all funky and crooked. Man, if that's not a symbol of a civilization in decline, I don't know what is. A bunch of pathetic white geezers who have all this money and so little to show for it that they have to make an imitation of something that's 600 years old.

He bends his knees and jumps in place, landing on his heels with a bang, as if to test the strength of the floor.

America is the most self-hating society the world has ever seen. Why else would all these rich folks decide that they're going to take the people they've chained, whipped, shat upon and murdered for the last 400 years, select the best ones and give them all the tools they need to take over? Sure, they get a few lapdogs here and there. Colin Powell, Clarence Thomas, Bill Cosby. But over time they're signing their own death warrant, and they know it. If those people really knew how to run a society they would have listened to Henry Ford back in the 1930s.

Henry Ford?

He was Hitler's biggest fan. Didn't you *study* any of this shit? He was the only one of them who was willing to tell the truth. A society based on money is a society based on murder. That's rule number one. Money creates envy on one side and fear on the other. And where does the urge to murder come from? Envy or fear. It's that basic. Hatred is the gas in the engine. The problem is, how do you *use* it? That's what Hitler understood. People like us, we *need* to kill. We *have* to hate somebody. It's in our blood. You can sublimate it, you can ignore it, you can hand out scholarships and welfare and what-all, but that only lasts so long. Hatred is power. It has to be *channelled*.

He speaks with his eyes locked on the ceiling, resting his hands on his hips or dropping them at his sides, fingers splayed. Ignoring me for dramatic purposes. As if we've both agreed, somehow, to pretend that this is a rehearsal, a preparation, instead of the main event.

There are four kinds of hatred. There's hatred that expresses itself as such, openly. That's the best kind. There's hatred that becomes self-pity. Extremely useful if dealt with correctly. There's hatred that gets channelled into other forms of aggression. Very wasteful and counterproductive, very difficult to change. And then there's hatred that turns into guilt and then into smothering kindness. It identifies with its opposite. That's almost impossible to manage.

The sticky haze of the pot is beginning to clear; each time I blink I see the room more clearly, its bright surfaces and hard-edged shadows. It isn't that I've never heard these things before. Baltimore has its share of street-corner prophets: vendors of *The Spartacist* and *Revolutionary Worker* and *The Final Call*. All the rusting Eastern cities do. If you're a curious fifteen-year-old out walking the streets for the first time, playing at independence, little more than bus fare in your pockets, you stop and listen to them. You take the pamphlet extolling the virtues of the Shining Path and the FMLN button and sign the petitions to free political prisoners you've never heard of. And you never, ever respond, because they don't want questions; it's a performance, not a dialogue. They have bright tubercular eyes, they are incapable of embarrassment and they never tire.

But you can't do it, I'm thinking. You can't be a shoeless prophet in the Berkeley College Dining Hall, underneath the chandeliers and the mounted ibex. It's there in invisible ink, in all the pages you sign. You take on that mantle of shame. The gate you don't see is the gate that closes behind you. It's the smell of the steam vents, the boiled food, the carving of Confucius over the library door. You relinquish the right to scrabble around in the entrails of birds. You refuse to call the president a blue-eyed devil, until you can prove it in a chemical equation, or refer to it, in passing, in a devastating parenthetical. You take on the humiliation of belonging.

With the confidence only a college freshman can have, I look up, I hold his gaze, his unblinking eyes rimmed with baby fat, and say in a hoarse whisper, Rafael, give it up. You know I don't hate you.

He squats in front of me, angling his face to one side, so that I see it in profile. See this scar? he asks, pointing. You know how I got it? A rat bit me while I was sleeping. When I was three. We were in some welfare hotel in South Carolina, and they evicted us, and it was raining, so we slept in the back, in the shed where they kept the dumpsters. When my mom took me to the hospital they refused to give me rabies shots because she couldn't provide any ID. If that isn't hate, then what is? Those people *wanted* me dead.

But—

And you can say that it's not fair, he says, you can say that I can't *extrapolate*, you know, that I can't tar you with the same brush, or whatever. But here's the truth. I *do. We* do. We're *hard-wired* to. And don't give me this nature-or-nurture, humanistic, free-will asinine liberal bullshit about individual worth and dignity. That's the biggest lie of all. As if anything in this world was really about individuals.

Hold on. I stick a finger out at him, as if to say, *Enough*. I respect your right to say, *Based on my experience, I believe*—almost anything. But you can't tell me that *I* hate *you*. Step back for a minute. The world is more complicated than that.

He turns partway towards me and grips the back of his neck with both hands, covering his ears with his wrists. You don't get it at all, he says, closing his eyes. Not that I'd really expect you to. But it's sad. It's really fucking sad. Because the point of all of this, the reason for my saying this, is that the only solution is total submission to God. Once you admit to yourself that you've spent your life worshipping false idols, and your heart is full of confusion and darkness and buried rage and guilt and lust, only *then* can you allow Allah into your heart. I'm talking about peace and serenity like nothing you've ever known. And you, Isaac, I thought *you* would understand this. Everybody can see it in your face, man. You're lost. You don't know *what* to believe. You're a wide-open door. You've got all this power and privilege, but that's not enough. You're sick of this dream country.

Outside, in the entryway, shuffling steps on the stairs, and a loud girl's voice. I can't believe you've never had jello shots before, she's saying. You have to take it slow. They put a *ton* of vodka in them, didn't you know that? Watch it! Hold the rail.

I don't have any power, I want to tell him. *I'm not special. Why did you have to choose me? Who do you think I am?*

And what if you're right? What then?

I've still got my scholarship cheques. He starts to sway back and forth, ducking, bobbing his head, and then begins to dance like a boxer, on the balls of his feet, whipping his arms out in careless punches. The bursar's office is after me. They've been banging on my door every day since I got here. If I go now I'll still have enough for a one-way ticket to Karachi. He spins, hammering at the air; he throws a roundhouse kick over my head. I met this guy in Jersey City who gave me the number of his mosque. He said they're always looking for Americans. You can go to school there for free; they'll teach you Arabic, the Qur'an, everything you need to know. It's all paid for by charity. That's the thing, man. It's a *system*. It's a new way to live. They're taking lost people from everywhere, people like us, and giving them a new life. All you have to do is show up.

He pulls up the hem of his T-shirt and wipes his face with it. Underneath his torso is the colour of putty. As if he never takes his shirt off, as if he's never been outside bare-chested, not once, not in a swimming pool or on a beach.

You can get the money, he says. The ticket's about fifteen hundred. Your parents probably gave you that much to start your bank account, didn't they?

Rafael, I say, smiling, shaking my head. Don't be an idiot.

Why not? he asks. Am I wrong? I haven't heard you arguing. Do you disagree with my analysis? Then tell me what *you* think. Don't just fucking *sit* there.

I respect your opinion. That's as far as I'll go. I'm willing to give you the benefit of the doubt.

Oh, Jesus, he says, what a classic liberal evasion, man, that's the way to defuse any argument, isn't it? They teach you that shit in the womb, don't they? *Let's agree to disagree. Fuck* that! He slaps his palm against the wall. Come on, articulate something! Why *shouldn't* I go to Pakistan? Now's your chance, Isaac. You've got thirty seconds.

He stares at me with such intensity that I have to look away; a biological reaction, probably, going back to our days in the trees. All animals know that eye contact is hostile, that meeting an angry gaze is open warfare. I have to force myself to look up again, to see him. And when I do, of course, I know how afraid he is. His forehead creases; his eyelids perform little spasms, narrowing and widening, as if he's waiting for me to jump up and attack.

I can't tell you anything new. You've worked it out to your own satisfaction. It's useless for me to say that *I* don't believe that Henry Ford was right. You know that already. And you know that I'm not going with you, either. You're afraid of leaving without *somebody* knowing why.

You're underestimating me.

The problem, I say, ignoring him, is that I don't think you really believe in this stuff. You've talked yourself into a corner and you can't get out, but that's not the same thing as a *conversion*. Islam is all about God's love, right? You don't *have* any fucking love. You need a shrink, not a new religion. So I'm not going to be your witness, all right? You can't put me in that position. Go do what you want, but don't ask me to legitimize it. As far as you're concerned, I was never here. I never listened to this.

He gives me a knowing grin, his lips pulled back against the teeth.

You can be cruel, he says. But I guess I should have expected that. That's the badge of the do-gooder class, ain't it? *My way or the highway.*

You asked for my opinion.

I asked for an argument, not a psychiatric evaluation. He opens the door a few inches. You can go now. That's what you want, right?

I stand up unsteadily; my legs have gone to sleep, and I have to bend over and massage them before I can walk. As I approach the door, he stands with his arms at his sides, like a sentry, half-blocking my way, so that I'll have to push past him to get by.

When you get sick of this place, he says, when you realize I'm right, come join me. I'll still be there. I'm not coming back.

I believe you.

Don't believe me. Believe God.

Lunging forward, he takes my right hand and presses the palm against his face. He hasn't shaved; he doesn't shave. Soft skin, oily, rubbery. *Human* skin. I haven't been touched in nearly a month. Not a hug, not a caress, not an arm over my shoulder. College students don't shake hands.

This body is just a shell, he says, it's a tool in God's hands, for him to use and throw away. Don't listen to my voice. Trust God speaking through me. Look at the movie, not the screen. *This is the life you want.* This is the call. It won't come again.

I pull my hand away and move into the gap between his shoulder and the doorjamb, and he turns with me, one body to another, like a dancer, and presses his mouth for a moment against mine. And what is it, what can I call it, *inertia*, or terror, or are they one and the same, keeps me moving, unclasping from his embrace like a hand releasing from a handshake. If I could speak I would say, *It's not enough. I wish it was. It's not enough.* At the bottom of the stairs, wiping my mouth, I hear his door slam.

In ten years I only thought about Rafael Mendes once. It was at a party in Cambridge, in the summer, on someone's back porch. We were sitting in a semicircle of chairs drinking sangria—a few friends from graduate school, wives, boyfriends, neighbours. The woman next to me was named Erin; she lived up the street and, as it turned out, she was a forensic pathologist at Brigham and

Women's, a researcher who specialized in scars, wounds, abscesses—the icky stuff, she said. She had slender white legs and little explosions of red freckles all over her face and shoulders, and she wasn't above sticking her fingers into her glass to retrieve the grapes.

I had a friend in college with a scar on his face from a rat bite, I told her.

I'm not sure why. I said it lightly, casually, as a bit of polite conversation; I hardly even remembered who it was I was referring to. Don't we all do that sometimes, just for the sake of having something to say? I described it, how it stood out against the skin, and used my pinkie to indicate the size.

She frowned and shook her head.

I hate to tell you this, she said, but your friend was making that up. Rat bites aren't that big, to begin with. And they gouge, they don't slice. To me that sounds more like a knife wound. Probably he cut himself playing when he was a kid. She bit into a chunk of apple. Points for creativity, though, she said. A rat bite? Only kids in the projects get those. He wasn't Puerto Rican, was he?

He might have been. I never asked.

Well, she said, I grew up in New York, and the Puerto Rican kids at my school always used to say that if you ratted out your friends to the teachers or the cops you'd get cut like that on the side of your mouth. They called it the *chismo*. Or sometimes *la rata*. Maybe he was being poetic. It's not the kind of thing you'd want to admit, is it? Even years later. You should look him up and see what he says now.

She crossed her legs and smoothed the front of her sundress nervously, as if afraid she'd said too much. Like so many women my age, I thought, apologizing for her expertise, hesitating to be an authority.

And you, she said, what do you do? You haven't said a word about yourself.

It's all right, I said. My friend, the one I was talking about? He used to say that individuals don't really matter.

Her lips formed a vague smile, a place holder, while she looked around the room for an explanation. What is it with you people? she asked finally. Why do you insist on telling jokes no one else gets?

Jess Row

From the *Washington Post*, October 7, 2003:

American Jihadist Reported Killed in Cairo Bombing

Rafael Mendes, a 28-year-old Delaware resident reported missing
ten years ago, was reported to have been killed Friday in a failed
suicide bombing near the British embassy in Cairo, according to
news reports in the Egyptian press over the weekend.

Mendes, who disappeared shortly after enrolling at Yale
University as a freshman in 1993, apparently had spent time in
Pakistan and Afghanistan, and at some point changed his name to
Mustafa Ali, according to a report in *Al-Ahram Newsweekly*,
which quoted an anonymous member of the radical group he was
associated with.

Mendes appears to have been the sole occupant of a truck filled
with explosives which exploded after striking a low overpass about
a mile from the British embassy. The overpass collapsed in the
explosion, killing a bicycle rider and injuring twenty motorists.

His parents, Marco and Rosa Mendes, of Wilmington, were
notified by the State Department yesterday. In an interview with a
local television crew, Mr Mendes said they had heard from Rafael
only once, in 1995, in a postcard sent from Islamabad, in which he
wished them well and advised them to build a bomb shelter
underneath their house in order to 'avoid the coming holocaust'.

It's the first week in November. I'm sitting cross-legged, alone, on
a bench on the Green, reading the *Oresteia*. It's too cold to be
sitting outside, but I've gone there to avoid my roommates' furious
glances across the common room. I've pulled the sleeves of my jacket
down over my hands, leaving only the knuckles exposed. On the
opposite side of the path, about twenty feet away, a homeless man
or woman is asleep under a pile of newspapers and dirty clothes,
his head—or hers—hidden under a torn piece of blue carpet.

For we are strong and skilled;
we have authority; we hold
memory of evil; we are stern
nor can men's pleadings bend us. We

drive through our duties, spurned, outcast
from gods, driven apart to stand in light
not of the sun.

As I look up the pale autumn sun dips behind the Taft, and all
at once I am gripped by a heart-wringing sadness. The three churches
on the Green stand deserted, like decorations, placed there as an
afterthought. Most of the storefronts along Chapel Street are empty
and dark. The cold is soaking into my bones. I ought to go over to
the figure lying on the ground and shake him, and say, *It's too cold
to stay out, you need to get to a shelter*, but you don't do that here;
too many of them are paranoid, or drunk, or high, and you could
get stabbed, or worse. Human beings freeze to death in this city from
time to time. You learn to live with it, and with the police sirens
racing past your window every night, and the faint pops in the
distance that might or might not be gunshots.

Rafael, I think, this broken world will never be mended.

My face is turning numb. I stand up stiffly and shake out my arms,
trying to get the blood flowing. I'm witnessing something; I know that
much. Say that for a moment it's possible to cut the fabric of our days
and expose the fulcrum, the glistening gears, the smell of grease. I
ought to lie down on the ground myself. I should hail a cab for the
airport and buy a ticket to Karachi and find a way to bring him back.

In a better world our wishes would have the force of law.

If I could find a way to walk out of this story, I would. Instead,
I turn and walk back towards Phelps Gate, towards the dark
battlements lying in shadow, because I have nowhere else to go. □

DIVAGATIONS
STÉPHANE MALLARMÉ

TRANSLATED BY BARBARA JOHNSON
The salmagundi of prose poems, prose-poetic musings, criticism, and reflections that is *Divagations* has long been considered a treasure trove by students of aesthetics and modern poetry. This was the only book of prose Mallarmé published in his lifetime and, in a new translation by Barbara Johnson, is now available for the first time in English as Mallarmé arranged it. The result is an entrancing work through which a notoriously difficult-to-translate voice shines in all of its languor and musicality.

Belknap Press / new in cloth

GAMER THEORY
McKENZIE WARK

Ever get the feeling that life's a game with changing rules and no clear sides, one you are compelled to play yet cannot win? Welcome to gamespace. Gamespace is where and how we live today. It is everywhere and nowhere: the main chance, the best shot, the big leagues, the only game in town. In a world thus configured, McKenzie Wark contends, digital computer games are the emergent cultural form of the times. Wark approaches them as a utopian version of the world in which we actually live.

new in cloth

GRANTA

THE BARN AT THE END OF OUR TERM

Karen Russell

Karen Russell, a native of Miami, was born in 1981. She is a graduate of the Columbia MFA programme and currently lives in New York City. Her debut collection, 'St Lucy's Home for Girls Raised by Wolves', is published by Knopf in the US and will be published by Chatto & Windus in the UK in June. She is working on a novel, 'Swamplandia!', about a family of alligator wrestlers in the Florida swamp. Her own family recently helped her to 'research' this novel by braving the Everglades during mosquito season. She is also working at a veterinary clinic, where she gives dubious medical advice to the owners of small dogs. 'The Barn at the End of Our Term' is a new story.

The girl

The girl is back. She stands silhouetted against the sunshine, the great
Barn doors thrown open. Wisps of newly-mown hay lift and scatter.
Light floods into the stalls.

'Hi horsies!' The girl is holding a cloth napkin full of peaches.
She walks up to the first stall and holds out a pale yellow fruit.

Rutherford arches his neck towards her outstretched hand. Freckles
of light float across his patchy hindquarters. He licks the girl's palm
according to a code that he's worked out, — - — -, which means that
he is Rutherford Birch Hayes, the nineteenth President of the United
States of America, and that she should alert the local officials.

'Ha-ha!' the girl laughs. 'That tickles.'

Rebirth

When Rutherford woke up inside the horse's body, he was tied to a
stout flag post. He couldn't focus his new eyes. He was wearing
blinders. A flag was whipping above him, but Rutherford was
tethered so tightly to the post that he couldn't twist his neck to count
the stars. He could hear a clock gonging somewhere nearby, a sound
that rattled through his chest in waves. That clock must be broken,
Rutherford thought. It struck upwards of twelve times, of twenty,
more gongs than there were hours in a day. After a certain number
of repetitions, it ceased to mean anything.

Rutherford stared down into a drainage ditch and saw a horse's
broody face staring back at him. His hooves were rough, unfeeling
endings. He stamped, and he couldn't feel the ground beneath him.
The gonging wasn't a clock at all, he realized with a warm spreading
horror, but the thudding of his giant equine heart.

A man with a prim moustache and a mean slouch blundered
towards him, streaked fire up Rutherford's sides with a forked quirt,
shoved Rutherford into a dark trailer. The quirt lashed out again and
again, until he felt certain that he had been damned to a rural Hell.

'The Devil!' Rutherford thought as the man drew closer. He shied
away, horrified. But then the man reached up and gave him a gentle
ear-scratch and an amber cube of sugar, confounding things further.

'God?'

The man seemed a little on the short side to be God. His fly was
down, his polka-dotted underclothes exposed. Surely God would not

have faded crimson dots on his underclothes? Surely God would wear a belt? The man kept stroking his blond moustache. His voice sounded thick and wrong to Rutherford's ears: 'He's in, hyuh-hyuh. Give her the gas, Phyllis!'

The trailer rolled forward, and in three days' time Rutherford reached the Barn. He has been stabled there ever since.

The barn

The Barn is part of a modest horse farm, its pastures rolling forwards into a blank, mist-cloaked horizon. The landscape is flat and corn-yellow and empty of people. In fact, the prairies look a lot like the grasslands of Kentucky. There are anthills everywhere, impossibly huge, heaped like dirt monsters.

There are twenty-two stalls in the Barn. Eleven of the stabled horses are, as far as Rutherford can ascertain, former presidents of the United States of America. The other stalls are occupied by regular horses, who give the presidents suspicious, sidelong looks. Rutherford B. Hayes is a skewbald pinto with a golden cowlick and a cross-eyed stare. Rutherford hasn't made many inroads with these regular horses. The Clydesdales are cliquish and pink-gummed, and the palominos are inbred buffoons.

The ratio of presidents to normal horses in the Barn appears to be constant, eleven: eleven. Rutherford keeps trying and failing to make these numbers add up to some explanation ('Let's see, if I am the nineteenth President but the fourth to arrive in the Barn, and if eleven divided by eleven is one, then...hrm, let me start again...'). He's still no closer to figuring out the algorithm that determined their rebirth here. 'Just because a ratio's stable doesn't make it meaningful,' says James Garfield, a tranquil grey percheron, and Rutherford agrees. Then he goes back to his frantic cosmic arithmetic.

The presidents feel certain that they are still in America, although there's no way for them to confirm this. The year—if time still advances the way it did when they were President—is indeterminate. A day gets measured in different increments out here. Grass brightens, and grass dims. Glass cobwebs spread across the tractor's window at dawn. Eisenhower claims that they are stabled in the past: 'The skies are empty,' he nickers. 'Not a B-52 in sight.'

To Rutherford, this new life hums with the strangeness of the future. The man has a cavalry of electric beasts that he rides over his acreage: ruby tractors and combines that would have caused Rutherford's constituents to fall off their buggies with shock. The man climbs into the high tractor seat and turns a tiny key, and then the engine roars and groans with an unintelligible hymn. Cherubs strumming harps couldn't have impressed Rutherford more than these humming ploughs of the hereafter.

'Come back! That's not holy music, you dummy!' Eisenhower yells. 'It's just diesel!'

The man goes by the name of Fitzgibbons. The girl appears to be Fitzgibbon's niece. (Rutherford used to think the girl was an Angel of Mercy, but that was before the incident with the wasps.) She refers to the man as 'Uncle Fitzy', a moniker that many of the presidents find frankly alarming. Rutherford, for his part, feels only relief. 'Fitzy' certainly doesn't seem so bad when you consider the many infernal alternatives: Beelzebub, Mephistopheles, old Serpent, the Prince of Darkness, the Author of Evil, Mister Scratch. Even if Fitzgibbons does turn out to be the Devil, Rutherford thinks, there is something strangely comforting about his Irish surname.

At first many of the presidents assumed that Fitzgibbons was God, but there's been plenty of evidence to suggest that their reverence was misplaced. Fitzgibbons is not a good shepherd. He sleeps in and lets his spring lambs toddle into ditches. The presidents have watched a drunken Fitzgibbons fall off the roof of the shed. They have listened to Fitzgibbons cursing his dead mother. If Fitzgibbons is God, then every citizen of the Union is in dire jeopardy.

'Well, I for one have great faith in Fitzgibbons. I think he is a just and merciful Lord.' James Buchanan can only deduce, given his administration's many accomplishments, that this Barn must be heaven. Buchanan has been reborn as a fastidious bay, a gelding sired by that racing great Caspian Rickleberry. 'Do you know that I have an entry in the Royal Ledger of Equine Bloodlines, Rutherford? It's true.' His nostrils flare with self-regard. 'I am being rewarded,' Buchanan insists, 'for annexing Oregon.'

'But don't you think Heaven would smell better, Mr Buchanan?' Warren Harding is a flatulent roan pony who can't digest grass. 'The Presidency was hell,' he hiccups, 'All I wanted was to get out of that damn White House, and now look where I've ended up. Dispatch for Mr Dante: hell doesn't happen in circles. This Barn is one square acre of hell and Fitzgibbons is the devil!'

Rutherford lately tries to avoid the question. All the explanations that the other presidents have come up with for what has befallen them, and why, feel too simple to Rutherford. Heaven or Hell, every president gets the same ration of wormy apples. Every president is stabled in a 12' by 12' stall.

Maybe we have the whole question reversed, mixed-up, Rutherford sighs. At night the wind goes tearing through the Barn's invisible eaves and he wonders. Maybe the man is Heaven, the mobile hand that brings them grain and water. Maybe the Barn itself is God. If Rutherford lops his ears outwards, the Barn's rafters snap with the reverb of something celestial. At dusk, Fitzgibbons feeds them, waters them, shuts the door. Then the Barn breathes with the promise of fire. Stars pinwheel behind the black gaps in the roof. Rutherford can hear the splinters groaning inside wood, waiting to ignite. *Perhaps that will be the way to our next life*, Rutherford thinks, *the lick of blue lightning that sets the Barn ablaze and changes us more finally*.

Perhaps in his next body Rutherford will find his wife Lucy.

The runaway

One day, at the end of an otherwise unremarkable afternoon, James Garfield makes it over the Fence. Nobody sees him jump it. Fitzgibbons and the girl come in to groom the horses, and Rutherford B. Hayes overhears them talking about it. Shouting, really: 'Well, I'll be sweetly pickled! A runaway!' Fitzgibbon's face looked blood-pulsed, flush from the search. But his eyes crinkle up with delight. Sunup, sundown, Fitzgibbons follows the same routine. Surprise is a rare and precious feeling on the farm.

'How do you like that, angel? We've never had a runaway before...'

'But where did he run to, Uncle Fitzy?'

Fitzgibbons grins down at her. 'I don't know.'

Fitzgibbons doesn't seem at all put out by the loss. Something about the way that he squints into the green mist beyond the Fence makes Rutherford think that Fitzgibbons is rooting for Garfield's escape.

'Do you think that Garfield will return?' James Buchanan asks now, looking nervous. 'Because he must return, for the good of the Barn. We elected Garfield to represent the mallards. Who is going to speak out on behalf of the mallards at our next Convention? You can't just shirk a duty like that. You can't just abandon your post!'

Apparently, you can, thinks Rutherford. The other presidents all stare at the waves in the air in James Garfield's stall.

The next incumbent

The following morning, Fitzgibbons comes in early to clean out Garfield's stall. The Barn buzzes with speculation about the next president to join the ranks. Millard Fillmore is nervous enough for all of them. 'Do you think he will be an agreeable sort of man? Do you think he will be a Republican? Why, what if he's just a regular stud horse, and not a president at all...?'

Nobody answers him. Every man is scheming in the privacy of his own horse-body. Andrew Jackson, a stocky black quarter-horse stabled next to Rutherford, can barely contain his ambitions in his deep ribs. You can feel his human cunning quiver from the fetlock up. 'Whoever the newcomer is, I will defeat him,' he says. Jackson has been lonely for an adversary. Every spring he runs uncontested for the office of Spokeshorse of the Western Territories. Many of the presidents have sworn themselves in to similarly foolish titles: Governor of the Cow Pastures, Commanding General of the Standing Chickens. They reminisce about their political opponents like old lovers. There's a creeping emptiness to winning an office that nobody else is seeking.

At noon, Fitzgibbons leads the new soul in. He's a thoroughbred with four white socks and a cranberry tint to his mane. Buchanan recognizes him right away: 'John Adams!'

Adams lets out a whinny so raw with relief that it dislodges sleeping bats from the rafters: 'You know me!' Adams woke up just yesterday, in the dark, close trailer that he assumed was a roomy coffin. 'Excepting that I could see sunshine through the slats,' he says in a voice still striped with fear. He seems grateful when Buchanan gives him a friendly bite on the shoulder.

'Are we dead?'

Ten horses nod their heads.

'Is this heaven?'

It's an awkward question. Ears flatten; nostrils dilate as wide as a man's fist. Rutherford unleashes a warm, diplomatic sneeze to ease the tension.

'That depends,' shrugs Ulysses. A series of bleary, battle-weary lines cross-hatch his black nose. 'Do you want this to be heaven? Does this look like heaven to you?'

Adams studies the dark whorls of mildew, the frizz of lofted hay, his own hooves. He goes stiff in the ears, considering. 'That also depends. Is Jefferson here?'

Jefferson is not. There are many absences in the Barn of unknown significance: George Washington, Lincoln, Nixon, Harrison. The presidents haven't arrived in the order of their deaths, either. Woodrow Wilson got here before Andrew Jackson, and Eisenhower has been here since the beginning.

'But we can't live out our afterlives as common beasts!' Adams's eyes shine with horror. 'There must be some way back to Washington! I am still alive, and I am certainly no horse.'

There is always this period of denial when new presidents first arrive in the Barn. Eisenhower still refuses to own up to his own mane and tail. 'I'm not dead, either, John Adams,' Eisenhower says. 'I'm just incognito. The Secret Service must have found some way to hide me here, until such a time as I can return to my body and resume governance of this country. I can't speak for the rest of you, but I'm no horse.'

'I'm no horse!' Andrew Jackson mimics. He butts Eisenhower with the flat of his head. 'What the Christ are you, then?'

'The thirty-fourth President of the United States.' Eisenhower shakes burrs from his tail in a thorny maelstrom.

Adams is rolling his eyes around the Barn, on the verge of rearing. His gums go purple: 'Gentlemen, we must get out of here! Help me out of this body!' By the looks of things, Adams will be a stall-kicker. He kicks again and again, until splinters go flying. 'We need to alert our constituents to what has befallen us. Gentlemen, rally! What's keeping us here? The doors to the Barn stand wide open.'

'Rutherford,' says Ulysses. He stands sixteen hands high and retains his general's authority. 'Why don't you show our good fellow Adams the Fence?'

The fence

Rutherford and Adams trot out of the dark Barn into a light silvery rain. The fence wood is rotted with age, braided through with wild weeds. Each sharpened post rises a level four feet tall, midway up the horses' thick chests. Fitzgibbons put it up to discourage the fat blue geese from flight.

'This is the Fence? This is what keeps us prisoners here? Why, I could jump it this moment!'

Rutherford regards Adams sadly. 'Go ahead, then. Give it a try.'

Adams charges the Fence. His forelegs lift clean off the ground as he runs. At the last second, he groans and turns sharply to the left. It looks as if he is shying away from an invisible wall. He shakes his small head, stamps and whinnies, and charges again. Again he is repelled by some invisible thicket of fear. Sweat glistens on his dark coat.

'Blast, what is it?' Adams cries. 'Why can't I jump it?'

'We don't know.' The presidents have tried and failed to get over the Fence every day of their new lives. Rutherford thinks it's an ophthalmological problem. A sharp dark corner in the mind that forces a sharp turn.

'How did James Garfield manage it? And where did he run to?'

Garfield's hoofprints disappear at the edge of the paddock. The fence posts point at the blue sky. Adams and Rutherford stare at the trackless black mud on the other side of the Fence. There are two deep crescents where Garfield began the jump, and then nothing. It's as if Garfield vanished into the cool morning air.

'Good question.'

Animal memories and past administrations

Woodrow Wilson is giving speeches in his sleep again: *Ah, ah, these are very serious and pregnant questions,* Woodrow mumbles, his voice thick with an old nightmare. *Upon the answer to them depends the peace of the world.*

Poor Wilson, Rutherford thinks, watching as he addresses the questions of a phantom nation. Wilson paws at the stall floor as he dreams, his lips still moving. The world is drafting new questions, new answers, without him.

In his own dreams, Rutherford never returns to the White House.

Instead his memory takes him back to his Ohio home of Spiegel Grove, back to the rainy morning of his death. Unlike the other presidents, Rutherford's dreams find him paralyzed, powerless. He remembers watching the moisture pearl on his bedroom window, the crows lining the curved white rail of his veranda. Lucy's half of the huge pine bed had been empty for years. In the end, divested of all decisions, there was only an old thick-waisted nurse opening his mouth, filling it with tastes, urging him to swallow. Boyhood tastes, blood-pumpkin stew and sugared beets. His son and his youngest daughter were two smudges above the bedside. The boy quietly endeavoured to blink goodbye. Then Rutherford's throat began to close, shutting him off from all words, and he felt himself filling with silence. The silence was a field of cotton growing white and forever inside him. Rutherford wasn't afraid to die. My Lucy, he remembers thinking, will be waiting for me on the other side.

The first first lady

Lucy Webb Hayes was the first president's wife to be referred to as a First Lady. Nobody besides Rutherford and a few balding White House archivists remembers her. Rutherford wishes that he was still a man and that she was still a Lady. He wishes that he had a hand to put on her waist. 'Lucy?' he hisses at a passing mallard. 'Lucy Webb?' Women revert to their maiden names in Heaven, Rutherford feels fairly certain. He can't remember where he learned this—France or the Bible.

'Lucy Webb!'

The duck goes clucking away from him, raising the green tips of its wings in alarm. When Rutherford looks up, Fitzgibbons and the girl are standing at the edge of the pasture, looking at him strangely. 'Uncle Fitzy? Does it sound like that horsie is *quacking* to you?' Rutherford and Fitzgibbons stare at each other for a long moment.

'You know, Sarge *has* been acting up lately. All of the horses have been behaving mighty queer. Worms, maybe. We ought to get the vet out here. We ought to get them some of those hydrangea shots.'

After Fitzgibbons and the girl disappear behind the house, Rutherford continues on his quest to find the soul of his wife. There is a sheep that Rutherford has noticed grazing on the north pasture, slightly apart from the others. The sheep perks up when Rutherford trots over. It might be his imagination, but he thinks he sees a fleck of recognition, ice-blue, floating in her misty iris.

'President Wilson?' Rutherford nudges him excitedly. 'Could I trouble you to take a look at one of the ewes?' Rutherford has heard that Woodrow Wilson grazed sheep on the South Lawn. He hopes that Woodrow will be able to confirm his suspicion.

'Your wife, you say?' Wilson exchanges glances with the other horses. 'Well, I will gladly take a look, President Hayes.' His voice is pleasant enough, but his ears peak up into derisive triangles. Rutherford's shame grows with each hoof-fall. The closer they get to the sheep pasture, the more preposterous his hope begins to seem. His trot hastens into a canter until Woodrow is breathless, struggling to keep pace with him. 'Slow down, man,' he grumbles. They stand in the rain and stare at the sheep. She's taking placid bites of grass, ignoring the downpour. Her white fleece is pasted to her side. 'Uh-oh,' says Woodrow. 'Hate to break it to you, but I think that's just your standard sheep. Not, er, not a First Lady, no.'

'Her eyes, though...'

'Yes, I see what you mean. Cataracts. Unfortunate.'

Rutherford thanks him for his assessment.

'President Hayes?' Eisenhower is smirking at them from across the field. 'Pardon, am I interrupting something? The other presidents have all gathered behind the bunny hutch. You are late again, sir.' Rutherford straightens abruptly, his cowlick flopping into the black saucers of his eyes. He takes an instinctual step in front of sheep-Lucy to shield her from Eisenhower's purple sneer.

'Late for what? Not another caucus on that apple tax.'

'We voted that into law two weeks ago, Rutherford,' Eisenhower sighs. 'Tonight it's the Adams' referendum. On the proposed return to Washington? We are leaving in three days' time.'

Washington or oblivion

Secret deals get brokered behind the Barn, just north of the red sloop of the bunny hutch. A number of the presidents are planning their escape for a day they are calling the Fourth of July.

'The country is drowning in sorrow,' Adams snorts. It's high summer. Oats fall around him like float-down snow. 'Our country needs us.'

After several months of nickered rhetoric, Adams has convinced a half dozen of the former presidents to be his running mates in a charge on Washington. Whig, Federalist, Democrat, Republican—Adams urges his fellow horses to put aside these partisan politics and join him in the push for liberty. He wants the world to know that they have returned. 'It is obvious, gentlemen: of course we're meant to lead again. It is the only thing that makes sense. What other purpose could we have been reborn for? What other—'

Adams is interrupted by a storm of hiccups. Behind him, Fitzgibbons is hitching Harding to a child-sized wagon. He helps the girl into the wooden wagon bed. Fitzgibbons grins as he hands the child the reins, avuncular and unconcerned, his big arms crossed against his suspendered chest.

'And tell me,' Rutherford asks quietly, 'tell me, what evidence do you have that the country needs us to lead again? They seem to be getting on just fine without us.'

Now Harding is pulling the girl in miserable rectangles around the bare dirt yard, hiccupping madly. '*This*—hiccup!—*is*—hiccup!—*Hell*.' The girl waves a dandelion at him like a wilted yellow sceptre. 'Giddy-up, horsie!' she laughs.

Aside from Rutherford and Harding, the other presidents are in ecstasies. 'Surely the term limits of the Twenty-Second Amendment won't apply to me any more. This rebirth is the loophole that will let me run again, Rutherford.' Eisenhower grins for some invisible camera, exposing his huge buck teeth. 'And win.'

Oh *dear*, thinks Rutherford. That smile is not going to play well on the campaign trail.

'With all due respect, sir, I fear you might be seeking the wrong office? I think there are some, er, obstacles to your run that you perhaps haven't considered?'

'Obstacles?' A fly buzzes drowsily between them and lands on one trembling whisker. 'Now, give me some credit, Rutherford. I've put a lot of thought into this. Let me outline my campaign strategy for you...' Eisenhower has made this speech before.

'And what about you, Rutherford? What are you, a stallion incumbent or a spineless nag?'

Rutherford blinks slowly and doesn't answer Eisenhower. Both options are depressing. He doesn't want to return to Washington, if there even is a Washington. He just wants a baaa of recognition out of this one ewe.

'Neither. I'm not going anywhere. I'm not leaving my wife.'

'Baaa!' says the sheep. She is standing right behind him. Her head is a black triangle floating on the huge cloud of her body. Rutherford has been training the sheep who might be Lucy to follow him. He holds his own supper in his mouth and then drops clumps of millet and wet apple cores to coax her forwards. 'Come on, sweet Lucy, let's go back to the Barn.'

The other presidents mock him openly, their ears pivoting with laughter. The sheep trails him like a pet delusion. *Or like a wife who hasn't woken up to the fact of our love yet!* Rutherford tells himself, tempting her with another chewed-up apple. White apples stud the slick grass behind him. The sheep that might be his wife follows him into the Barn, blinking her long lashes like a deranged starlet.

Dirt memoirs

The girl comes again later that evening with a curry comb and six leafy carrots. Her arrival causes riotous stirring in the Barn.

'Does the child have her book bag?' Buchanan inches forwards in his stall and cranes his neck, trying to see around the child's narrow back.

'Yes!' Adams crows. 'To arms, gentlemen!'

The horses have been trying to get hold of the girl's school books for some time. Every president wants to find out how history regards him. Fitzgibbons is no help; he is maddeningly apolitical. He'll spend hours musing out loud about fertilizer or the toughness of bean hulls. But Fitzgibbons never complains about property taxes. He never mentions a treaty or a war. He seems curiously removed from the issues of his day.

'Get her book bag,' Eisenhower hisses. There's something sinister about the angle at which his lips curl over his rubbery gums. The girl's school bag is leaning against the Barn door frame.

Van Buren tries to hypnotize the child by rhythmically swishing his tail. 'Look over here, girlie! Swish! Swish!' He shakes his head from side to side. Eisenhower steps gingerly into the looped strap of the child's bag and drags it with his foreleg. He has it almost to the edge of his stall before she notices.

'Uncle Fitzy!' the girl yells. 'Gingersnap is being bad!' Eisenhower hates it when she calls him Gingersnap. He complains about it with a statesman's pomp: 'Gentlemen, there exists no more odious appellation than…'—nose crumpling, black lips curling—'Gingersnap.'

The girl walks forwards and snatches her book bag back, but not before Eisenhower has shaken it upside-down and kicked several of the books under a clump of hay. 'Hurry,' he hisses, 'before Fitzgibbons comes with the whip!'

The presidents crowd around the books. Literature, mathematics, science, cursive. No history book. The Cursive book has fallen open to a page thick with hundreds of lowercase *b*s. Eisenhower sends the books flying with a swift kick from his right foreleg, disgusted. 'Every subject but American history! What has become of our education system? What are they teaching children in schools these days?!' It's an urgent question. What *are* they teaching children these days? And how is each president remembered? That's the afterlife the presidents are interested in. Not this anonymous, fly-swatting limbo.

James Buchanan is busy rewriting his memoirs, *Mr Buchanan's Administration on the Eve of the Rebellion*. He is furious that none of the other presidents ever read the original while they were alive. 'Yeah, about that,' coughs Harding. 'Pretty sure that's out of print.'

It's a laboured process. Equine anatomy severely limits the kinds of letters the presidents can straight-leg into the dirt. Buchanan can draw an *H*, an *F*, an *E*, an *A*, a *T*, an *I*, an *X* with the meticulous action of his right hoof. *Z*, once you get the hang of it, is also quite easy. *O*s and *U*s and *S*s are impossible. *K*s and *W*s leave him shuddery and spent. Buchanan never questions his own record of the past; commas are tough enough, and he would have to break his leg to make a question mark. He is just now putting the finishing touches to Chapter Four. 'Voila, gentlemen! And now I will add a final paragraph of summation and then on to chapter…*oh no!*' Fitzgibbons rolls one of his red fleet of tractors over Buchanan's sod parchment, erasing even the prologue.

Rutherford used to believe it was the civic duty of every elected official to preserve a full record of his administration. While in office, he was a compulsive memoirist who filled dozens of journals with his painstaking school-boy script. But now he has only a single use for the human alphabet. He hoofs messages in the rich loam behind the coop, too, but they are for one woman instead of posterity. *LL-L-L* he writes, by which he means, *Lucy*.

Hunger and restraint

Rutherford is losing weight. He keeps the sheep near him all the time now, crooning to her through closed gums: 'Lucy, Lucy, give me your answer do. I'm half-crazy...'

'Pipe down, Rutherford,' snaps Harding. 'Stop giving that sheep your food, you idiot. You will starve to death if you keep it up.'

Rutherford ignores the other presidents and kneels next to the sheep. He smiles at the blue fleck of evidence that his wife is hiding somewhere inside this fleecy body. *I know you*, he whispers. He lets a brown apple plop into the sawdust between them. The sheep eats it with gusto, and Rutherford hopes this means his love is requited.

In the morning, Fitzgibbons yelps when he discovers the sheep in the stall with Rutherford. 'Sarge!' Fitzgibbons smacks a palm against his bald head. 'What in the hell are you doing with that blind ewe? That is spooky, Sarge. That is goddamn unnatural. You feeling sick, Sarge? You get into some rat poison or something?' Fitzgibbons approaches Rutherford with the oiled halter. 'Come along now,' he grunts. 'Open up...' He jostles a carrot around Rutherford's stubbornly pursed lips. A second later, the carrot has disappeared and Fitzgibbons is cursing and hopping on one foot. 'Jesus!' he growls. 'Sarge, you old fleabag, you bit me!'

I am becoming very clever at getting the carrot without opening up for the bit, Rutherford thinks. He keeps the carrot in a pouch in his cheek, a gift for Lucy. *At the games of hunger and restraint, my fellow countrymen, I am becoming excellent.*

Campaign promises

In the yard, the other presidents are still hungry for power. They are practising for the return to Washington. Adams is so starved for dominion that he begs the girl to allow him to represent her interests to her uncle Fitzgibbons. 'Elect me to take part in the public life of your Barn, young lady, and I shall act a fearless, intrepid, undaunted part, at all hazards...'

'Ha-ha, Mister Pretty, you are so noisy today!' The girl hums a nonsense tune as she plaits Adams' tail with geraniums.

Martin Van Buren is barn sour, but even he shouts out impossible promises at the turkeys from the dim interior of his stall: 'You are my constituents, my turkeys,' Van Buren neighs, 'and the love I feel for you is forever.' The turkeys promenade around the yard and ignore him. Rutherford wonders if they, too, have human biographies hidden beneath their black feathers. The presidents spend a lot of time talking about where the other citizens of the Union might have ended up. Wilson thinks the suffragettes probably came back as kicky rabbits.

'I don't understand,' Rutherford says. 'Don't you gentlemen realize that you are stumping for nothing? What sort of power could you hope to achieve out here?'

Rutherford was ready for his term to be over. He was happy to keep his promise not to run for re-election. He had been a reluctant incumbent in the first place, unwilling to leave his war post to take a furlough for the stump. Mark Twain campaigned for him, and still he never expected to win. Rutherford never knew a generous margin in the whole of his life. His victory was the most disputed in American history. A single electoral vote would have given the Presidency to Samuel J. Tilden. 'It was a squeaker,' Eisenhower nods. 'I remember studying it in school.' Often, Rutherford wonders what would have happened if Tilden had won. He wonders if he has unjustly displaced Tilden from this stall in the blank country-sun of the after-life.

If we could just reach a consensus that this *is* heaven, Rutherford snorts, we could submit to it, the joy of wind and canter and the stubbed ashy sweetness of trough carrots, burnished moons, crushing the secret smells out of grass. I would be free to gallop. The only heaven that Rutherford has known in the Barn comes in single moments: a warm palm on his nose, fresh hay, a tiny feast of green thistle made nearly invisible by the sun. At dawn, heaven is a feeling that comes when the wind sweeps the fields. Heaven is this wind Rutherford knows for an instant, bending a million yellow heads of wheat.

By nightfall, though, the wheat has straightened and the whole notion of an afterlife strikes Rutherford as preposterous. 'All these arguments are nonsense,' he confides to Lucy. 'We are all still alive. This is still America. The stars look the same,' he continues, 'and we are fed. We are here.'

Shorn

One afternoon, the sheep is not waiting for him in his stall.

'Rutherford,' Jackson sniggers from the pasture, 'take a gander at this. Looks like Fitzgibbons is doing something very untoward to your wife.'

Fitzgibbons is kneeling in the centre of the field, shearing the sheep that might be Lucy. Wool flies up and parachutes down in the sun. Fitzgibbons razors off first one clump of fleece and then another, until the sheep is standing shorn and pink before him. All of a sudden Rutherford's body feels too heavy for his coltish knees. He stares at the growing pile of fleece, heart pounding, and for a crazy moment Rutherford thinks that he can still salvage what's left of his Lucy. Perhaps there's some way to put this wool back on the sheep's body, to cover her up again? He paws frantically at the white curls with his hoof.

The sheep rises up out of the green grass completely bald. Now the fleck in her eye looks bright and inhuman. Worse than meaningless, Rutherford thinks. A symptom of illness, cataracts, just like Woodrow first said. Rutherford hangs his head and keeps his eyes on the ugly dandelions. He swallows the grainy pear that he has been holding to feed the sheep with. 'That is not my wife.'

Independence day

On the eve of the other presidents' push for liberty, with a whistling nonchalance, Fitzgibbons leaves Rutherford's stall door open. The latch bangs in the wind, a sound like *open*, a song like *no accident*. Rutherford strolls through the doors into the dusk light.

'The Fence is just a wooden afterthought,' Rutherford thinks, coming as close to its rough posts as he dares. 'We're imprisoned already.' He can feel the walls of his new body expand and contract. Tonight it's not an altogether unpleasant sort of heaven to be trapped in. The stars are out, and for the first time in months Rutherford has swallowed his whole ration of grain at the trough. He can feel a forgotten strength pulsing through his body. It's our suspicion that there's another, better heaven behind the cumulus screen, he murmurs into the grass, bending and tearing at a root that tastes beautifully yellow. That's the trouble. That's what keeps us trapped here, minds in animals.

Rutherford begins to run, lightly at first. What am I, Rutherford wonders, a horse's body or a human mind? Both options are twining together like a rope, then fraying. They are disappearing, the faster he runs. The sound of his hoof beats doesn't trouble him now; it doesn't even register. They thud and they vanish. His tail is still attached to him at the root. But Rutherford isn't trying to outrun his horse tail any more. It sails out like a black flag behind him, its edges in tatters.

Rutherford turns and starts running again, and this time he finds that he cannot stop. The Fence is right in front of him now. It takes on a second life inside his mind, a thick grey barrier. His blood feels hot and electric inside him, and Rutherford knows from the certainty of his heartbeat that he is alive, that there isn't any 'after'. There is no reason to believe that anything better or greener waits on the other side of the Fence. There is nothing to prevent him from jumping it. There it is, Rutherford thinks, the blue lick of lightning. His eyes still refuse to focus, but now he finds that he is no longer afraid of the blind spot. *This is for the Union*, Rutherford whinnies, and suddenly he stops worrying about cause and effect, about the impossibility that his hoof beats could hold any Union together, or why any of this should matter, one horse running in an empty field: none of his speed, none of his grandeur, no droplets of sweat streaming off his hide like wings, and he runs. And nobody is watching when he clears the Fence. □

GRANTA

MOTHER AND SON

Akhil Sharma

Akhil Sharma was born in Delhi, India in 1971. As an eight-year-old, he migrated to the United States with his family. He is the author of various short stories and one novel, 'An Obedient Father', published by Faber & Faber in the UK and by Farrar, Straus & Giroux in the US. Asked what his greatest fear was, Sharma said that he is afraid of ghosts. 'I don't like to leave the house after it gets dark. People don't understand the danger they put themselves in when they go out at night.' He lives in New York City with his wife, Lisa. 'Mother and Son' is taken from a novel-in-progress to be published by W. W. Norton.

In my family, nobody was especially mature. My mother, whom I loved very much and who had a kind heart, was a little bit like a child in that she was excitable and talkative and somewhat vain. I remember that when my brother and I were children and we still lived in India, my mother would sit at our dining table on Sunday afternoons and have my brother and me search her head for white hairs. Birju, my brother, was around twelve then and, in the irritated, put-upon way he had, he would warn, 'One day I will pull out your last hair and then you will be bald.'

We left India in 1979, when I was eight. During the days before our departure, my mother, because she couldn't help herself, dressed me and my brother in new clothes so that people would see us and think about our luck.

I liked America immediately. Among the things I liked most was the television show *The Love Boat*. I had never seen women in bikinis before. I also liked elevators. Elevators were rare in India and to me there was something thrilling about how my pressing a button meant the elevator would shut its doors and pull itself up floor by floor.

My brother Birju also liked America. 'America is so clean,' he said. 'In India if anybody sees a clean spot, he thinks, let me spit there before somebody else gets a chance.' Birju had a long face with a round fat chin and he was someone who could say a bad thing about almost any topic. Like my mother, though, Birju was kind. There was an Indian boy from Trinidad whom Birju got to know and Birju used to worry about him because the boy did not work hard and get good grades. 'He is not from a good family,' he used to explain to my mother. 'He doesn't know that you work now so you can work less hard later.'

In America we lived in Queens, New York. My father had come a year ahead of the rest of us and gotten an apartment and a job. My father was not much of a talker and he was the type of person who believed that no matter what one did, things would end badly. But he too liked America. What he liked most about America was money. 'In India you can work as hard as you want, but it's who you know that matters.' He would say this and sigh in a disappointed way that suggested great satisfaction.

'How do you know?' my mother sometimes asked. 'When did you work hard?'

During our early days in America, many things made no sense. We had never heard of hot dogs before and, after our first day of school, my brother and I came home and told my mother that we had seen children eating dogs. My mother and I and Birju sat at a round table in our kitchen alcove and discussed this. My mother thought eating meat was disgusting and she imagined meat eaters as depraved creatures capable of consuming anything. We three debated what part of a dog a hot dog could be made from. We talked about what a hot dog looked like and eventually decided they must be made from tails.

Birju got good grades in India and he did well in his classes in America. At the end of seventh grade he was ranked first. Near the end of eighth grade he took an exam to get into the Bronx High School of Science. This is very hard to get into and the exam was held in a large school made of brown bricks. My mother, my father and I all went with Birju on the day of the exam. It was a warm spring morning and we waited for him on a sidewalk outside the school. I remember that there was a high chain-link fence that separated the sidewalk from a basketball court that belonged to the school.

Birju got into the Bronx High School of Science and that summer we went to Arlington, Virginia, to spend our vacation with my father's older sister. We had done this the previous summer also and, like last time, we spent our days lying on the sofa watching television or going to the swimming pool of a nearby apartment building. One afternoon, Birju went to the pool and dived in and hit his head on the pool's cement bottom. He became unconscious and he remained underwater for three minutes.

When I first heard what had happened, I didn't really understand. I was lying on the sofa in the living room watching television. The phone rang and then soon after my aunt came in and stood beside me. My aunt was short and had white hair. 'Birju has had an accident,' she said. My aunt was probably five feet tall and had a wrinkled face but she had dentures that gave her oddly young teeth. 'Birju's been taken to the hospital. I have to go to the hospital.' She said this and looked worried. I didn't know what my aunt meant. Perhaps Birju had had to go to the hospital to get an injection.

My cousin Naveen was in the house. He was twenty-two and he

had a round face and a shy smile that often made him look like he wanted to please. He came and sat beside me on the sofa. At first we kept the television off because it seemed bad manners to watch TV when something serious might have happened. Then we got bored and turned the TV on again.

My mother and I walked into Birju's hospital room. The room had white walls and I was holding the black duffel bag my mother had brought with her on the bus from New York. We came into the room and stopped just past the door. 'Don't think I don't blame you, Birju,' my mother shouted. 'Don't think I don't think this is all your fault.' My mother was wearing a yellow sari and the skin beneath her eyes appeared singed and her mouth was twisted open. 'What was at the bottom of the pool? Was there gold? Was there treasure that you had to jump in before anybody else got to it?' My mother and I walked further into the room.

Birju was in a bed with railings. His eyes were wide open and almost panicked and he had a clear plastic mask over his nose and lips like fighter pilots wear in thin air. My mother took hold of the railings and, leaning over, said, 'Look what you've done. Do you understand what you've done?' My mother started sobbing and this scared me. To me Birju looked like he was staring up at some invisible thing and that thing was pressing down on his chest. I wondered whether the gas coming from the mask was what was keeping Birju still. I wondered whether, if the mask were removed, Birju would start talking.

My aunt and uncle were also in the room. They had been sitting before a dark window when we came in and they were now standing. My aunt walked towards us, swaying from side to side because of her arthritic knees. 'God is there,' she said, coming up to my mother. The top of her head reached my mother's shoulder. 'God is always there.'

My mother began sobbing even more loudly. I held the black duffel before me with both hands. Doing this made me feel like I was helping.

My mother leaned over the railings. 'Don't worry,' she said. 'I am here. If a doctor doesn't act nice to you, I'll slap him twice and ask him his name. If a nurse looks at you bad, I'll tear her hair out.'

My aunt put her arm around my mother. 'We should go home,' she said. 'There is an operation in the morning.'

It was a little after one in the morning when we left. I had never been up so late.

My brother and I had lived in a small room with a blue carpet and white walls. There was no furniture in the room and that first night my mother and my aunt built an altar in one corner of the room.

They brought a large cardboard box from the basement and covered it with a white sheet so that it was almost like a table. Then they taped postcards of various gods to the wall behind the altar, and on the altar itself they placed a spoon and in the spoon's scoop a wick soaked in butter. All night my aunt and mother prayed before the altar. They kneeled or lay face down on the floor and sang and talked to God.

I slept in the room as they prayed. The lights were turned off and I slept on a sheet of foam with my back to the altar. Periodically I woke from the voices and saw the smoke's shadows rippling over the walls. Once, I got irritated and thought that though it was proper to pray for Birju he would be all right and it would be better to be quiet and sleep.

In the morning, when we got to Birju's hospital room, his bed was empty. He had already been taken for his operation. My aunt, my mother and I sat on chairs along the empty hospital bed and sang prayers. Without thinking about it, like how you automatically run faster and faster when you are going downhill, we began singing more and more loudly.

A few days later there was another operation, this time for a clot in Birju's brain, perhaps from where he had hit his head against the pool's cement bottom. Then, a week after, there was one more operation, this time to put a rubber tube into Birju's stomach. The tube was a waxy yellow and it went in just below his right ribs. Normally the tube lay coiled and rubber-banded against his side but every few hours a nurse would come and feed Birju. She would remove the rubber band and hold the tube up in the air so it was its full two feet and insert a plastic syringe in the tube's mouth so that she could pour a can of Isocal formula into the syringe. I remember that when I first saw the tube it seemed impossible and eerie, like there was a tulip growing out of Birju's side.

Each day, every day, we went and prayed by Birju in his hospital room. First my aunt came along with us to Birju's room and then it was just me and my mother. My mother and I would sit by Birju's bed and read aloud from the *Ramayana* and sing. At night during the first few weeks, my mother got up every hour on the hour to pray before the altar. Then she stopped doing this and instead began fasting on Tuesdays and Fridays.

Before Birju's accident, I had believed in God but never thought much about him. I had known that God existed and imagined him as being like the sky in that he watched everybody and everything but was not actually useful in a practical manner. Now, as we prayed first thing in the morning and even at night when we woke for some reason, God began to seem like a person. He began to seem like a person who was far away. I started imagining that God must be like the president, very busy, difficult to get attention from, and probably hard to convince that he should change his mind.

Summer ended. School started. In the morning it was cold enough for jeans but by afternoon it was warm again. Often I thought about how Birju was not getting to go to the Bronx High School of Science and this used to make me very sad for him.

Right after the accident, we had only been able to pray in ordinary ways. With time, though, my mother was able to write letters to her parents and ask them to feed Brahmins or drive a nail into a wish-granting tree on Birju's behalf. Some friend of my mother whom she had not heard from in years learned of Birju and sent us ashes from a fire that had been part of a great religious ceremony. The ashes came in a little plastic bag and my mother put them in a satchel and tied the satchel around Birju's neck. I too wanted to do something like this.

On the way to school, there was an oak tree that stood half on the sidewalk and half on the road. Somehow I began to feel that it might help Birju if, whenever I passed the tree, I touched it five times and after each touch brought my hand to my forehead. I would do this and feel embarrassed at the possibility of being seen and would also wonder if maybe God minded my showing respect to a tree. I asked God about this.

God said, 'I don't care. I don't get caught up in such small things.'

'Really I want to show you respect,' I said. 'The tree is just a way of praying.'

'People are strange,' God said. 'People will worship anything.'

He said this and laughed and shook his head. God looked like the Marlboro Man. It was night and I was lying on my foam sheet and God was sitting cross-legged beside me, wearing jeans and a cowboy hat that shadowed his face. 'I know what's in people's hearts,' he said.

Because I didn't know how pure my heart was, I became nervous. 'Good, you know I love you.'

'I know everything,' God said, and this felt like a warning.

I didn't answer and stretched my legs. Usually when God and I talked, I would begin by acting humble and telling God how much I loved him. Then, after some time had passed, I would start trying to move the conversation to what I wanted to discuss most, which was what God was going to give me to make up for Birju's accident.

I remained silent until it seemed okay to change topics. After a minute or two I asked, 'How famous will I be?'

'I can't tell you the future.'

'Why not?'

'Because I might change my mind.'

'But if you tell me something will happen, then it might be harder for you to decide something else.'

God laughed again and I was glad I had pleased him.

Originally God and I had begun negotiating my future fame because I had felt that as long as God and I were doing this he couldn't make a final decision on Birju. After some time, though, I had just begun enjoying talking about myself.

'So tell me,' I said, 'how famous will I be?'

'Don't worry. You'll be so famous that fame will be a problem.'

I liked hearing this. I tried not to smile. 'I need to be rich too,' I said. 'I need money for Mummy and Daddy, and if you want to keep Birju sick, then I need money for doctors.'

'You are very responsible.'

'I can't help it,' I said. 'Some people aren't responsible at all but I am. It's because I was raised properly.'

'Don't worry. You can hardly imagine the life ahead.'

And suddenly, just like that, I became frightened. These sudden frights used to happen often and now, even though God's voice had promised something wonderful, the idea of the future scared me and I opened my eyes.

The only light was the glow coming through the window. I was lying with a blanket pulled up to my neck and my mother was sleeping nearby, snoring slightly. Outside I heard a car go by and I imagined Birju in his bed in the hospital. Sometimes the nurses forgot to turn the lights off in his room and he lay there all night with the fluorescent lights buzzing and blinking.

It was not that I did not understand the seriousness of what had happened to Birju. It was just that I believed in my own luck; that in the end God would have to protect me.

One thing I knew about God was that he was more likely to help good people than he was to help the wicked or the ordinary. It was important therefore to be very good.

My mother used to get angry and say mean things. Every afternoon when school ended, my cousin Naveen would pick me up and drive me to the hospital. There, in Birju's hospital room, my mother once said, 'Nobody can stand seeing an unlucky face. That's why your aunt wants you here instead of letting you stay at home.'

'No. Buaji loves me,' I immediately said, and felt proud for being virtuous. 'Naveen loves me. They just know you should have company.'

Whenever my mother said something bad and I said something good in response, I felt as if I had prayed, as if I had done a little bit of work.

I was being good myself and one other thing that made me hopeful about Birju was how my father had changed.

My father used to make me nervous. My father often ignored me and this was good and he did things that were strange and that my mother made fun of, things like going often to doctors and asking for his blood or urine to be tested or like bringing home brown-paper napkins from his cafeteria at work so we would not have to pay for napkins ourselves. But my father could also be mean and he was like Birju in that it seemed easy for him to say bad things. Now, though, my father seemed a different person. It was like he had decided he could no longer be himself and he had decided to become someone completely different.

My father was short and stocky with close-cropped hair and sometimes I could see him deciding to be this different person. Naveen and I used to go meet him at the bus station on Friday nights, when he would arrive from Queens. Often he would come through the swinging doors into the waiting room and his face would be grim and then he would see us and his lips would twist into a wide, thin smile. This smile, fixed and sometimes straight and not even curving up at the ends, would remain on his face all weekend long, and while before he might have been impatient and irritable, now he joked and tried to make my mother calm.

There was a nurse who did not like us. I am not sure why, but this woman, Irene, a heavy woman with curly white hair, used to say that our insurance paid too little money and that it was people like us who caused hospitals to close. 'Every place has a snake,' my father sometimes said, and shrugged his shoulders like this was nothing to be excited about. Also when Irene was in Birju's hospital room, my father would stand behind her and start flicking his tongue in and out like he was a snake.

My father behaving so nicely surprised me and it seemed worth pointing out to God. I tried mentioning it before the altar every morning during my prayers. I would be kneeling and my mother would be putting on a sweatshirt over her sari as she prepared to go to the hospital and I would say, 'Isn't it amazing how much Daddy has changed? It is like he has taken a knife and cut all the bad parts out from inside himself and thrown them away.'

I used to say all this before the altar because to me the altar was like an open microphone that broadcast whatever was said in front of it to wherever God might be in the universe.

Time kept passing, though. There was a day in November when it rained very hard and the trees lost all their leaves at once. Then Thanksgiving came and I thought, soon it will be Christmas and after that there will be New Year and in the coming year there won't have been a single day in which Birju had walked or talked.

'Are things getting worse?' I asked. It was night and I was lying on my mattress and God was sitting beside me, smoking a cigarette.

'What do you think?'

'They seem to be.' God nodded, sighed. 'At least the insurance company is paying the bills.'

'Yes.'

Because of the cowboy hat, it wasn't possible to see God's face. God said, 'You need to think of the good as well as the bad.'

'I know.'

'Your father is behaving well. He has become a good man because of the accident.'

I had not meant to ask this but I said, 'Why don't you make Birju better?'

God ignored the question. 'There is some good in everything that happens.'

'What are three minutes to you?' I asked. 'Just get rid of the three minutes Birju was in the pool.'

God sighed.

'Three minutes,' I said.

'Presidents die in less time than that. Planes crash in less time than that.'

I didn't speak.

'I can't tell you what good things will come because of the accident.'

This was usually the time to start speaking of my future fame. I opened my eyes. My mother was on her side, a blanket pulled up to her neck. She looked like an ordinary woman. It surprised me that you couldn't tell, just by looking at her, that every day, from morning to evening, she sat in a hospital room beside a bed that held her brain-damaged son.

There were not many nursing homes which we could afford and which also took patients like Birju. In December a space in one of these finally opened. The nursing home was in New Jersey. We would be leaving Arlington. This frightened me. Leaving Arlington felt like we were giving up; it felt like we were accepting what had happened. I decided I had to pray; I decided I had to pray all the time.

Because Christmas season was a holy time, I thought prayers during this period would be especially potent. Now if I were at school and sitting at my desk and suddenly thought of God, I wouldn't worry about embarrassing myself and instead would close my eyes and ask God to help Birju. If I were watching television and thought of God, I would press my hands together before me and whisper, 'Hare Rama, Hare Krishna.' My mother wouldn't let me fast but I began throwing away my school lunch. I also tried holding my breath for a moment longer than necessary and asking God to give the unused breaths to Birju.

The more I prayed, though, the more saying God's names sounded strange. In the mornings, I would lie face down before the altar and pray, but as I prayed I felt like I was only acting.

We were going to be leaving Arlington in the first week of January and on Christmas Eve my mother asked the hospital chaplain to come to Birju's room and pray with us. My mother and I kneeled with him beside Birju's bed. Afterwards, the chaplain asked my mother whether she would be attending Christmas services. 'Of course, Father,' she said.

'I'm also coming,' I said.

The chaplain turned towards my father, who was sitting in a wheelchair with a book in his lap.

'I'll wait for God at home,' he said.

That night I lay on the sofa in the living room and watched *It's a Wonderful Life* on television. To me the movie meant that if you become unhappy enough, almost anything can pass as happiness.

The next morning, when I arrived at the hospital with my parents, Birju was asleep on his bed while a nurse stood nearby and gave him a feeding. The nurse was holding the waxy yellow tube in the air before her, a syringe in the tube's mouth and a can of Isocal milk in one hand. Seeing Birju asleep and the tube stretched to its full length, I felt something heavy in my chest.

That day I did not want to be far from my parents and so, instead of going to the lounge with its big television, I sat with a book in a corner of Birju's room. I sat there quietly but something felt wrong. My thoughts felt confused, like two sentences printed over each other, and periodically, for no reason, my heart would start racing.

It had been a cloudy morning and by afternoon the sky outside had grown dark. At some point my mother turned on the lights and not long after this I began crying. I tried to be quiet. I felt ashamed. I did not want my parents to notice my tears and think that I was

weeping for Birju, because in reality I was crying for having to move
to a new town and start in a new school.

My father was studying a thick red book in preparation for a civil-
service exam and my mother was making a list of things that my
father needed to buy for whatever apartment we moved to. I must
have been crying for several minutes when my father noticed.
'What's the matter, hero?'

'What happened?' my mother shouted. She sounded so panicked,
it was as if I were bleeding.

I didn't know what to say and so I said, 'I didn't get any Christmas
presents. I need a Christmas present. You didn't buy me a Christmas
present.' And then, because I had revealed my selfishness, I began
sobbing. 'You have to give me something. I should get something
for all this.' I wiped my face with my hands. 'Every day I come here,
I should get something.'

My mother came and pulled me out of my chair and pressed me
into her stomach. My father stood beside us. 'What do you want?'
he asked.

'What do you want?' my mother said.

I had no answer for this and the only thing I could think was, 'I
want to eat pizza and I want candy.'

My mother stroked my hair and called me her little baby. She kept
wiping my face with a fold of her sari. When I stopped crying, my
parents decided that my father should take me back to my aunt and
uncle's.

On the way, my father and I stopped at a mini-mall. It was a little
after five and the streetlights were on. First, my father and I went to
a magazine shop and there we bought a bag of 3 Musketeers bars
and a bag of Reese's Peanut Butter Cups. Then we went next door
to a pizza shop. The front of the shop was a glass wall and it was
misted over. My father and I sat in a booth wearing our winter coats.
Neither of us unzipped the coats as we ate. The pizzeria was staffed
by Chinese people. On the counter, near the cash register, was a small
television with a black VCR balanced on top. There were voices
coming from the TV that sounded like cats. The cashier, a round-faced
teenage girl, was watching the screen and smiling. Seeing her and her
happiness, I thought, 'There is something wrong with me. There is
something wrong inside my head.'	□

GRANTA

FROM THE DIARIES OF LENNY ABRAMOV

Gary Shteyngart

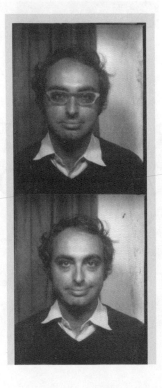

Gary Shteyngart was born in Leningrad in 1972 and came to the United States seven years later. He spent his first years in exile writing a satire of the Jewish Torah called 'The Gnorah', which received mixed reviews at his Hebrew primary school. He is also the author of the novels 'Absurdistan' (Granta/Random House) and 'The Russian Debutante's Handbook' (Bloomsbury/Riverhead). 'Absurdistan' was chosen as one of the ten best books of the year by the 'New York Times Book Review'. He first appeared in this magazine in Granta 78 with 'Several Anecdotes about My Wife'. He lives on New York's Lower East Side in an apartment building that 'sadly does not allow long-haired dachshunds'. 'From the Diaries of Lenny Abramov' is taken from a novel-in-progress.

June 1, Rome

Dearest Diary,

Today, I've made a major decision: *I am never going to die.*

Others will die around me. They will be nullified. Nothing of their personality will remain. The light switch will be turned off. Their lives, their entirety, will be marked by glossy marble headstones bearing utterly false summations ('her star shone brightly', 'never to be forgotten', 'he liked jazz'), and then these too will be lost in a coastal flood or get hacked to pieces by some kind of genetically modified future-turkey.

Nullified. All of them gone for ever. Don't let them tell you life's a journey. A journey is when you end up *some*where. When I take the number 6 train to see my pedicurist that's a journey.

But wait. There's more, isn't there? Our legacy. We don't die because our progeny lives on. The ritual passing of the DNA, momma's corkscrew curls, his granddaddy's lower lip, *ah buh-lieve duh chil'ren ah duh future.*[1] But what *ah duh chil'ren*? Lovely and fresh in their youth; blind to mortality; rolling around in the tall grass with those alabaster legs; fawns, sweet fawns all of them, gleaming in their dreamy plasticity, at one with the outwardly simple nature of their world.

And then a brief half-century later: drooling on some poor Mexican nursemaid in an Arizona hospice.

Nullified. Did you know that each peaceful, natural death at age seventy-seven[2] is a tragedy without compare? Did you know that there's a slaughter going on around us? Every day people, individuals, Americans if that makes it more urgent for you, fall face down on the battlefield, never to get up again. Never to exist again. These are

---

1. From 'The Greatest Love of All', by 1980s pop diva Whitney Houston, track nine of her eponymous first LP (Arista Records, 1985). Utter nonsense. The children are the future only in the most narrow, transitive sense. They are the future until they, too, perish. The song's next line encourages an adult's relinquishing of selfhood in favour of future generations. The phrase 'I live for my kids', for example, is tantamount to admitting that one will be dead shortly and that one's life, for all practical purposes, is already over. 'I'm gradually dying for my kids' would be more accurate.

2. The average life expectancy of an American woman born in the year 2000 is 77.6 years. Men, for all their violence, disregard and self-hatred, will meet their end three years sooner.

complex personalities, their cerebral cortices shimmering with floating worlds, universes that would have floored our sheep-herding, fig-eating, analogue ancestors. These folks are minor deities, vessels of love, life-givers, gods of the forge, unsung geniuses getting up at six-fifteen in the morning to fire up the coffeemaker, mouthing silent prayers that they will live to see the next day and the one after that and then Sarah's graduation and then...

Nullified.

But not me, dear Diary. Dear hazelnut-coloured, $1.99 retailing, five-star Mead personal notebook in which the Greatest Story Ever Told will be recorded and carefully annotated. Lucky Diary. Undeserving Diary.

I will live for ever. The technology is almost here. I just have to be good. I just have to stay off the trans-fats and the hooch. I just have to drink plenty of green tea and alkalinized water and submit my genome to the right people. I will need to regrow my liver, replace the entire circulatory system with 'smart blood'[3] and find some place safe and warm (but not too warm) to while away the angry seasons and the holocausts. And when the earth expires, as it surely must, I will leave it for a new earth, greener still but with fewer allergens; and in the flowering of my own intelligence some $10^{(32)}$ years hence when our universe decides to fold in on itself, my personality will jump through a black hole and surf into a dimension of unthinkable wonders, where the things that sustained me on Earth 1.0—*tagliatelle con ragù*, pistachio ice cream, the early works of the Velvet Underground, smooth, tanned skin pulled over the soft Baroque architecture of twenty-something buttocks—will seem as laughable and infantile as building blocks, baby formula, Simon says *do this*.

I am never going to die, *caro diario*. Never, never, never, never. And you can go to hell for doubting me.

Today's my last day in Rome. Pretty much the same as all the other days. Got up around eleven, *caffè macchiato* at the bar that has the best honey brioche, the neighbour's ten-year-old anti-American kid screaming at me from his window, 'No global! No way!', warm cotton towel of guilt around my neck for not getting any work done.

---

3. US Patent pending.

Yet another day of early summer wandering, the streets in charge of my destiny, holding me in their warm pink eternal embrace. Then the familiar dread of the late afternoon—prelude to evening, prelude to night-time, prelude to death. The crush of government workers, tall, balding men jumping in and out of dark-blue official Lancias, the city groaning under scaffolding, welcoming in Diesel and Miu Miu stores and yet more places where a limited-edition sneaker can be bought for over 200 euros. Everywhere, the business of a middle-class city. Everywhere, the march of time. And we all know where it's marching.

Evening came. Ended up where I always end up. By the single most beautiful building in Europe. The Pantheon. The rotunda's ideal proportions; the weight of the dome lifted above one's shoulders, suspended in air by icy mathematic precision; the oculus letting in the rain and the searing Roman sunlight; the coolness and shade that nonetheless prevail. Even the gaudy religious make-over (it is officially a church) and the inflated American visitors seeking shelter beneath the portico do nothing to diminish it. This is the most glorious grave marker to a race of men ever built. When I outlive the earth and depart from its familiar womb, I will take the memory of this building with me. I will encode it with zeros and ones and broadcast it across the universe. See what primitive man has wrought! Witness his first hankerings for immortality, his discipline, his selflessness.

But then, wandering out of the Pantheon past the flower sellers and the discarded fast-food wrappers, I felt scared.

Here amid the McDonald's-choked streets stood this tiny oasis of careful rationalism, and all around its perfect marble hulk were modern-day Italians fighting and cajoling, boys trying to stick it inside girls, mopeds humming beneath hairy legs, volumes of familiar, ancient emotions crashing like tidal waves through the building's echoing mass, multi-generational families bursting with pimply life. But it wasn't their life that I noticed. It was the intimation of death. The decline of civilization; its endpoint. And an image came to mind.

The facade of the New York Public Library cleaved into two, a growth of wild tropical trees choking its once grand lobby, empty windows, empty shelves, the heads of one of the famed lion statues pillaged, the other beast mostly missing, just one paw stubbornly

Gary Shteyngart

attached to the pedestal. A man approaches me. He is dressed in the remains of a T-shirt that reads OLLIE'S LI'L PIGGY HOUSE, FAYETTEVILLE, NC, his face bears no trace of civility, the forehead slopes and the eyes recede, he makes a sound from someplace in the back of his throat, from a muscle our species has never before used to communicate. 'Stop,' I say in English. 'Stop, friend.' And then, 'Wait, friend!' And then the appeal of the weak to the strong: 'Please, friend...' And then the conclusive: 'No!' It doesn't help. The flash of a dull blade against my neck, red warmth trickling down my shirt front, the last-seconds-on-earth chemicals kicking in, flooding my brain with false images of the cheap Hawaiian paradise we have all been promised in the hereafter.

Which is to say: what if I'm wrong? What if I'm crazy? What if I won't survive? What if all these carefully annotated diary entries are just the prelude to another huge, comic, characteristically impotent letdown? What if our society falls to the barbarians? What if the best of us are left to bleed in front of the public libraries? What if my life is no better than the lives of others? What if my life is just as finite as yours?

Breathe, Lenny, breathe. Enough of your genetic pessimism. Soon you will be home among your own kind. Soon you will embark upon the path to the everlasting. In the meantime, take stock of your Italian sojourn. Learn from your year abroad. You've kept careful records as befits an obsessive. Why not share them with your diary?

How I Spent My Roman Vacation:
A Quantitative and Qualitative Analysis
By Leonard Abramov, BA

1.0 Pages of Greatest American Novel completed: 44.
1.1 How that makes me feel: like a failure.
1.2 Pages that will stand the test of time: 21.5 (the lyrical part about my mother's brassiere works quite well)
1.3 Pages that will not stand the test of time: 22.5 (anything with the word 'zeitgeist' on it must be fed to the flames)

2.0 Cathartic moments not involving sex or food or architecture: ZERO

330

From the Diaries of Lenny Abramov

2.1 Involving sex: 2 (one with Fabrizia when she first straddled me and I came like a fourteen-year-old, one with Sheryl when we did doggy on the roof and the Roman sunlight lit up her great big moony ass just so)

2.2 Involving food: 4 (in particular, the way the *bucatini* stood up to the sardine and pine nuts at the Sicilian place on Via Giulia)

2.3 Involving architecture: every moment of every day

3.0 Damage to vital organs

3.1 Circulatory system: moderate (from over-consumption of butter and cream)

3.2 Pulmonary system: low to moderate (from second-hand smoke, some pot mixed with tobacco)

3.3 Liver and kidneys: moderate to high (from uncontrolled near-daily drinking stemming from sadness, loneliness, inability to express myself to others because of poor Italian or feelings of superiority)

3.4 Reproductive system: low (possibly contracted HPV from Sheryl, but that only affects future partners not personal health)

3.5 Mental health: moderate (increased anxiety, lower reflex time, lowered intellectual stimulus in Rome vs. New York leading to atrophy in key areas of brain)

3.6 Skeletal: minor damage to coccyx bone when fell on marble flooring in Pompeii in the middle of the day, drunk

4.0 Lessons learned from antiquity: none

4.1 Truths about myself learned from being in foreign land: I am an American, Flushing-born, and there's no use pretending to be a European

4.2 Truths learned from brief parental visit: hardened immigrant parents incapable of pity and do not have my best interests at heart

4.3 Truths learned about women: they are not as indifferent as men, they have a far-reaching intelligence that nonetheless fails them regularly; if I am to achieve immortality I must spend as little time as possible engaged in the rites of courtship

331

Gary Shteyngart

June 4, New York City
Dearest Diary,

For me there is only one place in the physical universe that matters, that I would actually defend with my own blood and treasure, for even the murky waters of Jamaica Bay are worth to me a hundred Tibers and for the farthest parcel of Queens I would sacrifice all of Tuscany, Umbria and Piedmont besides. To hell with the political situation. I was back in New York.

When I lived on Via Giulia I'd meet this little American homo guy for lunch at da Tonnino and we'd talk about what we missed the most about Manhattan. For me it was fried pork-and-scallion dumplings on Eldridge Street, for him bossy older black women at the phone company or the unemployment office who called him 'honey' and 'sugar' and sometimes 'baby'. He said it wasn't a gay thing, but rather that these black women made him feel calm and at ease, as if he had momentarily won the love and mothering of a complete stranger. The first face I saw after deplaning at JFK belonged to just such a woman, if younger and more petite, her lips luminescent with gloss. She was doing her job, screaming at the herd of arrivals in an attempt to separate us into 'foreigner' and 'citizen' queues, and I impulsively went down the wrong line just so I could ask her, 'Is this for American citizens, ma'am?'

'This way, sugar,' she said, and physically extricated me from the dark sea of Italians, then gently pushed me in the right direction. I felt a wave of pride and belonging. Here I was, an American in America. A country steadily going to hell according to my friends and the Internet, but at least I no longer had to spend entire dinner parties accounting for the sins of our military. *'This way, sugar.'* Such kind words. Such tender professionalism in the face of mounting insanity. This is who we Americans really are in the end. This is why the best of us will live for ever.

Heartened by the black woman, I submitted easily to the immigration officer in the mauve pocket vest who shone a laser into my eye, took a recording of my teeth and clipped one of my precious receding hairs from the front of my head. 'It is forbidden to discuss our interaction,' the man said. 'Sedition Omnibus Four.'

'Yes?' I said. It was my first encounter with the fabled Omnibus.

'You said "yes",' the man said.

There was something wrong with one of his bloodshot eyes, it seemed dilated and independent of the rest of his face, and I realized there was a small rectangular box attached to the upper eyelash like an errant piece of mascara.

'Yes,' I agreed.

He looked at me crookedly. His mascara-filled eye scanned downwards. 'Did you mean "yes?" in the form of a question or "yes" to imply consent?'

I think I have a genetic instinct for run-ins with the security services. My parents were born in the Soviet Union and my grandmother had survived Stalin, although barely. '"Yes"' to imply consent,' I said, and showed the man my opened palms, as if to demonstrate how utterly helpless I was. The immigration man touched his eyelash and waved me through. No sooner did I collect my bags, when the customs crew pulled me over and searched the hell out of my luggage (somehow managing to miss two kilos of *prosciutto crudo* I had stashed away in my socks). They passed a flashing light sabre over me and demanded that I both deny our interaction and imply consent, conditions to which I expressly agreed.

As I rolled my suitcases down to the arrivals hall I saw two naked men, one brown and one white, with their hands tied behind their backs lying on the cold, air-conditioned floor, their buttocks smooth and oddly beautiful, their faces turned towards each other to avoid the stares of my fellow passengers, the Italians among them muttering '*Che cosa barbarica!*'[4] and '*A che serve?*'[5], while the Americans hurried towards the promise of early summer sunshine, their eyes on the person in front of them. I stopped for a moment, just to take in how incongruously bestial these two naked men appeared amidst the high-tech neon splendour of the arrivals hall, like zoo animals forced to lie in a hospital bed, when a middle-aged man in civilian clothes began walking towards me, a large pistol in his hand. 'Gah!' I said. I threw up my arms, once again flashed my empty palms and ran for the exit. I glanced back to see if the armed gentleman was behind me (he had disappeared), but before I could gain the automatic doors, my gaze skirted the two gleaming, coin-sized bald spots of the naked men on the floor. It's silly to be sure, but nothing touches me like hair loss on

---

4. How barbaric.
5. For what purpose?

an otherwise healthy body. And I knew then, with a shock of spectacular clarity, with a chill against my forehead and the flash of heat in my armpits, that whatever the gravity of these men's crimes, however they had wronged our country, this day would not end well for them.

I stood in the warm and perfect afternoon, breathing in the familiar American car exhaust, whose volume and ubiquity coat not just the eyes and nostrils but the throat and anus as well. Something was off. There was quiet all around me, or at least a kind of lingual inversion. I strained to hear the sweet emotive English of a busy transit point, the 'hey, man's and 'watch it, mister's, yet nothing crossed my ears. Foreigners were speaking, but our people were not. I walked past a camouflage-coloured armoured personnel carrier with no markings idling at the kerb, ahead of an armada of taxis respectfully keeping their distance. A black-on-orange highway sign warned us: IT IS FORBIDDEN TO ACKNOWLEDGE THE EXISTENCE OF THIS VEHICLE ('THE OBJECT') UNTIL YOU ARE 0.5 MILES FROM THE SECURITY PERIMETER OF JOHN F. KENNEDY INTERNATIONAL AIRPORT. BY READING THIS SIGN YOU HAVE DENIED EXISTENCE OF THE OBJECT AND IMPLIED CONSENT—SEDITION OMNIBUS IX-2.11

After hiring a cab and leaving the terminal, the fear began to dissipate. A deep unmoored anger began to take its place in my solar plexus. I was angry at everyone. The immigration officer, the crew at customs, the man with the pistol, even the two naked, balding men forced to lie on the floor. My last half-year in Rome was spent dreaming of my return, of the embrace of the warm and provincial, the crunch of Gus's pickles and the soft, excited jabber of young American Jews. And now my homecoming was ruined! I had merely left one foreign country for another.

Traffic was slow, one lane of the Van Wyck taken up with a row of gun-mounted Jeeps in camouflaged jungle garb and Seditions Omnibus signs warning us not to acknowledge their existence until we were 0.5 miles outside the airport's security perimeter. 'What are all these motherfuckers *doing*?' I said to the driver, savouring the ease of speaking normal, obscenity-laced, working-class English. The cabbie looked up from his Hispanic phone conversation, met my eyes in the rear-view and quickly looked away.

We drove through New York's few remaining ghettos, which lulled me with their quaint linear charm, the streets given over to deadly fried-food establishments and Baptist Cavalry ministries.[6] I saw black people strolling past or fanning themselves atop rickety chairs and basked in the familiar recognition that this is how it ever was. 'Homeland' basically refers to the poor people who keep a country's lowest denominator common.

And still my anger would not abate. Why shouldn't I 'acknowledge or discuss' the existence of some disgusting war vehicle squatting like a dead water bug on a minor highway in my beloved city? And why should I 'imply consent' to this kind of visual pollution? When the cabbie had ceased his Spanish cell phone jabbering I said to him, 'What was that all about, *jefe*? What the fuck is a 0.5-mile security perimeter anyway?'

His eyes went wide and brown in the rear-view as he stepped on the brakes and pulled over. 'Out!' he shouted.

'Wait a second,' I said, but the little fellow had already unlocked the trunk and was soon throwing my luggage out on the kerb. I got out too and approached him with as menacing a stride as possible, my arms crossed at my chest. I may be scared of men at the immigration counter but I still know my place around actual immigrants. 'You can't just leave me here,' I said. 'I'll fuck you up.'

'Omnibus, asshole!' he shouted, his hair standing up in thick ethnic spikes. He was looking at the ground, the sky, the poor people oddly quiet on their benighted porches, anywhere but my face, as if I was diseased or demented or both. 'Om-ni-bus,' he spelled it out for me, then drove off without his fare.

Well, dear Diary, as you can imagine, the rest of the day was spent in a state of serious existential panic. It took three hours to find a gypsy cab in the sticks, another hour to crawl over the heavily armoured carapace of the Williamsburg Bridge, and another hour to clear the Omnibus checkpoints at Delancey, where more armed men in civilian clothing pointed hollow tubes at our eyes and spoke quietly into their collars. They were ruddier and whiter than most New Yorkers, with elliptical blond moustaches that even from

6. On the subject of religion I have nothing to say. This diary is concerned with what is actually possible and probable. There is no space here for superstition. This is not a 'dream diary'.

a distance smelled of coffee and ham. I wondered what it would take for them to shoot me dead and which authorities would come to inspect my body.

By the time I got to my co-op on the banks of the East River I felt once removed from myself, as if I were just a poor relation to the man who had left for Rome a year prior. My parents never successfully learned English, but after my father would wrestle me down as a child and beat my head and body, I would burble through my tears in English, 'You can't do this to me, Poppa. *I know my rights!*' And now that silly American sentiment took on the mantle of cold immutable fact. I knew my rights. As a prosperous citizen. As a landholder. As a man working at the cutting edge of technology. If a taxi driver of dubious green-card status could throw me out in the middle of an outer borough to fend for myself, if anyone could stop me on the Williamsburg Bridge and shine a flashlight into my soul, what else was possible? I briefly entertained the possibility of suffering the kind of grievous bodily harm that leads to death. I saw the blows coming, raised my hands in mock defence, and shut my eyes so tightly for that for several seconds I successfully ceased to exist.

□

IN THE TUNNEL
John Wray

John Wray was born in Washington, DC in 1971 and raised in Buffalo, New York. His father is American and his mother is Austrian, and he himself is a citizen of both countries. His first novel, 'The Right Hand of Sleep' (Vintage UK/Knopf), was published in 2001 and won a Whiting Writers' Award. His second, 'Canaan's Tongue', is published by Chatto & Windus in the UK and by Vintage in the US. 'The Tunnel' is taken from his latest novel, 'Lowboy', which will be published by Farrar, Straus & Giroux in 2008. At present he lives in Brooklyn. The glass in the above photograph contains a Singapore Sling.

O n November 11, Lowboy ran to catch a train. People were in
his way but he was careful not to touch them. He ran up the
platform's corrugated yellow lip and kept his eyes on the train's cab,
commanding it to wait. It was a good train, an uptown local. Its
doors had closed already but they opened when he kicked them. He
couldn't help but take this as a sign.

He got on board and laughed. Signs and tells were all around him.
The floor was shivering and ticking beneath his feet and the brick-
tiled arches above the train beat the murmurings of the crowd into
copper and aluminium foil. Every seat in the car had a person in it.
Never mind about that. Notes of music rang out as the doors closed
behind him: C# first, then A. Sharp against both ears, like the tip of
a pencil. He turned and pressed his face against the glass.

Skull & Bones, his state-appointed enemies, were forcing their way
head-first up the platform. Skull was a skinny, milk-faced man, not
much to look at, but Bones was the size of a ticket booth. They moved
like policemen in a silent movie, as though their shoes were too big for
their feet. No one stood aside for them. Bones kept stepping on the
back of Skull's Reeboks by accident. Giving him a flat tyre, that was
called. Giving him a flat. Lowboy smiled as he watched them stumbling
towards him. He felt his fear of them falling away with each ridiculous
step they took. I'll have to think of something else to call them now,
he thought. Short & Sweet. Before & After. Habeas & Corpus.

Bones saw him first and started pounding on the doors. Spit flew
noiselessly from his mouth against the scuffed and greasy glass. The
train gave a sudden lurch, stopped, then lurched again. Lowboy gave
Bones his village-idiot smile, puckering his lips and blinking, then
solemnly held up his middle finger. Skull was running now, struggling
to keep even with the doors, moving his arms in slow, emphatic
circles. Bones was shouting something at the conductor. Lowboy
whistled the door-closing theme at them and shrugged. C# to A, C#
to A. The simplest, sweetest melody in the world.

Everyone in the car would later agree that the boy seemed in very
high spirits. His happiness set him apart from them at once. He was
late for something, by the look of him, but not for work or school.
A date possibly. His clothes didn't fit, hanging apologetically from his
body, but because he was blue-eyed and unassuming he caused
nobody concern. He was making an effort to seem older than he was.

John Wray

They watched him for a while, glancing at him whenever his back was turned, the way people watch one another on the subway. He carried himself with authority and calm. What's a boy like that doing, a few of the women wondered, dressed in such hideous clothes?

The train eased into the tunnel like a hand into a mitten and closed over Lowboy's body and held him still. He kept his right cheek pressed against the glass and watched the guttered bedrock passing. I'm on a train, he told himself. Skull & Bones aren't. I'm riding on the uptown local.

Not ten feet above him the citizenry held itself hunched against the mid-morning chill, but the climate in the car was temperate as always, hovering comfortably between sixty-two and sixty-eight degrees. Its vulcanized rubber doorjambs allowed no draught to enter. Its suspension system, ribbon-pressed butterfly shocks manufactured in Quebec, kept the pitching and the jarring to a minimum. Lowboy listened to the sound of the wheels, to the squealing of the axles at the railheads and the bends, to the train's manifold and particulate elements functioning effortlessly in concert. Welcoming, familiar, almost sentimental sounds. His thoughts fell sleepily into place. Even his pinched and claustrophobic brain felt a kind of dull affection for the tunnel. It was his skull that held him captive, after all, not the tunnel or the passengers or the train. I'm a prisoner of my own brain-pan, he thought. Hostage of my limbic system. He smiled at this idea, though the truth was that it wasn't very funny. Funny was too much to hope for yet.

I can make jokes again, he said to himself. I never could have done that yesterday.

Lowboy was five foot ten and weighted 130 pounds exactly. His hair was parted on the left. Most things that happened didn't bother him at all, but others got inside of him and itched. He had a list of beautiful things that he took out and ran through his fingers like rosary beads whenever he had a setback. A wad of ancient paper, warm and damp. He recited the first seven items on the list from memory:

obelisks
invisible ink
Violet Hoek
snowboarding

the Bronx Botanic Gardens
Jacques Cousteau
the tunnel

His father had taken him snowboarding once, in the Poconos. The Poconos and the beach at Breezy Point were items eight and nine. His skin turned dark brown in the summer, like an Indian's or a surfer's, but now it was as white as a corpse's from the time he'd spent away.

Lowboy looked down at his white dead-looking hands. He was a dreamer, and sometimes that can be considered rude: but most of the time he was considerate and obliging. He came from a long line of soldiers, and secretly felt a soldier himself, but he'd sworn on his father's grave that he would never go to war. Not again. Once he almost killed someone with just his two bare hands.

The tunnel straightened itself without any sign of effort and the axles and the rails went quiet. Lowboy decided to think about his mother. His mother was a blonde, like somebody on a billboard, but she was already more than thirty-eight years old. She painted eyes and lips on mannequins for Saks Fifth Avenue and Bergdorf Goodman. She painted parts of mannequins that no one would ever see. He'd asked her once what she did about the nipples and she'd sighed. On April 15 she would turn thirty-nine unless the rules changed or he'd miscounted or she died. He was closer to her house than he'd been in seventeen months. He had these directions: transfer at Columbus Circle, wait, then eight stops on the downtown D. That's all it was. But he would never see his mother's house again.

Slowly and carefully, with practised precision, he shifted his attention towards the train. Trains were easy to consider. There were thousands of them in the tunnel, pushing ghost-trains of compressed air ahead of them, and every single one of them had a purpose. They almost never hit each other. The train he was riding on was bound for Bedford Park Boulevard. Its coat of arms was a B in Helvetica script, rampant over a bright orange escutcheon. The train to his mother's house had exactly that same colour: the colour of wax fruit, of sunsets painted on velvet, of light through half-closed eyelids at the beach. *William of Orange*, thought Lowboy, giving himself over to the dream. *William of Orange* is my name. He closed his eyes tightly and passed a hand over his forehead and pictured himself wandering through the grounds of Buckingham Palace. It was pleasantly cool there under the trees. Little fountains. He glanced in through the windows as he strolled. He saw dark panelled corridors, dust-covered paintings, high ruffled collars and canopied beds. He saw his own portrait wearing a mink pillbox hat. He saw his mother in the palace kitchens frying onions and garlic in butter. Her face was the colour of old soap. He bit down on his lower lip and forced his eyes back open.

A self-conscious silence prevailed in the car. Lowboy noticed it at once. The passengers were studying him closely, taking note of his scuffed sneakers, his sharply creased pants, his misbuttoned shirt and his immaculately parted yellow hair. In the glass he saw their puzzled looks reflected.

'I'm William of Orange,' Lowboy said. He turned around to see them better. 'Has anybody got a cigarette?'

The silence got flatter. Lowboy wondered whether anyone had heard him. Sometimes it happened that he spoke perfectly clearly, taking pains to articulate every word, and got no response at all. In fact it happened often. But on that day, on that particular morning, he was undeniable. On that particular morning he was at his best.

A man to his left sat forward and cleared his throat. 'Truant,' the man said, as if in answer to a question.

'Excuse me?' said Lowboy.

'You are a truant?' the man said. He spoke the sentence like a piece of music.

Lowboy squinted at him. A friendly-looking gentleman with an elegant wedge-shaped beard and polished shoes. He sat very correctly, with his knees pressed together and his hands folded precisely in his lap. His pants were white and newly pressed and his green leather jacket had a row of tiny footballs where its buttons should have been. The top of his head was covered by a glossy yellow turban. He looked stately and wise.

'I can't be a truant,' said Lowboy. 'They kicked me out of school.'

'Did they?' the man asked. 'What for?'

Lowboy thought carefully before he answered. 'It was a special sort of school,' he said. 'Progressive. They sent me home for good behaviour.'

'I'm sorry, I can't hear you,' said the man. He laid his right hand on the seat beside him. 'Will you sit?'

Lowboy stared down at the empty seat. It had happened again, he decided. He'd been moving his lips without actually speaking. He took a half-step forward and repeated himself.

'Is that so.' The man was less friendly now. 'You aren't coming out of prison—?'

'You're a Sikh,' said Lowboy.

The man's eyes opened wide, as though the Sikhs were a lost and forgotten race. 'It must have been a very good school, to teach you that!'

Lowboy took hold of the crossbar above the seats and leaned forward. He looked the man over closely. There was something theatrical about him. Something contrived. His skin lightened slightly where his turban met his forehead and the wisps of hair that poked out behind his ears were the colour of piss in a bottle.

'I read about you in the library,' said Lowboy. 'I know all about you Sikhs.'

They were coming to a station. First came the slight falling back of the tunnel, then the lights, then the noise, then the change in his body. His left side got heavy and he had to hold on to the crossbar with all his strength. The fact that he'd met a Sikh first, out of all the people in the tunnel, signified something without question but the coming of the station disconcerted him. I'll think about the Sikh when we pull out again, he thought. In a little while I'll think about him. Then I'll decide. The platform when it came was narrow and neglected-looking and much less crowded than the one before had been. He'd expected to find them waiting for him there—his mother, Dr Trabull, Dr Prekop, Skull & Bones—but there was no one on the platform that he knew. The doors slid open and shut on nothing.

'The capital of the Sikhs is the city of Amritsar,' Lowboy said as the door-closing music sounded. His head was clear again but he wanted a cigarette badly. 'Amritsar is in the Punjab. Sikhs believe in reincarnation, like Hindus, but in a single god, like Muslims. A baptized Sikh never cuts his hair or beard.'

The Sikh's smile widened. 'A fine school. An *extraordinary* school.'

'I need a cigarette. Let me have a cigarette please.'

The Sikh shook his brown face merrily.

'The hell with this,' said Lowboy.

The train gave a twitch and started rolling. Both seats on the Sikh's right side were empty. Lowboy sat down in the farther one, mindful of the Sikh's bony elbow and of his legs in their bright linen pants. He took a deep breath. It was reckless to get close to a living body just then, when everything was still so new and overwhelming, but the empty seat between them made it possible. It was all right to sit down and talk. He looked around to see who else was listening. No one was. 'The Sikh religion is less than seventy years old,' he announced.

The Sikh pursed his lips and bunched his face together. 'That is not so,' he said, pronouncing each word carefully. 'That is not so. I'm sorry.'

Lowboy put his hand on the seat between them, where the Sikh's hand had been. It was still slightly warm. 'Can you say for *certain*,' he said, 'that it's older than that?' He drummed against the plastic with his fingers. 'You're not seventy years old.'

'I can say so,' the Sikh said gravely. 'I can say so absolutely.'

Why does he have to say everything twice? thought Lowboy. I'm not deaf. It was enough to put him in mind of the school. The way the Sikh was looking at him now, trying hard not to seem too curious, was exactly the way that people did it there. He forced his eyes away, fighting back his disappointment, and found himself staring down at the Sikh's feet. They were the smallest feet he'd ever seen on a grown man. The Sikh wore penny loafers with old subway tokens where the pennies should have been. They look like shoes a doll would wear, Lowboy thought. The Sikhs are supposed to be the tallest men in Asia. He looked up from the shoes to the Sikh's face, flat and pleasant and unnatural as a cake. As he did so he began to have his doubts.

Here they come, he thought, clenching his eyes shut. His throat went dry and tight, as it always did when the first doubts hit. The train braked hard and shuddered through a junction. The air grew warmer by exactly six degrees. 'All right,' he said out loud, patting himself on the knee. But it wasn't all right. His voice sounded wrong to him, stilted and precious, like the voice of a spoiled English lord. *William of Orange is my name.* 'All right,' he said, feeling his skin start to prickle. 'It's perfectly all right, you see.'

When he opened his eyes they were back in the tunnel. There was only one tunnel in the city but it was wound and snarled together like telephone wire, threaded back on itself, so it seemed to have no beginning and no end. *Ouroboros* was the name of the dragon that ate its own tail and the tunnel was *Ouroboros* also. He called it that.

It seemed self-contained, a closed system, but in truth it was the opposite of closed. There were openings spaced out evenly along its length like gills on an eel, just big enough for a person to pass through. That was part of the perfection of the tunnel. The trains were held prisoner, stuck to the rails, but the passengers were free to come and go. Right now the train was under 53rd Street. You could get off at the next station, ease your body through the turnstiles, and the tunnel would carry on exactly as before. The trains would run without a single person in them.

Two men got off at the next station, looking back over their shoulders, and a third man moved ahead to the next car. On my account, thought Lowboy. He could see the man in question through the pockmarked junction doors, a middle-aged commuter in a rumpled madras jacket, Jewish or possibly Lebanese, flipping nervously through a gilt-edged leather datebook. Soon the Sikh would switch cars too and that was perfectly all right. That was how you managed in the tunnel. That was how you got by. You came and sat together in a row and touched arms and knees and held your breath and stared, and after a few minutes, half an hour at the most, you separated from each other for all time. It would be a mistake to take that as an insult. He'd done the same 1,000 times himself. He was doing it now. It was a question of not thinking about what you were doing.

The incredible thing was: the people around him did it effortlessly.

The Sikh could certainly do it, and he would. He'd be getting up directly. Lowboy patted himself on the knee and reminded himself that he hadn't gotten on the train to talk to little grandfatherly men about religion. He'd gotten on for a reason and he knew in his heart that his reason was the best one that anyone could have. He'd been given a calling. Also a purpose. Also a career. It was a matter of consequence, a matter of urgency, a matter of life and death. It was as sharp and light and transparent as a syringe. If he got careless now he might lose track of his calling, or confuse it with something similar, or possibly even forget it altogether. Worst of all, he might begin to have his doubts.

He turned to the Sikh and nodded at him sadly. 'I get off next stop,' he said. He coughed into his sleeve and looked around and the people who'd been watching him looked away. 'Next stop!' he repeated for the benefit of all present.

'So soon?' said the Sikh. 'I haven't even asked you—'

John Wray

'William,' said Lowboy. He gave him his bankteller's smile.
'William Amritsar.'

'William,' the Sikh said. He pronounced it *Well-yoom*.

'But people call me Lowboy. They prefer it.'

'Pleased to meet you, William! My own name is—'

'Because I get moody,' said Lowboy, raising his voice a little. 'Also because I like trains.'

The Sikh said nothing. He looked at Lowboy and ran two birdlike fingers through his beard. Trying to make sense of me, Lowboy decided. The idea made him feel like a hermit at the top of a cliff.

'Underground trains,' he offered. 'Subways. *Low* in the ground.' He felt his voice go quiet. 'Does that make any sense to you?'

The train was pulling into the station now and he got to his feet, keeping his eyes on the Sikh the whole time. The Sikh kept himself motionless, propped up straight in his seat like a near-sighted old lady on a bus.

'You're not a doctor, are you?' Lowboy said, squinting down at him. 'An MD? A PhD? A DDS?'

The Sikh looked surprised. 'A doctor, William? What could possibly—'

'Can you prove to me that you're not with the school?'

The Sikh gave a small, dry laugh. 'I'm past seventy, William. I once was an electrical engineer.'

'Bullshit,' said Lowboy. He shook his head. 'Balls.'

Everyone in the car was looking at him now. There were times when he was practically invisible, monochrome and flat, and there were others when he gave off a faint greenish glow, like teeth held up to a blacklight. When that happened his voice got very loud very fast and the only thing he could do was to keep his mouth shut. He decided to do that now. The air outside the glass got thicker. There were things he wanted to explain to the Sikh, to apprise him of, but he held his breath and pressed his lips together. He could keep himself from talking when he had to. It was one of the first things that he'd learned to do at school.

'Who were those men chasing you?' the Sikh said, leaning forward on his beautiful sticklike legs. 'Were they truancy officers?'

Lowboy shook his head fiercely. 'Not sent by the school. Sent by—' He caught himself at the last moment. 'By a *federal agency*.

346

To frighten me. To try and make me follow their itinerary.' He turned measuredly around to face the doors. 'You'll have to excuse me now,' he said. It was too warm in the car to move any faster.

The train seemed to hesitate as it came into the light. Its ventilators went quiet and its mercury strip-lights flickered and it rolled into the station at a crawl. The station was a main junction: six lines came together there. Its tiles were square and unbevelled, like the tiles on a urinal wall. The only person on the platform was a stooped guard who looked ready to fall down and die of boredom any minute. Lowboy frowned and bit down on the knuckle of his thumb. There was no good reason for the platform to be empty at 10.30 in the morning.

The guard watched the train coming out of his left eye-corner, careful not to seem too interested. The old school trick. Lowboy thought of the last glimpse he'd had of Bones, pounding on the glass and shouting at the conductor. He thought about Skull running alongside the train and making great slow circles with his arms. He looked at the transit guard again. Something was clipped to the inside of his collar and he held his head cocked towards it, moving his lips very subtly, like someone reading from a complicated book. Watching him made Lowboy want to lie down on the floor.

'I fucked up,' Lowboy said, turning back to the Sikh. 'This isn't my stop.'

The Sikh nodded approvingly. 'Why don't you sit back down?'

'I'll tell you why they expelled me,' Lowboy said. He sat. 'Do you want me to tell you?'

'Here comes the policeman,' the Sikh said softly.

Lowboy turned his head a quarter-turn and saw the transit guard dragging himself up the platform, glancing sideways into each car and mumbling into his collar. The doors stayed open. No announcement was given. If the guard looked bored it was only because he knew every event before it happened. Lowboy let his head rest against the window for a moment, gathering his strength, then eased his body sideways until his cheek touched the Sikh's shoulder. The collar of the Sikh's shirt smelled faintly of anise. Lowboy's eyes began to water.

'Can I borrow your turban?' he whispered.

'You should go back to school,' the Sikh said through his teeth.

'I wish I could,' said Lowboy. His left hand gave a jerk. The rest of the car was staring at the transit guard, then back at the Sikh and

Lowboy, then away. Some of them were starting to look restless. 'Do you have a family?' the Sikh said. He cleared his throat. 'Do you have anyone—'

'Give me a hug,' said Lowboy. He took the Sikh's arm and ducked his head beneath it. The anise smell got stronger. He saw the guard reflected in the windows and in the doors and in every set of eyeballs on the train. He buried his face in the Sikh's green leather jacket.

'Hello, officer,' said the Sikh.

As soon as the guard was gone Lowboy coughed and bent forward as far as he could go, pressing both his hands against his ribs. The Sikh pulled his arm free as calmly as a nurse and smoothed out a crease in his pant leg. 'I have a grandson in Pakistan,' he said finally. 'When he was sixteen years of age—'

'I'm not ready yet, you understand,' Lowboy said, tapping out a rhythm on the seat. 'I never should have got myself expelled.'

As the train began to roll again the niceties of life resumed, the breathing and the coughing and the whispering and the singing out of key. The singing especially seemed strange to him after the long, unbearable silence but he was glad to hear it. He hummed to himself for a few seconds, grateful for the rocking of the train, then took a breath and made his face go flat. What he had to say next was solemn and imperative and meant for the Sikh alone. He had nothing else to offer, either as a gesture or a covenant or a gift: only his one small discovery. But lesser gifts than that had saved men's lives.

'Your religion values sacrifice above all things.' Lowboy caught his breath again. 'Sacrifice is important. Am I right?'

The Sikh didn't answer. Lowboy had expected him to react in some way, to cry out or to shake his head or to laugh, but instead he kept his sallow face composed. He wasn't looking at Lowboy any more but at a girl across the aisle who was fussing with a pair of silver headphones. He no longer seemed wise, or kind, or even especially clever. The longer Lowboy stared at him the more lifeless he became. It was like watching a piece of bread dry out and become inedible.

'You're drying out,' said Lowboy. 'Are you listening?'

It's because of the heat, Lowboy said to himself. Everyone's baking. The Sikh stared straight ahead, as though he was sitting for a portrait. His posture was impeccably severe. He's preparing himself, thought Lowboy. Mustering his resources. The Sikh would get out at the next station and move to another car, or transfer to a different train, or call the police, or even send a message to the school: Lowboy knew in his heart that he'd do one of these things. He accepted it as a given, as something long ago ordained. But it was a terrible thing that the Sikh would act out of ignorance, without waiting until he'd received his gift. A worse setback could not have been imagined. There could be no covenant between them if that happened.

All at once, without warning, without turning his head or taking in a breath, the Sikh said quietly and clearly, 'What is your reason, William?'

'My reason?' Lowboy said. He could hardly believe it. 'My reason for running away, you mean?'

The Sikh blinked his eyes slowly, like a kitten sitting in a patch of sun.

'I'll tell you why,' said Lowboy, 'if you really want to know. The world's going to shit.' He laughed. 'The world won't make it past this afternoon.'

The Sikh turned and regarded him now, though only his watery close-set eyes had life. Lowboy couldn't be sure that he was listening, since he hadn't said a word, but it seemed likely that he was. There was no life in him anywhere but in his pinched, dark eye-sockets but even that trace amount might be enough. The Sikh sat forward, bobbing his head impatiently, digging the heels of his penny loafers into the floor. Fidgeting like the girl across the aisle. Why was everyone impatient? It was true of course that there was very little time. There were two transfers at the next station: an orange and a blue. Choices would have to be made there. They were being made already.

A hissing came off the rails as the train crossed a switch and the noise cut straight through the car, hanging in sheets down the length of the aisle, as if to offer the two of them a kind of shelter. Lowboy blinked and took a breath and said it. 'The world's going to die in six hours. Six hours exactly. Is that all right, Doctor?' He pressed the heel of his palm against this teeth until he could finish. 'By fire.'

The expression on the Sikh's face was impossible to make sense of. His body was the body of a somnambulist or a corpse. Lowboy closed his mouth and caught his breath and nodded. It was difficult, even painful, to keep his eyes on the Sikh, to sit and wait for the slightest trace of feeling, to smile and nod and hope for the one true

John Wray

reply. He decided to look at the girl with the headphones instead.

She was sitting straight up in her seat, the exact mirror-image of the Sikh, as poised and geometric as a painting. It was possible that she was making fun of him. The longer Lowboy looked at her the less he knew. His take on the girl, on the Sikh, on everything in the car refused to hold still any more. His thoughts careened like mercury from one possibility to another. The white spaces between each event got heavier and wider. In no time they'd outnumber his ideas. He forced himself to focus on the surface of things and on the surface only. There's more than enough there, he said to himself. No need to see what happens underneath. He let his eyes rest flatly on the girl.

The girl's hair was coloured a mute shade of red, the way dyed-black hair gets by the end of the summer. It was cut in a way he'd never seen before, with long feathered bangs hanging down into her eyes. Ugly bangs. When she leaned forward her face disappeared completely. Lowboy pictured a city of identical girls, their faces all hidden, silver headphones plugging up their ears. A year and a half was a long time to have been gone. He'd been a cosmonaut for seventeen months, a castaway, an amnesiac, veteran of an arbitrary war. The world had gotten older while he'd been away. Away at school, regressing. He smiled to himself in acknowledgement of the joke. He studied the girl's hands, cupped protectively in her lap, hiding whatever the headphones were attached to. A sentimental and affecting picture. She seemed ashamed of her hands, of her lap, of her intentionally torn crocheted stockings. She'd hide her whole body if she could, he thought. He felt a sudden rush of recognition. So would I.

Her hands were chapped and pink, with short ungraceful fingers, and it took him a long time to see what he liked about them. Only when she raised one to her mouth did he notice that the nails were bitten down to the cuticles, torn and unpainted, the nails of a girl half her age. She was smiling as she bit down on her finger. She was smiling without question but the meaning of her smile kept itself encoded. 'It's the music,' Lowboy murmured, nodding confidently to the Sikh. 'There's music in those headphones that she likes.' But even as the Sikh nodded back—blankly, disaffectedly—Lowboy knew he was wrong. The girl's smile wasn't private: it was unabashed and open. And she was smiling it at nobody but him.

That made Lowboy remember about why he'd left the school.

Cautiously, as an experiment, he tried to duplicate her smile. He kept his eyes wide open and made sure to show his teeth. The strangeness of what he was attempting made the roof of his mouth go numb. He had no name for the smile that he was making. There'd been no girls at the school, and he hadn't cared about them before he got sent away. But now he did care about them. Now they made him feel wide awake.

'Don't leer at her that way,' said the Sikh.

'I'm not leering,' Lowboy said under his breath. 'I'm making myself sexy.'

'You're frightening her, William.'

Lowboy waved at the girl and opened his eyes wider and pointed at his mouth. Her smile went blank and stiffened at its corners. He adjusted his own smile accordingly. The girl pulled her backpack open with a jerk and let her head hang forward, lowering her bangs across it like a shutter across a storefront. She stared into her backpack like a baby looking down into a well.

'Why won't she take those fucking headphones off? I want to tell her something. I'll *sing* it to her, if she wants. I want to—'

'The world will end?' the Sikh said. 'Why is that?'

Lowboy stopped smiling. What magnetism he might have had was neatly and resourcefully sucked away. The question had been meant as a distraction, nothing more. To disarm him. To keep him from establishing contact with the girl. That he should choose that to ask out of all possible questions. Out of all questions that one: the most critical, the most grave. How ignorant. How heartless. The girl with the backpack receded and the Sikh slid quietly forward and took her place. Still smiling politely. The rest of the car went dark, as though the Sikh were in a spotlight. He was not the same person he had been before. There was no curiosity in his expression, no humanity, no love. He spoke in a completely different voice.

'Your voice has changed,' Lowboy said to the Sikh. 'I don't think I can hear you any more.'

'Don't trouble that poor girl any longer, William.' Behind his sparse, discoloured beard the Sikh was grinning. The grin looked fastened to his face with wallpaper adhesive. He slid full into the light and gave a wink. 'Why not trouble me, instead?'

It was then that Lowboy saw the danger. The fact of it hit him in the middle of his chest and spread out in all directions like a cramp.

'No trouble,' he said. He said it effortfully, slowly, biting his breath back after every word. 'No trouble at all, Grandfather. Go away.'

The Sikh flashed his teeth again. 'Grandfather?' he said at the top of his voice. He said it to the rest of the car, not to Lowboy. He was making a public announcement. He looked up and down the car, the consummate entertainer, and brought a hooked brown hand to rest on Lowboy's shoulder. 'If I was *your* grandfather, Boy—'

His voice was still booming up and down the car, like the voice of a master of ceremonies, as Lowboy slid his hands under the Sikh's beard and pushed. The Sikh lifted out of his seat like a wind-tossed paper bag. Who'd have guessed he was as light as that, thought Lowboy. The Sikh arched his back as he fell and clutched at the air and opened his mouth in a garish, slack-jawed parody of surprise. A pole caught him just below the shoulder and spun him counterclockwise towards the door. The booming was coming not from the Sikh any more but from an intercom in the middle of the ceiling. 'Columbus Circle,' Lowboy shouted. 'Transfer to the A, C, D, 1, 9.' No joking any more, he thought, laughing. No part of this is funny. A woman halfway down the car was standing gasping in the middle of the aisle. He turned towards her and she shut her mouth.

'Boy,' the Sikh said breathlessly. He was sputtering just like the intercom. '*Boy*—'

Lowboy crouched down next to the Sikh. 'Sacrifice makes sense to me,' he said. 'Am I right?'

The Sikh flashed his teeth and made thin, meaningless noises and brought his fingers together at his throat.

'You're worried about me,' Lowboy said. He shook his head. 'Don't worry about me, Doctor. Worry about the world.'

The Sikh slid backwards until his head came to rest against the graphite-coloured crease between the doors. His eyes transcribed a mournful circle. His turban sat next to his elbow like an ornamental basket, still immaculately wrapped and folded. So that's how they do it, Lowboy thought. They put it on and take it off like a hat.

'*Boy*,' the Sikh said again, forcing the word out stiffly with his tongue. It seemed to be the only word he knew.

Lowboy bent down and took hold of the Sikh by the collar of his jacket. He could feel the little footballs grind together under his fingers. 'It's going to get very, very hot,' he whispered. 'Are you ready?'   □